GROWING UP IN HOLLYWOOD

Growing Up in

HOLLY-WOOD

ROBERT PARRISH

Harcourt Brace Jovanovich
New York and London

Library of Congress Cataloging in Publication Data
Parrish, Robert.
  Growing up in Hollywood.
  Includes index.
  1. Parrish, Robert.   I. Title.
PN1998.A3P27 1976   791.43'023 [B]   75-29174
ISBN *0-15-137473-2*

First edition
B C D E

To Reesie

Contents

Part I

Part II

Part III

List of Illustrations

"The Big Trail"/Author's Collection
Johnny Indrisanno/Author's Collection
Chalky Wright/Wide World Photos
American Legion Stadium/Robert Belcher
    Collection
Jack McHugh/Author's Collection
"Harold Teen"/Author's Collection
Cecil B. DeMille/Author's Collection
"Having Wonderful Time" Poster/Author's
    Collection
RKO Tower/Author's Collection
Sonja Henie/Author's Collection
Billy Hamilton/Author's Collection
"One In A Million"/Author's Collection
Santa Monica State Beach/History Division,
    Natural History Museum of Los Angeles County
Santa Monica State Beach/History Division,
    Natural History Museum of Los Angeles County

Between pages 182 and 183
Author and Mother/Author's Collection
John Ford, Author/Author's Collection
OSS Field Photo Farm Chapel/Clarence Inman
    Collection
Parrishes and John Ford/Author's Collection
Universal Studio/Author's Collection
John Wayne, Mark Armistead. John Ford, Ward
    Bond/Clarence Inman Collection
"Body And Soul" poster/Author's Collection
Screenplay/Author's Collection
"Body And Soul" still/Author's Collection
Author and Anne Baxter/Author's Collection
Oscar nomination/Author's Collection
Robert Rossen/Author's Collection
Broderick Crawford/Author's Collection
Cecil B. DeMille/Author's Collection
Paramount Release/Author's Collection
Variety/Author's Collection
Joseph L. Mankiewicz/Author's Collection
John Ford/Author's Collection

PART

1

1

The Black Pirate

I N THE city of Columbus, Georgia, there used to be three movie theaters: the Lyric, the Royal, and the Dream. The Lyric had a piano over on the left side, down in front near the screen. The Royal had an organ that came up from a pit, complete with organist, as the lights went down in the theater. A magic moment. I don't know what went on in the Dream over on First Avenue because that was a Negro theater and whites were not allowed, not even seven-year-old whites.

The Lyric had a Saturday matinee where my mother deposited me and my older brother while she did the shopping for the week. We usually saw a comedy or a western and one episode of a serial. The comedy stars I remember are Charlie Chaplin, Buster Keaton, Our Gang, Lloyd Hamilton, Fatty Arbuckle, Harold Lloyd, and Larry Semon. The western stars were Buck Jones, Harry Carey, William S. Hart, Hoot Gibson, and Tom Mix.

From time to time, if our parents were staying in town and if we had saved enough money from our chores or from selling peanuts at the football games at nearby Fort Benning—"Peanuts! Ground peas! And Goobers! Five cents a bag!"—we were allowed to see the grown-up feature picture. The first one I remember is *The Black Pirate*, starring Douglas Fairbanks.

He slid down the mast and balanced on the top spar of the mainsail just long enough to flash that wonderful smile and draw a ten-inch knife from a leather sheath. He wore boots that came almost to his knees, and he had a large ring in one ear. He put the knife crosswise in his mouth and looked around to see if he was being followed. After glancing right and left, he looked down to the deck of the ship.

We saw what he saw far below—fifty frantic pirates slashing at each other with cutlasses, swords, scimitars, and various other lethal weapons. The ship was in full sail. The bow rose and fell in the foamy sea and the sails ballooned like white sheets in the wind.

Douglas Fairbanks took the knife out of his mouth, grasped it firmly in his right hand, and sprang to the top of the billowing mainsail, plunging the knife into the canvas as he made contact. He rode the knife down to the deck, smiling out at us all the way. I don't remember exactly what he did when he got there, but whatever it was, I remember him smiling all the time he was doing it.

I also remember trying the knife stunt that afternoon in Jack Dimon's back yard. Jack Dimon's uncle was the mayor of Columbus. His father owned the wholesale grocery store that supplied most of Muscogee County. Jack was ten, older and richer than the rest of the kids in the vicinity. He was the leader of our gang. We tried to please him so that he wouldn't beat us up, and also because we hoped for some of the fallout from his opulent household. He told me to get a long curtain. I looked at the ones in our living room, but they were too short, so I went across the field at the back of our house to our closest friends, the Zacharias family.

On this day, I went in the kitchen door as usual. Mattie, the Zachariases' black cook, was kneading some dough for sweet rolls. She looked up over her steel-rimmed spectacles and said, "Whatchall want?" I said I wanted to see Miss Hortense or Miss Eva or Miss Rebecca, the three grown daughters of the house. Mattie stopped kneading her rolls and went to the cookie jar. She started muttering, "How'm I goin' get my work done with y'all bustin' in here botherin' me all day?" She carried on this complaint while she laid out some cookies and a glass of milk for me. "Lawd, I don't know how come these chillun keep on botherin' me when I'se tryin' my best to do my work. . . ." The monologue continued as I started on the cookies and milk and she went out to get one of the three daughters.

I once referred to Mattie as a "nigger lady" and promptly had my mouth washed out with soap, twice, by my aunt Nell— once for calling Mattie a "nigger" and once for calling her a "lady." ("Nigras are never referred to as niggers and they are never ladies, Robert, you know that.")

We were allowed to say "Negro" or "colored" or "nigra" in those days in Georgia, but my mother would not permit us to call them "nigger," "coon," "jungle bunny," "tar baby," "jigaboo," "spook," "darkie," "chocolate drop," "snowflake," etc. We used these words behind her back, especially in conversations with black children. They, in turn, called us "white trash," "redneck," "gray boy," "pink eye," "cracker-ass," "pa-ley," "ghost boy," "white ass," and so on. They called my father Massa or Boss or Capt'n, and he called them by their first names, or just "boy." My mother also forbade calling them "blacks," because she said it called attention to the color of a person's skin and might embarrass him.

Aunt Nell was the mouth-soaper in our family. She used Octagon kitchen soap because the shape made it easy to stuff into the victim's mouth. The main thing in these mouth-soapings was to take the offender by surprise. As soon as he said the forbidden word he was grabbed by the arm and dragged into the kitchen or laundry room, whichever was closer. If he was howling, Aunt Nell's job was easy—she just grabbed the base of the skull at the top of the neck, just below the ears, with one hand and stuffed the soap in the mouth as far as it would go with the other. Then she twisted the soap around to be sure some of it stuck to the back of the teeth. If the victim had had his mouth soaped before, he usually kept his lips tightly closed as soon as he had said "shit" or something and before Aunt Nell made her move. In these cases Aunt Nell simply exerted pressure on the neck until the mouth opened—the same way I had once seen her do with a three-foot water moccasin.

On that occasion she had found the poisonous snake stealing eggs in her chicken coop. She trapped it against the ground with a forked stick and picked it up, her tough, farm-calloused thumb and forefinger pressing at the base of the head until the mouth sprung open. As soon as this happened I discovered why water moccasins were sometimes called "cottonmouths." With the mouth fully hinged open, white puffs of translucent flesh protruded, making it look like a boll of fresh-picked cotton.

Aunt Nell took the straight end of the forked stick and rammed it into the snake's mouth and down through his squirming body until she could feel it with her other hand through the flesh and skin. Then she put the whole mess on the ground and stomped the head to a pulp. The rest of the snake's body kept writhing around as though it were still alive. My brother and I huddled in the corner of the chicken coop, scared but fascinated by the whole spectacle. The chickens that had not run out into the yard were squawking and half running, half flying around like crazy. Aunt Nell's old rooster sat up on the chicken roost, quite still, watching, his neck arched and his neck feathers bristling the way they did when he jumped on the hens.

Aunt Nell said, "He won't finish dying until sundown. You boys stay here and see that the rooster doesn't peck around the head. That's where the poison is. I'll be back in a minute. Keep your hands off him." She left, and my brother dared me to touch the snake. He was still squirming, but I touched him with my big toe.

Aunt Nell came back with a pair of tweezers, a shovel, and a bucket. She put her foot on the snake's still-moving body and retrieved her forked stick. She poked the end of it around in the smashed head, spotted what she was looking for, and said, "You boys come here and look." With her tweezers she picked out two small, almost transparent, needlelike teeth and said, "These are the fangs. The poison shoots out of these into your blood stream when he bites you." She shoveled the rest of the snake into the bucket and told us to bury it by a crepe myrtle tree behind the chicken coop.

My brother thought we should just dig a hole and throw him in, but I said that was all right for burying cats or dogs or possums but snakes were different and deserved special treatment, especially poisonous snakes, so we dug a slit trench about four feet long, six inches wide, and a foot deep. My brother dumped him in and I straightened him out with the shovel. The tail end was still moving, so I put a rock on it. We filled in the trench, except for the part over the tail. Over that section we put a piece of broken glass.

During supper, we watched the sun set through the kitchen window. As soon as it disappeared, we both said, "Can we be excused?" My mother nodded approval and said not to forget to do our chores. We said, "Yes'm," and dashed to the tool shed in the back yard. We lit a kerosene lamp and took it to the snake's grave and looked through the glass window. The rock was off the snake's tail, but the tail was no longer moving. We watched it for a long time, hoping to prove Aunt Nell's theory wrong, but the tail never moved again.

I was washing down the last cookie when Mattie came back with Eva, the middle Zacharias daughter. I told her I needed the curtain for a sail, but I didn't tell her about riding down it on a knife. She didn't have a curtain long enough, so she gave me a linen bed sheet instead. I picked it up and Mattie said, "Miss Eva, you know I done jes' ironed them sheets. That boy's goin' bring it back all rumpled." I made it to the door without waiting to hear Eva's answer.

The Dimons lived in a large gray house about a half mile from us, at the end of Cedar Avenue. The house had served as a Confederate hospital during the Civil War, and in one of the cellars were eight unmarked graves. Grandma Dimon used to hide her "blackberry acid" (blackberry wine) in the cellar. Jack's father also used the cellar to store surplus groceries. It was a treasure house for rats and seven-year-olds. The rats liked the sacks of grain and sugar, but our favorite was the peanut butter. There must have been five thousand jars of peanut butter in that cellar. We were too clever to take a full jar. Jack made a rule that no one could take more than a double-fingered scoop from any one jar. That way, we spread the theft around and avoided detection.

As soon as I got to Jack's house with the sheet, we attached it to the limb of an oak tree about ten feet from the ground. Jack got a butcher's knife from the kitchen and told me to climb up the tree and put the knife in my mouth. He said I could be the first to try it because I had furnished the sheet. I was also the smallest and would offer the least resistance. Jack and the other kids got some sticks and fashioned them into swords. While they were doing this, I carved a skull and crossbones in the limb of the oak tree.

When Jack shouted, "Ready," I put the handle of the knife in my mouth and looked around the way Douglas Fairbanks had done. Jack and the others started flailing away at each other with their weapons, screaming like banshees.

I looked down. They seemed a mile away, much scarier than in the movie. I felt sick to my stomach, and Jack yelled up, "Smile, you asshole! You're supposed to smile all the time!" I made a brave attempt and cut the corner of my mouth. When I tasted the blood, I felt even sicker. Jack screamed, "JUMP!" I took the knife out of my mouth and clutched it in my hand. The other pirates now took up the cry, "Jump, Jump, Jump." I just stood there, petrified, and they changed to a rhythmic chant— "Jump, or you're chickenshit! Jump, or you're chickenshit! Jump, or you're chickenshit!"

When I could take it no longer, I decided to try to do it exactly like Douglas Fairbanks, come what may. I grinned down at my tormentors through bloody lips, pointed the knife at the sheet, and took off. The sheet crashed down, enveloping me like a deflated parachute. The knife flew out of my hand and I landed on the ground, still smiling, with a broken arm, blood pouring from my mouth, and unable to breathe for about three agonizing minutes. The other kids went screaming to the house for help. All of them. I was left completely alone and so out of breath that I was unable to call anyone. The Dimons' black retainer, Mose, finally came along and carried me into the Dimon kitchen. Dr. Wooldridge and my mother were summoned, explanations were given (mostly lies), and Grandma Dimon brought out some ginger cookies and sent Mose to the "coolhouse" for a pail of fresh milk.

I was the hero of the day, coddled by the grownups and admired by my peers. As Dr. Wooldridge drove me off in his Model T Ford to set my arm, I heard Carl Hurst, one of my tormentors of a half hour before, say to Jack Dimon, "Gee, did you see that? He was smiling all the time. Just like Douglas Fairbanks."

2

A New Hero

I HAD never been to the movies with my mother before I broke my arm. In our gang, going with your mother was not considered the best way to go, although it was better than not going at all. So I jumped at the chance when my mother said, "Robert, you've been very good about your broken arm. I'm going to reward you with a trip to the movies."

I thought she would drop me at the Lyric while she did her shopping. I didn't realize that the main reason for the trip was that she wanted to see *Broken Blossoms* and that my father, who thought all movies were a waste of time, had refused to take her. My mother loved me and might have wanted to reward me for sticking a butcher's knife through the Zachariases' sheet and breaking my arm, but she also wanted an excuse to see *Broken Blossoms* again. She had already seen it three times. When she told my father she wanted to take me to the movies, he guessed she wanted to see *Broken Blossoms* again and they had an argument about it. He said it wasn't fit for children, and my mother said how did he know when he hadn't seen it. He said he didn't have to see it to know it was harmful, and in any event, he didn't want her to spend money on anything but necessities because his territory had been changed and he would be making less money until he built up the new territory.

My mother said, "What about your cigars? Are they necessities?" My father said, "I smoke C.H.S.'s—five cents apiece, the cheapest cigar you can buy. That's only thirty-five cents a week." My mother said, "That's exactly what it will cost for me and Robert to go to the movies," but my father didn't hear her. He had put on his straw hat and stomped out of the front door.

He worked for the Columbus Coca-Cola Bottling Company and went to work every morning in a Model T Ford furnished by the company. It had a Coca-Cola sign and bottle painted on each side and an Orange Squeeze sign on the back. We called it "the Orange Squeeze car." I watched my father through the window as he reached inside, pulled out the choke, and retarded the spark. Then he came to the front of the car, turned the crank over twice, and when the engine started, he scrambled into the seat, adjusted the throttle, released the hand brake, and drove off. The whole performance seemed to me like a Keystone Kops routine at the Lyric. I had seen aviators in leather helmets and goggles go through practically the same motions, but their machines finally took off into the sky. My father's Orange Squeeze car rattled off down a dusty road, and he was wearing a straw hat instead of a helmet and goggles.

My mother said, "I've saved some money from my millinery work, Robert, so get ready. I'm not going to break my promise to you." She gave me a clean shirt and told me to wash my feet, which meant she expected me to wear shoes and socks. We always had shoes but we only wore them on special occasions, and then reluctantly. If we argued we could sometimes wear her down, but I didn't want to chance it this time or she might cancel the whole operation. I put on the shoes, thinking that I would slip them off in the theater as soon as it was dark.

We took the streetcar to downtown Columbus. My heart sank as we passed the Lyric, where *Riders of the Purple Sage* was playing. The streetcar churned around the corner into Broad Street and we got off at the stop in front of the Springer Opera House. For a terrible moment I thought my mother had changed her mind and was going to take me to a "Legitimate Stage Show." I didn't know exactly what they were, but I knew that's what happened at the Springer Opera House and I knew I liked the movies better.

My mother went into the millinery shop next door and told me to wait for her outside. There was a wooden sign with gold letters on the wall of the Opera House which said, "Opened by Francis J. Springer Feb. 1871. Edwin Booth, Oscar Wilde, William Jennings Bryan, and John L. Sullivan have appeared on the Springer stage." I had heard of John L. Sullivan, but the other fighters were unknown to me.

When my mother came out, I asked her if we were going to see John L. Sullivan and she said no, that we were going to the Royal, where *Broken Blossoms* was playing. I said couldn't we go to the Lyric and she said no, that she wanted me to start learning to appreciate the finer things of life. As we crossed Broad Street and turned into Talbotton Road, I could see the lights flashing BROKEN B OSSOMS on the Royal. The L was not functioning, and for about five years after that I thought we had seen *Broken Bossoms* that afternoon.

Aside from the programs they showed, the Lyric and the Royal themselves were entirely different. The Lyric was plastered inside and out with lurid posters of serials, westerns, and comedies—past, present, and future. Everywhere you turned, you could see William S. Hart or Tom Mix pointing a gun at you or Charlie Chaplin or Mack Swain or Hank Mann getting hit in the face with a pie or Lloyd Hamilton adjusting his checkered cap.

The Royal was a masterpiece of theater construction, its seating capacity of over 2,700 making it one of the largest theaters in the South. Judging from the lobby, the specialty of the house seemed to be Lillian and Dorothy Gish. They were everywhere, smiling, crying; looking frightened, sad, happy, surprised. In addition to the Gishes there was an occasional still photograph of Theda Bara, Nita Naldi, or Pola Negri lying on a couch or a tigerskin. I asked my mother why those ladies were lying around with their eyes half closed. She said, "They're vamps." I started to question her further, but she said it with such conviction and with such finality that I accepted it as the definitive word. The next day, I bet Jack Dimon he didn't know what a vamp was and he said, "It's a bloodsucker," and I said, "Yeah, but with its eyes half closed."

The second difference between the Lyric and the Royal was the smell. The Royal smelled of perfume, cigars, sweat—grown-up smells. The Lyric smelled of unwashed clothes, stale candy, and pee—our smells. There were two toilets in the Lyric, but we were usually too engrossed in what was going on on the screen to use them. We only needed them when we got excited, and during those periods wild horses couldn't drag us out of our seats. During a fight or any kind of action on the screen, we would sit on the edge of our seats, bottom jaws hanging loose, and watch Jack Hoxie or somebody jumping over the Grand Canyon or gunning down Indians, or maybe it would be Harold Lloyd hanging on to the minute hand of a clock for dear life while the traffic of downtown Los Angeles crawled around far below. Our seven-year-old bladders were usually full to over-flowing. If the action on the screen was exciting enough, we would just watch the screen and pee, without opening our flies or looking down or anything—just pee. We didn't even know we were peeing until we got that nice warm feeling running down our legs as the pee trickled past our bare feet and onto the Lyric's wooden, uncarpeted floor. The soft-pine planks of the

Lyric were saturated and redolent with several generations of juvenile urine.

As soon as an action sequence finished and a subtitled dialogue or love scene appeared, we jumped up to act out what we had just seen, punching and fighting in the aisle and yelling at the top of our voices. Even when rolling on the floor, locked in deadly combat, we kept our eyes on the screen. There was an unwritten law that we had to stop fighting and scramble back into our seats as soon as someone in the film got hit or shot.

The Royal was completely different. As we walked through the Valley of the Vamps to the carpeted lobby, my mother said, "Robert, do you want to make the river run? If you do, go now." I said I didn't have to go, which was true. We never had to pee until the movie started.

We took our seats, and as the lights went down, a man and a pipe organ came up out of the floor in front of the screen. He was banging away at the keys and kicking his feet and I thought his name was Wurlitzer because that's what it said on the organ. It was the same man who played the organ at the First Baptist Church every Sunday morning. I eased my shoes off and looked up to see if my mother had noticed.

After the ads for Kirvens Department Store, Orange Squeeze, and the Chatahoochee River Excursion Boat had been flashed on the screen, they had a coming-attractions trailer for *Intolerance*. In one of the shots, a man sat in a wooden chair and yelled at thousands of people through a large megaphone. I asked my mother who he was, and she said, "He's the director, D. W. Griffith." I asked what he did, and she said, "He's in charge of everything. He tells everybody what to do and how to do it."

Mr. Wurlitzer's music rose to a crescendo as the coming attractions ended and *Broken Blossoms* started. My mother's eyes began to fill as soon as Lillian Gish's name appeared.

"Does he tell Douglas Fairbanks what to do?" I whispered.

My mother said, "Who, son?" Her watery eyes were glued to the screen. Nothing sad had happened yet, but she knew what was coming up and she wasn't going to be caught unprepared.

"The director."

"What about him?" she said as she felt for her handkerchief in her purse.

"Did he tell Douglas Fairbanks how to slide down the sail in *The Black Pirate*?"

My mother said, "Yes, Robert. Now watch the picture."

I watched for a while, but my mind wandered over to the Lyric. "Does the director tell Tom Mix and Charlie Chaplin and Hoot Gibson what to do?"

By now, the famous emotional scene in the closet was on and my mother was really enjoying herself. The tears were flowing freely. She said, "Yes, the director tells everyone what to do. Now I don't want to hear another word from you. You're disturbing the other people." I looked around. Most of the other people were women. They were all crying. They were disturbed, but not because of me.

I had never heard the word "director" before. I thought the actors just got up there and did it, whether it was throwing pies or sliding down sails. Now my mother had said someone else told them what to do and that his name was D. W. Griffith. From then on, I imagined Griffith, with his big megaphone, behind every scene. I believed that this one man directed every movie and told every actor what to do and how to do it. I had a new hero. I no longer wanted to be Douglas Fairbanks. I wanted to be D. W. Griffith.

3

Shall We Gather
at the River?

NINETEEN-twenty-six was a vintage year—the heart of the Roaring Twenties. The songs I remember from our Victor records were "All Alone," "Pretty Baby," "Always," "Remember," "What Can I Say After I Say I'm Sorry?," "In a Little Spanish Town," and "California, Here I Come." Calvin Coolidge was trying on Indian headdresses. It was the year of the first Dempsey-Tunney fight.

It was also the year the Coca-Cola Company transferred my father from Columbus, Georgia, to Hollywood, California. Well, not really Hollywood at the beginning. Our first stop was near Westlake Park (now MacArthur Park), between Los Angeles and Hollywood. My father was on the road most of the time, so my mother, my two sisters, my brother, and I settled into one large room in a boardinghouse just off Alvarado Street. My mother fixed it up with partitions between the girls and the boys and another partition between the children and grownups. The bathroom was at the end of the hall, and the kitchen, which we shared with the other boarders, was directly across from our room. I remember hearing my father tell my older brother, "You're the man of the family while I'm away, so I expect you to look out after your mother and your sisters and brother. We'll only have to live this way until we find a house in Hollywood."

My brother then told me not to worry, that we would soon move away from the Westlake district. I, in turn, told my sister Beverly, seven, the same story, and she told it to Helen, three. My mother overheard Beverly apologizing for our quarters to Helen in baby talk, "Don't ums worwie. We're all going to get out of this horrible room and move to a beautiful castle in Hollywood." My mother asked Beverly where she got that information. Beverly said, "From Robert." I told her Gordon had told me but that Dad had told him.

That night, coming down the hall from the bathroom, I heard my mother and father having a heated argument in the kitchen. I stopped and listened. My mother said, "Why are you trying to make the children ashamed of where they live?" My father said, "Six people shouldn't have to live in one room."

My mother said, "It's not a crime to be poor, but it's a crime to let children think they are poor, especially if they are warm and have enough to eat." My father finally agreed and put his arm around my mother and she burst into tears.

I tiptoed back to the bathroom, sat on the toilet without taking my pants down, and thought about being poor. I wondered how long we had been poor and how long it would last and how I would know when it was over. There were two mirrors in the bathroom, one across from me in back of the bathtub, and another on the medicine-cabinet door over the sink. I saw myself sitting there and stuck out my tongue. I then put my fingers in the sides of my mouth, pulled my cheeks apart, and stuck out my tongue again, this time pointing it straight forward instead of flapping it down over my lower lip. I decided to see if I could stretch it to touch my nose. I turned my head for a better view and caught a glimpse of the back of my head reflected from the other mirror. It was the first time I had ever seen the back of my head, so I lost interest in trying to touch my nose with my tongue and I concentrated on studying this fascinating new view of myself. As I put my fingers up like horns, my mother walked in without knocking and crossed to the sink to wash the tears from her face. She didn't see me until she looked in the mirror over the sink. She said, "What are you doing, Robert?"

I said, "I'm trying to grunt."

She wiped her face, and as she left she said, "I think you'll have better luck if you take your pants down."

For the next week, both parents kept telling us how wonderful it was living in the same room, stumbling over each other's clothes, waiting for the bathroom, etc. The fact was, we would have thought it was wonderful whether they told us so or not. That three months was the closest our family has ever been, before or since.

The house was owned by an old lady named Mrs. True. She was a giant, six feet three inches, and she and her invalid husband were dedicated followers of Aimee Semple McPherson, the evangelist. Mrs. True went to Aimee's Angelus Temple at least three times a week. On Sundays she wheeled poor old Mr. True down the twenty-four cement stairs in front of the house and over to Alvarado Street, where she hustled him and the wheelchair onto the No. 7 yellow streetcar. Twenty minutes later they were in the Angelus Temple on Glendale Boulevard, affectionately known in the press as "Aimee's Shack."

One Sunday, as I was wiping our dishes in the community kitchen, Mrs. True sneaked up behind me and asked me if I was a Christian. I was so startled I dropped the two saucers and three cups that I was trying to dry at the same time. While I was on the floor cleaning up the mess, Mrs. True followed me around and told me what it was like to be a true believer. She ended her sermon with the same question that had frightened me out of my wits five minutes before: "I ask you again, Robert —ARE YOU A CHRISTIAN?"

I looked up at the towering figure. Her finger was pointing at me accusingly. A "yes" or "no" answer was obviously called for, but I couldn't oblige because I honestly didn't know whether I was or not. Her old gray witch's eyes widened and she said, "ARE YOU?"

I told her I had won a Bible for learning the Lord's Prayer at the First Baptist Sunday School in Columbus and so I guessed I was. Once that was established, she offered to take me to church with her. She also offered to pay me ten cents to help her with Mr. True's wheelchair. I said I would like to help her with the wheelchair but that she didn't have to pay me. As I said this I was mentally saving up the dimes to buy some balsa wood to make a model airplane. Mrs. True said she insisted on paying me and I said OK and she said to go get my Baptist Bible and meet her on the front porch at eleven o'clock.

I was standing on the front porch, hair brushed, face washed, and Bible in hand, as Mrs. True wheeled Mr. True out. My mother had tied my tie so tight that I could hardly breathe. Mr. True was shaking like a chinaberry tree, but he seemed happier than usual. His eyes were looking at things instead of just rolling around in their sockets. He put his shaking hand on my head and tried to say something, but no words came out. The hand beat a tattoo on my head like a woodpecker drilling on a telephone pole. Mrs. True reached over, took his hand, and put it in his lap. It was still shaking. While she prepared him for the trip down the twenty-four cement stairs, I loosened my tie. She took my Bible and put it in her purse and said, "Let's go."

As we maneuvered the wheelchair down the steps, Mrs. True explained that we would take the streetcar to the Angelus Temple because it was uphill most of the way, but we would walk home. "No need to spend money if you don't have to, is there, Robert?" I said no, I guessed not, and I began to worry about my ten cents. She must have read my mind, because she said, "I'm going to let you put your ten cents in the offering plate at the church."

After all the jokes I had heard my father make about "Aimee's Shack," I was surprised to see a big dome-shaped building with marquee lettering like a movie theater. The flashing lights informed us that AIMEE LOVES GOD. On the top of the building there was a gold cross that lit up at night, and two giant radio towers with the letters KFSG in lights on each of them. At the main entrance there were posters and ads for the movie *The Ten Commandments*. On one poster was a picture of a bearded Moses with his tablet of commandments in one hand and a long stick in the other. He was pointing the stick at the ocean, which had parted to let thousands of Israelites walk across the ocean's floor. I had seen the same poster outside the First Baptist Church in Columbus when the movie was shown to our Sunday-school class. I knew it was Moses parting the sea, but the name above his head on the poster, both in Columbus and outside Aimee's Temple, was Cecil B. DeMille. I studied the poster carefully to see if I could find D. W. Griffith and his megaphone telling them all what to do, but he wasn't to be seen.

Hundreds of people were streaming into the building for the twelve o'clock service, and there was a festive feeling about the place, an anticipation. It reminded me of the feeling outside the stadium in Columbus at the Georgia-Auburn football game. Everybody seemed to know that somebody was going to win and somebody was going to lose, and nobody knew who was going to do what but everybody knew it was going to be exciting.

As I wheeled Mr. True along, I saw that most of the people were old and a lot of them were cripples. Mrs. True explained that this was "Healing Day" and that everyone expected to leave the church "healthy, wealthy, and wise." She told me about one old woman who had thrown her crutches away and danced in the aisle after Aimee had blessed her on the previous Healing Day. I looked at Mr. True and pictured him dancing up the aisle, his jaw flapping and his eyes floating around in his skull like peeled grapes in boiling water. I hoped Aimee's magic would work on him so that he could dance down Alvarado Street and I could ride the wheelchair home, downhill all the way.

Inside, an usher greeted the Trues like old friends and said, "Let's roll the Colonel right down in front to his regular place." It was the first time I had heard that Mr. True was a colonel. The usher took over the wheelchair and navigated it down to the front of the church, where a wheelchair parking area was marked off with garlands of flowers. Mrs. True and I sat right in back of him, in the front row. The parking area soon filled up with about fifty wheelchairs, and around the outside of the area a group of walking wounded settled into specially made chairs with racks for crutches and canes. Finally, when the giant auditorium was almost full, a trumpet blasted out from somewhere, and uniformed ushers wheeled about ten or fifteen stretcher cases down the aisles and into a favored position near the stage. A nurse in white followed and stood beside each stretcher.

The lights dimmed and an unseen chorus of several hundred voices started singing "Shall We Gather at the River?" I knew the song well. It was a standard at our church in Columbus. I had also heard it sung by blacks at their all-day baptisms and fish fries on the Upatoie Creek, near where we lived. (The white kids used to sneak in and watch from the bushes.) It was one of the few hymns I really liked. I had been singing it and hearing it sung all my life, but I had never heard it sung like this.

Perhaps it was the blast of sudden beautiful sound when I was thinking about cripples and pain and stretchers. Maybe it was because it took me back to the banks of the Upatoie and the blacks singing and eating while a white-robed black preacher stood waist-deep in the muddy creek baptizing small black children. As everybody sang "Shall We Gather at the River?" the preacher took the child from the parent and asked if Woodrow Wilson Tyler Franklin (aged six months) was ready to receive God. He timed his question so that the parents said, "Yes, Lord!" in rhythm just after the words "The beautiful beautiful ri-iv-ver." Then he held his hand above the face of the child and waited until the singers came to "that flows by the throne o-of God." When he heard the cue, he clamped his hand over the infant's nose and mouth, dunked him on the downbeat, and raised him on the upbeat as the singers started the second chorus in the next higher key: "Yes! We'll gather at the river, the beautiful, beautiful ri-iv-ver." As the shiny, kicking, squalling bundle was returned to the parent, some of the singers shouted, "Praise the Lord," or "I hear you calling, Lord," or "Yes, Lord!

Tell me, Lord!" The preacher declared Woodrow Wilson Tyler Franklin saved and asked if anyone else was ready to receive God, God could save everybody.

I looked at poor old Mr. True's head lolling in front of me and I wondered if God could save *him*. The choral voices reached a climax and finished with "that flows by the throne o-of God!" The mighty organ held a long sustaining note as all the lights went out and the vast auditorium was plunged into total darkness, except for some little luminous star-specks high up on the ceiling and one magenta spotlight, which was aimed at a corner of the stage. I looked up at Mrs. True's profile silhouetted against the star-specks. It reminded me of a Boy Scout ax. As the organ note diminished so that only dogs could hear it, I looked down at my feet and saw that one of my shoe-laces was untied.

Suddenly, the organ crashed out with a clap of thunder and all kinds of kaleidoscopic lights started flashing on and off. The unseen chorus burst forth with "Hallelujah," and from some-where there appeared on the stage the most beautiful woman in the world. She just appeared—BANG!—like some white-robed genie out of a magenta bottle, standing in front of the round radio mike with the letters KFSG on it. The flashing lights stopped and there she was, prettier than my mother, prettier than Lillian Gish, prettier than anybody I'd ever seen, just stand-ing there, bathed in colored light, her two arms raised like a cheerleader after a touchdown.

The chorus belted out another four or five *Hallelujah*s and then stopped cold. The organ stopped too, and there was the greatest silence I've ever heard, finally broken by Mrs. True mut-tering "Praise the Lord" through her transfixed, slack jaw. Mr. True applauded twice, the hollow sound cutting through the silence like two well-spaced rifle shots. Mrs. True touched him on the back of the head with her program. He stopped his hands before the third clap and docilely dropped his chin to his chest.

Aimee said, "Let us pray," and everyone in the auditorium closed his eyes except Mr. True and me. I lowered my head as Aimee asked God to bless us and make us "healthy, wealthy, and wise," but I kept my eyes on Mr. True. As Aimee got to the part about healing the sick and feeding the poor and anointing the wounded, Mr. True turned his head and winked at me. There was no doubt about it, it was a genuine, controlled wink, followed by a smile. I thought maybe he wasn't as ga-ga as he seemed. I winked and smiled back and Mrs. True almost caved in the left side of my chest with her elbow. Aimee said "Amen," and everybody echoed her, with a few adding "Praise be to Jesus," "Help us, Lord," and stuff like that. Then the organist started to play a song called "Jesus Loves a Cheerful Giver," and Aimee said we would have the "first offering."

The "first offering" was quite a ritual at the Angelus Temple. The ushers came down the aisles with ropes over their shoulders like lassos. As one of them reached our aisle, Mr. True wheeled his chair around and started to applaud again. The usher took the rope off his shoulder and I thought for a minute he was going to tie Mr. True up or hang him or something. Instead, he handed the rope to the man sitting on the aisle and asked him to pass it along. As it was handed to me, I noticed a large safety pin attached every two feet. When the end of the rope reached the next aisle, there was a safety pin in front of each person, and every fifth safety pin was gold. At first the gold pin stopped in front of me, but the usher spotted this, yanked the rope, and shifted the gold pin back to Mrs. True. Aimee said that God wanted us to pin our "offering" on the "Holy Rope" and that He expected us to give generously because it was all going to help her heal the poor unfortunates in front. When she said this, she pointed to the wheelchair parking area, and Mr. True started clapping his hands to the organ music.

When I looked around and saw everyone pinning paper money to the rope, I thought my ten cents were safe. You can't pin a coin on a rope, not even a Holy Rope. As I started to put the coin in my pocket, Mrs. True reached over and took it away from me. "I'll save it for you, Robert, and when you've earned ten dimes, you can pin a dollar on the Holy Rope." I thanked her and wished I were big enough to punch her in the nose. Mr. True stopped applauding, steadied his rolling eyes, and watched my dime go back in his wife's purse.

While the collection was going on, Aimee preached about money. She picked out some places in the Bible and read us her interpretation of what the Good Book really meant. It turned out that it meant to keep pinning money on the Holy Rope. She said you were one of God's chosen children if the gold safety pin stopped in front of you and that the gold pins were for five-dollar bills only, "no more, no less! The Good Lord says you can put as much or as little as you like on the other pins, but the golden pins are reserved for the 'golden fives.'" When she said that, Mr. True threw me another wink. I glanced up at Mrs. True and saw that she was busy pinning her five bucks on the Holy Rope, so I chanced a slight wink back at Mr. True. I thought it would pass as an eyelash flutter or a tic, but Mrs. True knew exactly what it was and gave me the old elbow again without taking her eyes off the Holy Rope. As I tried to recover my breath, she folded her five-dollar bill and jabbed the gold safety pin through Abraham Lincoln's left eye. I pretended it was Mrs. True's eye.

The unseen chorus started to sing "Bringing in the Sheaves" and the ushers started to roll up the Holy Ropes, now fluttering with bills of all denominations. In addition to the "golden fives," I caught glimpses of several tens and twenties passing in front of me and noticed that there were only a few one-dollar bills. I was so busy watching the money that I didn't see Aimee disappear. When I looked up, the magenta spotlight was gone, Aimee was gone, and the chorus suddenly appeared, stacked up all around the stage and bathed in golden-white light. They had been there all the time, singing in the dark until now. The women were in white robes like Aimee's and the men wore tuxedos. As they belted out, "We will come re-joic-ing, bringing in the sheaves," the ushers hung the money-laden Holy Ropes around their shoulders and headed up the aisles looking like plain old ushers with wings of money. I wondered who was going to do the counting and who was going to watch the counters.

After that the chorus sang a lot of songs. From time to time there would be an interruption, like a radio commercial, while someone made a pitch for the Building Fund and the Missionary Fund and the Charity Fund, and so on. A man named Hutton sang "Nearer My God to Thee" in a deep voice, and finally Aimee came back, this time with a black satin cape over her flowing white dress and her hair combed down straight, businesslike. With the magenta spotlight gone she wasn't as pretty, but she still looked pretty good.

She said, "Let us pray" again. In the prayer she asked God to take all these unfortunate cripples under His wing or something like that and then she started the Twenty-third Psalm. I'd memorized the old Twenty-third years ago and parroted it every time I went to Sunday school, but the first line never made any sense to me—"The Lord is my shepherd; I shall not want" always meant to me that I wouldn't want the Lord to be my shepherd, especially if He "maketh me to lie down in green pastures." As Aimee droned on, I conjured up a picture of Mrs. True being made to lie down in a pasture full of cow cakes. I daydreamed that I came along and anointed her with a bucket of castor oil.

When the prayer was finished, the spotlight followed Aimee as she got down to the business of healing the sick. She went to two of the stretcher cases and asked them their names. They turned out to be an old couple from Whittier, man and wife, who had been bedridden for years but had only recently discovered God through Aimee's Four Square Gospel, and this was their wedding anniversary. All this information poured out despite the fact that Aimee had only asked their names. She then asked them if they would like to walk, and they both confessed that they would. She asked them if they would like to dance, and they giggled and said they would like to do that too. She asked them if they believed in Jesus and the Holy Spirit, and they admitted they did. Aimee then asked us all to pray for Mr. and Mrs. Cameron from Whittier, and while we were doing this the organist played "Jesus Loves Me, This I Know, For the Bible Tells Me So." The chorus picked it up, and when they got to "He will watch and o'er me keep," Aimee told the Camerons to get out of bed and walk. The nurses pulled the covers back and the Camerons from Whittier got out of bed— fully dressed, shoes and all, but that didn't seem to bother anyone. Aimee took Mrs. Cameron's hand and led her over to Mr. Cameron. She then motioned to the organist, and he started to play the "Wedding March." The Camerons started to dance, and the auditorium exploded in applause and cries of "Praise the Lord," "Hallelujah!," "Glory to God," etc.

Aimee went through the forest of crutches and canes like a white angel. Not everyone got the full Cameron-from-Whittier treatment but certain selected ones did, and after they were "cured," they tossed their crutches and canes on a pile marked NEVER AGAIN and sat together on a bench marked CHILDREN OF GOD.

After a while, Aimee came over to the wheelchair parking area and said the Lord would only have time to help a few more of His children. She headed for an old lady on the other side of Mr. True, but as she approached, Mr. True spun his wheelchair into her path and looked up at her. His head was rolling around, but his eyes looked directly into hers, very steady. Aimee saw there was no escape. She was obviously an old hand at this kind of thing, so she raised both arms to the heavens (i.e., to the star-speckled Angelus Temple ceiling) and asked God to help Colonel True. At first I was surprised that she knew his name. Then I thought that if Mrs. True decorated the Holy Rope every time they came to church, they must be considered pretty good customers and that the least Aimee could do was remember their names.

I didn't hear God answer Aimee's request, but she must have gotten a message from somewhere, because she really went to work for poor old Mr. True. She told God that it had been almost six years since Colonel True had arrived in the beautiful Golden State of California—God's country—from Kentucky, with his lovely wife, and that they had appealed to Him several times before on this matter (Mr. True held up four arthritic fingers), and that He in His infinite wisdom had not seen fit to come through with a cure so far. She explained that nobody was angry or anything like that and she knew that He had a lot on His mind, but she also knew that He sometimes worked in mysterious ways and she appreciated how He had handled the Camerons-from-Whittier case. But she said that Colonel True had suffered for a long time and his lovely wife had stood by him and comforted him (I thought, "She hit him on the head with her program and wouldn't let me wink at him"). Aimee went on about how Colonel True was one of God's Christian Soldiers (the organist segued into "Onward, Christian Soldiers") and that he was a pillar of the Angelus Temple and that she hoped God would see fit to let him rise up out of his wheelchair ("Arise Ye Children of God"—full chorus and organ) and join Mr. and Mrs. Cameron from Whittier and the others that He, in all His wisdom, had so generously cured.

I sneaked a glance up at Mrs. True. The handle of the Boy Scout ax had sunk back into her throat and she was staring at Aimee with such intensity that I thought maybe she was dead.

Aimee raised her arms to the ceiling and yelled, "Help him, Lord! Help him! He's one of Your children!" The organist started kicking his feet and banging the keys the same way Mr. Wurlitzer had done at the Royal movie house in Columbus. This produced an ominous rumble of organ thunder followed by a loud, explosive clap that actually shook the walls of the Angelus Temple. At the same time, the kaleidoscopic lights started flashing on and off again and the chorus whipped up another batch of *Hallelujahs*. When they had delivered four, Aimee dropped her arms and everything stopped, just as it had done for her first entrance. Everybody had gone all out: the organist, the chorus, the congregation, Aimee herself. It was a hell of a show, much bigger even than the one for the Camerons from Whittier. And now it was deathly quiet, except for Mrs. True's heavy breathing and Mr. True's hand beating its tattoo against the side of the wheelchair.

I looked up at Aimee and discovered that she wasn't prettier than my mother after all. She wasn't even prettier than Lillian Gish. Beads of sweat had popped out on her upper lip, and the mascara was completely out of control on the left side of her face. I could see where her pinkish-yellow make-up stopped and her white neck began. She was so close I could have reached out and touched her, which, indeed, I considered doing and would have done if I thought I could have survived another elbow from Mrs. True.

Aimee pointed to Mr. True and said, "ARISE!" The organ hit a big note, the chorus dredged up a few more *Hallelujahs*, the lights flashed. Mr. True met Aimee, eyeball to eyeball, for a moment, then he turned his head to me and gave me another all-out, "we're in this together" wink.

Aimee screamed, "DO YOU BELIEVE?! IF YOU DO, ARISE!"

Mr. True turned back to Aimee, looked hard at her for a moment, and then let his eyes go completely out of control. They rolled around like anchorless oysters. His chin dropped to his chest and he fell asleep. I knew he was asleep because he had stopped shaking.

4

Breakfast with Champions

W HILE we lived in the Trues' house, I sold the Los Angeles *Evening Express* on the northwest corner of Alvarado Street and Sixth. Julio Martinez had the southeast corner. We were good friends, except I thought Jack Dempsey was the greatest fighter in the world and Julio thought he was the second greatest, just after Fidel La Barba, the flyweight champion.

Our papers were delivered to us by a man named Jerry Langdon, who claimed he was related to Harry Langdon, the comedian. He didn't look anything like Harry Langdon and he didn't actually deliver our papers, he threw them at us. As his truck passed our corner, he would fling out a bundle of one hundred papers for each of us. When I first got the corner, he managed to hit me with them quite regularly, but Julio soon taught me to crouch between the mailbox and the traffic signal when Jerry swept by in his pickup truck. That way we avoided the bombing and were in a good position to yell obscenities at Jerry as he sped away to his next corner.

The papers sold for three cents and we got them for two cents. If there was an important headline—USC BEATS NOTRE DAME, or AIMEE CAUGHT IN LOVE NEST, or MOTHER CHARGES MURDER OF MISSING AIMEE MCPHERSON—we would have no trouble selling out early and could go to hunt duck eggs around Westlake Park before dinner. If the headline was unimportant —PRESIDENT COOLIDGE TO FIGHT FAMINE, or LEAGUE OF NA-TIONS VETOES PEACE PLAN—we would have trouble selling our hundred papers. When Jerry Langdon "gave" me the corner (for one dollar), he said, "I don't take no papers back, savvy? You either sell 'em or you eat 'em. If you don't sell 'em on the corner by six o'clock, take 'em to the residential streets and sell 'em as 'extras.' If you can't sell 'em there, take 'em home to your mother. She can boil 'em up for you and you can eat 'em. I don't care what you do with 'em—but I don't take no papers back. You take a hundert papers, you gimme two bucks, savvy?" He said "savvy" a lot. For a while, I thought he thought it was my

25

name. After I learned some Spanish from Julio, I realized it was American for ¿Sabe usted? ("Understand?").

A genuine "extra" was a special edition published for special crises: wars, ax murders, earthquakes, etc. On slow days, Julio and I would take our leftovers and hawk them through the quiet residential streets. We would find some scandalous story on the inside of the paper and start yelling "HEY, EXTRA, GET YOUR EXTRA PAPER—ALL ABOUT AIMEE!" (anything about Aimee Semple McPherson was a sure sale), or "READ ABOUT THE NUDE HOUSEWIFE MURDER!" (this usually brought the women in curlers out of their kitchens). Jerry taught us to fold the papers so that the customer couldn't see the real headline until after he had bought the paper.

One day, when we were cringing between the mailbox and the traffic light, Jerry stopped his truck and brought the bundles of papers to us instead of trying to hit us with them. Julio was apprehensive. Jerry was always telling us that other kids wanted to buy the corners, so from time to time he would try to squeeze a little tribute from us. Julio didn't trust Jerry for a minute and thought that's what we were in for this time. Instead, Jerry said, "How would you guys like to have breakfast with Jack Dempsey, the heavyweight champion of the world?"

Julio had known Jerry longer than I had and enjoyed a more intimate relationship. He said, "How would you like to kiss my ass?"

Jerry said, "No, thanks. It looks too much like your face." Then, having dispensed with the formalities, he said, "The mayor's running for re-election and he's giving his annual 'Breakfast with Champions' at the Breakfast Club tomorrow. He's having some spastic kids from the county hospital and they want some newsboys to fill up the tables. The mayor says Jack Dempsey and some other champions'll be there. If you wanna come, be on your corner at five in the morning. If you don't, you're gonna miss a free breakfast. The Express is picking up the tab."

Julio said, "Will Fidel La Barba be there?"

Jerry said, "It's called 'Breakfast with Champions,' not 'Breakfast with Bums.' "

Julio said, "Up yours, Jerry."

After Jerry left, I asked Julio if he was going to the breakfast. He said, "I dunno, probably not. Jerry's full of crap. Dempsey won't be there. Are you going?"

I said, "I dunno, probably not. Who wants to get up at five o'clock not to see Jack Dempsey?"

The next day, when I got to the corner at four-thirty, Julio was already there. My mother made me wear my tie and my best suit because I told her "the Company" (the *Evening Express*) had invited me to breakfast with some spastics. I didn't tell her anything about Jack Dempsey because she hardly knew who he was. My father was out of town and wouldn't be home until that night.

At six-thirty Jerry pulled up with his pickup truck full of spastics and newsboys. We started to climb in and he told us to take it easy, that we were to wait for the next pickup. As he drove off, the other kids yelled derisively and gave us the finger. Julio said, "I don't trust that sonofabitch," and I said I didn't either. Then Julio said, "We should kick the shit out of him," and I said he was too big.

The early-morning traffic was building up and the corner of Sixth and Alvarado seemed like a dumb place to spend Saturday. Julio and I debated about whether we should wait for the unlikely "next pickup" promised by Jerry or go duck-egg hunting at the lake. We did pretty well with this sometimes. There were plenty of ducks and a lot of nests around the lake. When I first brought some eggs home and told my mother where I had gotten them, she told me not to do it again. She then made a great omelet in the Trues' kitchen.

After that, Julio and I always took the eggs to his house. His mother never asked where they came from and the truth was that her omelets were even better than my mother's. She used peppers and tomatoes and Tabasco sauce and she usually gave us a Coke. My mother gave us milk, which I actually liked better but I never told Julio that.

We once caught a duck and brought it to Julio's and asked his mother to cook it for us. She didn't speak much English, but I knew enough Spanish to understand when she said if we didn't take it back to the lake pronto, she would call the police. We took it to the Trues' house instead and kept it as a pet. It was brownish-gray and followed my three-year-old sister, Helen, around the back yard as long as we lived there. She fed it and called it Duck, which seemed an appropriate, if unimaginative, name for a female mallard.

Just when we had decided to leave the corner for the lake, a black Cadillac limousine pulled up and a man with glasses got out. He looked like an owl. He said, "Are you the *Evening Express* kids?" We said we were and he said, "OK, get in." We got in the front seat with the driver. The man with the glasses got in the back seat, where another man was sitting, and said, "OK, let's go. The Breakfast Club out on Riverside Drive." The driver shifted into first and we eased into the northbound traffic. Julio and I sat like two scared rabbits, staring ahead, not daring to look back. It was the fanciest car I had ever been in.

I heard the man with the glasses say, "Jack, these are the two kids from the *Evening Express* that we want you to take up to the house after breakfast. We'll get our pictures of you showing them around the joint, introducing them to Estelle and stuff like that. I know you're meeting Kearns at the Brown Derby at twelve-thirty, so there should be plenty of time. Don't worry about the way they look. We'll fix 'em up before we take the pictures."

The other man said, "They look fine to me." I thought about the back of my head that I had seen in Mrs. True's bathroom because that was the view they had from the back seat.

Nobody said a word after that until we got to the Breakfast Club. The man with the glasses had mentioned Estelle. Jack Dempsey was married to Estelle Taylor, the actress, so I was almost certain we were riding down Riverside Drive with Jack Dempsey, the heavyweight champion of the world. I glanced over at Julio. He was still staring straight ahead. I think he knew too.

A bunch of photographers were waiting for us outside the Breakfast Club. When the Cadillac stopped, the man with the glasses jumped out and told the photographers to get ready to snap shots of the heavyweight champion of the world shaking hands with the winners of the Annual Los Angeles *Evening Express* Newsboys' Contest for the Benefit of Spastic Children. Julio said, "Jerry never told me about any contest. Did he tell you?" I said, "No," and was looking around for the winners when the man with the glasses opened the car door and said, "Come on, kids."

As we got out, he grabbed Julio's hand and said, "Congratulations!" Knowing Julio, I was afraid he was going to say "Up your ass" or something, as he would have done to Jerry, but the man with the glasses didn't give him a chance to say anything. He turned to the photographers and said, "Here they are, boys. The winner and the runner-up of the Annual Los Angeles *Eve-*

ning Express Newsboys' Contest for the Benefit of Spastic Children."

The photographers moved in. Owl Eyes said, "Wait a minute, boys—the Mexican kid's OK, but let's get the tie off the other one and mess him up a bit." The man in the back seat got out and the photographers forgot us and started to take pictures of him. They said, "Hi, Jack," and "You're looking great, Champ," and "Show us the one that got Firpo."

Jack Dempsey made his right hand into a fist, scowled, and pretended to punch the photographer on the chin. Another photographer said, "Which one did you get Willard with?" Dempsey held up his left hand and turned it around so that it could be photographed from all angles. We had indeed been riding down Riverside Drive with Jack Dempsey, the Manassa Mauler, himself, the man who had beaten Jess Willard, Carpentier, and Firpo, the man who soaked his hands in brine for hours before each fight to toughen them.

As I was looking at his hands for salt marks, Owl Eyes grabbed my tie and started to jerk it off my neck. Jack Dempsey asked him what he was doing and he said he was making me look like a newsboy. Dempsey said, "Why can't a newsboy wear a tie?" Owl Eyes said, well, he guessed the runner-up could, and Jack Dempsey put my tie back in place with his brine-soaked hands. I kept that tie pressed in a book called *Tom Swift and His Electric Runabout* for more than ten years. I never threw it away, it just disappeared the way things do.

A lot of pictures were taken, and then Owl Eyes led us into the Breakfast Club. Dempsey put his left hand (Willard) around my shoulder and his right (Firpo) around Julio's and took us with him as he made his way down the main aisle toward the mayor's "Table of Champions." The American Legion Band played "California, Here I Come," which seemed kind of dumb to me because we were already in California. There was a lot of red, white, and blue bunting hanging on the walls, and above the mayor's table there was a big board suspended from the ceiling. On it were stuck a sign, in gold letters, reading BREAKFAST WITH CHAMPIONS and the insignias of several civic organizations—the Lions Club, the Rotary Club, Pathfinders, and Kiwanis are the ones I remember.

There were a lot of other tables surrounded by businessmen wearing suits, and each table had its quota of spastics and newsboys. As we passed Jerry's table, Julio said, "Good morning, Mr.

Langdon," and Jack Dempsey said, "Who was that?" Julio said, "That was Harry Langdon's father."

The mayor had rounded up every champion and near champion in the Los Angeles area, and they were all at our table. They were mostly boxers—Jackie Fields, Jim Jeffries, Fidel La Barba (Julio kicked me under the table when he was introduced), Bud Taylor, Mushy Callahan, Johnny Indrisano, etc. They also had Bill Graber (the pole vaulter from USC), Charlie Paddock (the world's fastest human), Johnny Weissmuller, Jim Thorpe, Brick Muller, and a lot of other guys they didn't introduce. The only thing I remember about the mayor was that he talked too long, but I remember vividly every other face at that table, every cauliflower ear, every mashed nose.

A spastic kid was rolled in between each champion, but Julio and I were the only newsboys at the Table of Champions. After a breakfast of orange juice, sausages, and scrambled eggs, the mayor informed his "friends, champions, and fellow Angelenos" that Julio Martinez had won the Annual Los Angeles *Evening Express* Newsboys' Contest for the Benefit of Spastic Children and that Robert Parrish was the runner-up. He said we were both from the Alvarado and Sixth corner and that the prize was a trip to Jack Dempsey's beautiful home in Los Feliz Heights after breakfast. He never told us how we won the contest, and I wasn't particularly bowled over with the prize. It wasn't as though we'd won a trip to a summer camp at Catalina Island or something. Jack Dempsey's house was only about half a mile from where we were sitting.

As the speeches started and the downtown Los Angeles businessmen wearing suits started to tell us how lucky we were to have such a great mayor and how he ought to be re-elected, I looked over at Julio, who looked like an eleven-year-old Mexican who would rather be out duck-egg hunting in Westlake Park than being bored to death. As it turned out, the morning wasn't a total loss for him. He got Fidel La Barba's autograph and two tickets for La Barba's next fight at the Olympic Auditorium. We went together, and I had to admit that La Barba looked pretty good in the fourth round knocking out some guy whose name I can't remember. I said La Barba must have soaked his hands in brine. Julio said, "Bullshit. He soaks 'em in tequila and Tabasco sauce."

After the speeches, the mayor had his picture taken with each champion and a few spastics and Julio, the prize-winning newsboy. Then Julio and I got up with Dempsey and walked back down the aisle as the American Legion Band played "Happy Days Are Here Again." When we passed Jerry's table, Julio held up the two tickets to the La Barba fight and said, "Good-by, Mr. Langdon." Jack Dempsey said, "Who was that?" and Julio said, "That was Harry Langdon."

The limousine took us to Jack Dempsey's house, where we met Estelle Taylor. She had dark hair and dark eyes and gave us each a Coca-Cola. After we drank them she said, "You young people like Coca-Cola, don't you?" I said, "Yes, ma'am," and Julio said, "I like Orange Crush better." She got him an Orange Crush but didn't get me another Coca-Cola. I didn't care because I didn't really like Coca-Cola *or* Orange Crush.

The photographers snapped pictures of all this, then one of them turned to Owl Eyes and said, "We got plenty, Jimmy." Owl Eyes said, "OK. Let's get going. I want to make the first edition."

On the ride back, we sat in the back seat with Dempsey. Owl Eyes sat in the front seat. As we drove down Vermont Avenue, Owl Eyes said, "Let's let the kids out here, otherwise we'll keep Kearns waiting."

Dempsey said, "No, we'll take 'em where they want to go." I said we wanted to go to Westlake Park. Dempsey said, "What's at Westlake Park?" and Julio said, "Duck eggs." Dempsey asked where we went to school and we told him, and that's the only conversation we had until we pulled up on the Wilshire Boulevard side of the lake. As we got out, Dempsey said, "Congratulations on winning the contest." We thanked him for breakfast and the Coca-Colas and Orange Crush. Owl Eyes said to the driver, "The Brown Derby, opposite the Ambassador," and the limousine pulled off.

When it got about fifty yards away, it stopped. Dempsey leaned out and waved us to him. We ran up to the limousine and he said, "Mr. Doyle forgot something." Owl Eyes took out his wallet and gave us each a five-dollar bill. It was the most money I had ever had in one lump. We knew Jerry would ask us if we got any money, so we agreed to give him fifty cents each for letting us win the contest and to tell him that was half of what Owl Eyes gave us.

My father came home that night and, at dinner, announced he had found a fine house for us on Ridgewood Place between Melrose Avenue and Santa Monica Boulevard in Hollywood and that the boys and girls would have separate rooms and that

Mother and Dad would have a bedroom of their own. I said I had had breakfast with Jack Dempsey and my father told me not to interrupt while he was talking. My mother asked when we were going to move and he said on Monday, the day after tomorrow.

When Mrs. True heard this, she said we would have to pay another full week's rent if we didn't get out Sunday night. My parents agreed to borrow a friend's car and move on Sunday. My mother said the children would pitch in and help and she was sure we could do it. Mrs. True said it would be a shame if Robert didn't go to church on Sunday. It would have been my tenth trip to the Angelus Temple and she wanted to give me the pleasure of pinning my dollar to the Holy Rope. I had Owl Eyes's money in my pocket, so I couldn't have cared less about the Holy Rope. I said I would help wheel Mr. True down the steps, but after that I'd better stay and help with the packing.

The next morning, when I said good-by to the Trues at the bottom of the steps, Mrs. True patted me on the head and told me to be sure and get rid of Duck before she got home. Mr. True held out his shaking right hand and fixed his eyes on me. I shook his hand and told him I hoped Aimee would help him to-day. As Mrs. True wheeled him away, I felt something in the palm of my hand. I looked down and saw a dollar bill folded into a neat one-inch square.

I looked up and wished Mr. True would turn and give me a wink, but I don't know whether he did or not. Mrs. True's giant frame blocked him from my sight. Her legs looked as though they were screwed on upside down. They were bigger at the bottom than they were at the top.

5

Silent Star

WE MOVED into a five-room duplex bungalow in the heart of Hollywood. A bedroom for my mother and father, a bedroom for the two girls, and a bedroom for me and my brother. We spread out into the five rooms with solid walls between us and began to lead different lives. The Westlake Park days were over, but for a long time I kept thinking they might return, that the duplex with the walls between rooms would disappear and we would all be back in the wonderful, chaotic, big room with the partitions again.

I was enrolled in the fifth grade at Santa Monica Boulevard School, less than a mile from twenty-three film studios. It usually took ten minutes to walk from my house to school—unless I used a short cut through the Paramount and F.B.O. (later RKO) back lots, under the fence to the adjacent Hollywood Cemetery, a dash across four acres of marble slabs, headstones, and dead flowers, then through a secret hole in the surrounding high cedar hedge, across Van Ness Avenue and, panting, through the school gates as the bell rang. That way, I could make it in just under four minutes.

My first confrontation with the Hollywood star system occurred on September 7, 1926. The star was Rudolph Valentino. He was dead, but I guess he was more of a star dead than many stars are alive. Or, at least, it seemed that way to me as I made my sprint through the cemetery on that memorable Tuesday, the day of his funeral.

The Great Lover had died in New York's Polyclinic Hospital two weeks before and had lain in state for a week while millions of women throughout the world carried on with breast beatings, suicides, and other hysterics.

And that was only the beginning. After about a million women and eighty-seven men had viewed Rudy's body, it was transported to Hollywood in a silver-bronze casket, a three-thousand-mile train journey on the Southern Pacific's Golden State Limited. At whistle stops across the country, young women wept openly and older women prayed.

The newspaper accounts of the trip were discussed at our breakfast table, punctuated by my mother saying, "The poor man," and my father saying, "Nonsense." Then my mother said, "I feel sorry for Pola Negri," and my father said "Nonsense" again.

Pola Negri, Valentino's fiancée, was his leading mourner. Or, at least, she seemed to be getting the most mileage out of his death. She arranged the funeral train and accompanied the body from New York. She also promised to enshrine his memory in a $250,000 massive bronze statue, to be erected "somewhere in the Hollywood he loved."

My mother read aloud, " 'Rudy's sweetheart brings body. In the solemnity of the death car, with the blush of the desert morning against the windows on which the shades were partly drawn, the emotional Polish actress was alone with her dead.' "

My father said, "The toast is burning, Reesie."

My mother turned the toast off without looking up and continued reading, " 'It was, perhaps, the last time the lovers could be alone for days to come, for screenland begins its tribute this afternoon. Every great star and director will be at the Hollywood Cemetery to bid farewell to the star of stars.' "

I said, "Will D. W. Griffith be there telling them all how to bid farewell?"

My mother said, "Yes, of course he'll be there, and so will Lillian and Dorothy Gish."

"How about Hoot Gibson and Theda Bara?"

"Everyone will be there, Robert, and they'll all be in mourning. Now finish your oatmeal."

My sister Beverly said, "What's 'in mourning'?" and my mother said, "They'll all be wearing black." I said, "Will Theda Bara be wearing a black tigerskin and will D. W. Griffith be carrying a black megaphone?"

Before my mother could answer, my father said, "Have you fixed the children's lunches?" and my mother said, "They can buy their lunches today." My father said, "Why?" but instead of answering, my mother started to read the paper again—" 'Miss Negri, attired in a simple but striking black costume, was sobbing audibly. Although apparently on the verge of a nervous breakdown, she walked steadily forward to the car where the mortal remains of Valentino lay in the heavy silver-bronze casket.

" 'Many times she had trod that path in the transcontinental journey of the funeral train. Kneeling beside the bier, which stands at the base of a veritable mountain of flowers, Miss Negri enacted the greatest emotional scene of her life.

" ' "Ah, dear," she sobbed, as tears coursed down her cheeks in pitiable grief, "we will soon be home; home, my dear, where you were so happy and life and love were so sweet." ' "

My father stopped buttering the toast and looked at my mother. My mother continued reading.

" 'As she arose and bowed her head over the bier, a delicate little flower dropped from her hand to the draped casket.' "

My mother stopped to wipe her eyes. My father took the paper and said, "I think you're making all this up." My mother sobbed, "Read it yourself then."

My father read a bit to himself, then said, "Will you listen to this— 'Though few realized it, a great tribute was paid the dead star in the early-morning hours. In the massive, rolling sand dunes, just outside Yuma, is the location where, a few years ago, Valentino rode in gallant trappings before the camera in the memorable role of *The Sheik*.

" 'In memory of the famous part, which individualized Valentino in the films, the Golden State Limited bearing his remains slacked its speed as it rolled across the vast wastes.

" 'Then, as the train flashed down the rails outside Douglas, Arizona, a lone horseman, booted, spurred, and bronzed by western suns, topped a rise on his horse. The horseman straightened in his saddle for a moment, lifted a broad, white sombrero, and bowed his head as the train whipped around a curve and disappeared.' "

My father threw the paper in the wastebasket. My mother took it out.

According to the schedule published in the paper, a Solemn Requiem High Mass was to be conducted at 10:30 A.M. by the Reverend Michael J. Mullins at the Church of the Good Shepherd in Beverly Hills, "for the repose of the soul of Rudolph Valentino." All the studios would close for one hour during the Mass. Pallbearers would be Charles Chaplin, Norman Kerry, Mario Carrillo, George Fitzmaurice, Emmett Flynn, John W. Considine, Jr., Count Gradenigo, and Tullio Carminati. Richard Bonelli would sing *Ave Maria*. The funeral cortege would leave the church for the Hollywood Cemetery at 11:00 A.M.

At 11:30 A.M., the funeral service was to be held at Hollywood Cemetery. In a marble crypt (No. 1199), lent to the

Valentino family by June Mathis, the screenwriter, the Great Lover's body was to be slid into its temporary resting place until a new memorial, designed by Pola Negri, was completed. Some papers said it was to be made of bronze, others said Italian marble from Rudy's homeland.

When I arrived at school, at 7:55 A.M., weeping women were blocking Santa Monica Boulevard in front of the cemetery from Van Ness Avenue to Gower Street. The big red Pacific Electric streetcars crawled through the crowd, bells clanging, motormen cursing. Certain American impulses, it may be comforting to know, were flourishing in the midst of the mass hysteria. The entrepreneurial spirit, for example. Black-bordered stills of the great man from his latest picture, *Son of the Sheik,* were being hawked through the crowd. Also offered were "guaranteed genuine" swatches of the muleta from *Blood and Sand,* "genuine" copies of the Gaucho serape Valentino wore as Julio in *The Four Horsemen of the Apocalypse* (the part that had made him a superstar in 1921), silver Valentino slave bracelets (like the one his wife, Natacha, had given him and which had never left his right wrist, even now), gypsy earrings, hair grease, black arm bands, etc.

As the morning wore on, the tension built. At eleven o'clock an assistant fire chief arrived and advised the principal to close our school and send the children home, which she promptly did ("Go *straight* home!"). Then she and the other women teachers joined the mourners, who now numbered ten thousand by Los Angeles Police Department count. Russell J. Birdwell said there were "more than twenty thousand," but he was the press agent for *Son of the Sheik,* so he may have exaggerated.

We had been told to go straight home, so Ely Novic and I went straight to the cemetery. Trust two alert ten-year-olds to know where the action is. As we crawled through our secret entrance, we saw thousands of women, dressed mostly in black, being herded to the southeast corner of the cemetery, where the mausoleum was located. As the ladies trampled across the graves of various prop men, cameramen, extras, and other lesser Hollywood figures, we followed in their wake, hoping to get a look at whatever was going on. Long before we got anywhere near the mausoleum, we were caught by a black cemetery worker known to us as Bud, the Blue-Gum Nigger. His gums were actually blue, and he used to tell us that our balls would turn to blue rocks if he bit us. We half believed him, so when he bared his gums, we scurried through the fence to the Paramount back lot.

One of the standing sets was a square-rigged, four-masted schooner. We climbed to the crow's nest at the top of the tallest mast and had a bird's-eye view of the whole show. Every time Bud looked our way, we thumbed our noses, raised the middle finger of our right hand, and cried in unison, "Bud, Bud, Peter Pud! How do you like it? Fried, stewed, or barbecued?" To this day, I don't know why we did this, but it seemed like a sensational thing to do at the time.

Ely and I were having the time of our lives, but the rest of Hollywood was in a mood of deep sorrow. We watched all the glittering stars pay homage to the immigrant from the heel of Italy's boot. Then, while a low-flying airplane, piloted by someone named Earl H. Carlisle, dropped flowers from the sky, Rudolph Valentino was stashed away in a borrowed crypt, a dream put away from the world. Mussolini sent a wreath, which was placed on the marble floor next to twelve red roses and one white rose brought by Miss Ditra Flame, a fan who was to become known as "the Woman in Black."

Bud, who thought Valentino was an Arab because he had only seen him in *The Sheik*, told us later that the mysterious "Woman in Black" was an "A-rab" too. Actually, she was a pianist and dancer who had once been visited by Valentino when she was in the hospital.

Ely and I watched from our crow's nest until the last mourner left. There were a lot of ladies hiding their faces behind black veils, and I guess some of them could have been Lillian or Dorothy Gish or Pola Negri, but I didn't see a black tigerskin or a black megaphone, so I told Ely that Theda Bara and D. W. Griffith couldn't make it. He said, "What's D. W. Griffith?" and I told him that he was the director and that that's what I was going to be one day. Ely said he'd rather be the pilot of the plane that dropped the flowers.

As Bud cleaned up the debris around the mausoleum we speculated about what would happen to Valentino's balls if Bud sneaked in one night and bit *him*—an unlikely prospect because Bud was actually a kindly old fellow who wouldn't bite anybody, dead or alive. In fact, he took us into the mausoleum a few days later and let us help him take the dead flowers to the rubbish dump in the back of the cemetery, next to Paramount. There were a lot of wreaths and flowers, but the only ones I remember were from Jack Dempsey, Douglas Fairbanks, Buster Keaton, and the Western Costume Company.

That was forty-nine years ago. I went back recently to see if Rudy was still in his "temporary resting place." The pseudo-Roman marble temple is located in the cemetery on Rosemary Avenue, next to the sunken garden where Douglas Fairbanks is buried, and not far from Cecil B. DeMille, Marion Davies, and Tyrone Power. The D. W. Griffith memorial is across the lake, next to the Confederate Soldiers plot. The main interior hallway of the Valentino building is high-ceilinged and marbled, lit by sun through a stained-glass skylight. It's called the Hollywood Cathedral Mausoleum. After entering, I walked east down a long corridor lined with larger-than-life-size statues of the Apostles. Near the end, I turned left at St. John and continued down another corridor to St. Paul. Left at St. Paul and I found myself in a small wing, the walls of which contain vaults, or, as the cemetery attendant called them, "crypts." In front of a large, beautiful stained-glass woodland scene is crypt No. 1199.

It is now occupied by June Mathis Balboni. Next to it, on crypt No. 1205, is a bronze plaque with a vase on either side. The inscription on the plaque says "Rudolph Guglielmi Valentino 1895–1926." I don't know when they switched Rudy from crypt 1199 to 1205.

What I do know is that on September 6, 1973, the vase on the right held a withered yellow rose and a note saying:

> *This yellow rose is from John Ford's funeral,*
> *Wednesday morning, 5th September, 1973.*
> *[signed]*
> *Don   Schneider*

Now why do you suppose a fellow named Don Schneider would take one of John Ford's yellow roses and give it to Rudolph Valentino?

If Bud were here, I'm sure he could give me a perfectly logical explanation.

6

Charlie

C HARLIE Chaplin's casting director came right into our schoolroom. He asked who would like to work in a movie called *City Lights* and about half of us raised our hands, mostly girls. Then he asked how many could shoot peas through a peashooter, and the girls' hands went down. The casting director selected me and Austin Jewell and told the teacher to send our parents in to see him at the Chaplin Studio on North La Brea Avenue. Luckily, my father was out of town, so I went that afternoon with my mother. My father would not have approved. He was never interested in anything to do with the movies.

The casting director explained that I would have to go to the California Department of Child Welfare in downtown Los Angeles, have a medical examination, and, if found sound of mind and body and up on my schoolwork, I would be given a work permit. When that was done, I was to come back tomorrow and meet the director.

"D. W. Griffith," I thought. "Who else?" I would actually meet my hero, the man who told everybody what to do, the man with the big megaphone who told Douglas Fairbanks how to slide down the sail, told Tom Mix's horse, Tony, how to paw the ground when counting, told the Our Gang kids how to be naughty and Lillian Gish how to be sad.

My mother and I got on the Pacific Electric streetcar at La Brea and Santa Monica Boulevard. I was thinking about Griffith when she said, "Robert, you must do exactly as Mr. Chaplin says tomorrow." I said I would, but I knew Mr. Griffith would have the final word. Through his megaphone.

The next day, we went to the casting office at 7:00 A.M. My mother checked me in, showed the assistant casting director my temporary work permit, and told him she would leave me with him because she had to go home and get her other children off to school. I was given an extra's voucher and told to wait in the outer office.

After being alone for about fifteen minutes, I was joined by

Austin Jewell. He had worked in some movies before and already had a permit. He promptly told me the names of the movies, the stars, directors, and how much he had been paid: "*Quality Street,* starring Marion Davies; director, Sidney Franklin; three dollars. *Casey at the Bat,* starring Wallace Beery; director, Monty Brice; three-fifty and a box lunch. (We made that one at Wrigley Field.) *Sparrows,* starring Mary Pickford; director William Beaudine; five dollars."

As he gave me his list of credits, I noticed that he kept saying the word "director" but he never said "D. W. Griffith." After he didn't say "D. W. Griffith" about ten times, I wrote him off as a fake who had never worked in any movies. He didn't even know who the director was.

It turned out that I didn't either. When the assistant director came and took us out to the back lot where *City Lights* was being shot, I saw fifty or sixty people hanging around doing different things. A man was powdering another man's face and another man was powdering a very pretty lady's face. A man in overalls had a flat board about four feet square with silver paper pasted on one side of it. He was aiming it at the sun and reflecting the sun's rays onto Charlie Chaplin.

A man with a megaphone yelled, "QUIET!" which seemed like a dumb thing to yell because nobody was talking and the only sound I could hear was the soft pat-pat-pat of the powder puff on the beautiful lady's face. The man stopped patting and the man with the megaphone yelled "QUIET!" again. I kept my eye on him because I figured when he took the megaphone away from his face, I would finally see D. W. Griffith.

The assistant director with us whispered, "Quiet now, boys. They're ready to shoot." Austin Jewell and I whispered, "Yes, sir" in unison. The man with the megaphone turned it in our direction and yelled "QUIET!" at the top of his voice. I wondered if D. W. Griffith ever did anything but yell for people to be quiet when they were already quiet. I waited for him to yell at Charlie Chaplin and tell him how to twirl his cane or skid around the corner on one foot or wiggle his mustache or something. Instead, Charlie walked over to him, took the megaphone out of his hand, and said in a very soft voice, "If you are through yelling, we'll make the shot."

The megaphone man didn't look like D. W. Griffith at all. He didn't look like much of anything except a man being gently criticized by his boss. He said, "Yes, sir." Then he turned to the cameraman and said, "Roll the camera." Chaplin went back to his position on the street corner, the man beside the camera said, "Running," then, "Speed." The megaphone man said, "Start your background action!" Some people with powdered faces started to walk around in the background. Charlie Chaplin said, "Action, Virginia," and the beautiful lady with the powdered face walked toward Charlie, holding her hands out like a blind person. She touched Charlie. He jumped, tipped his hat, twirled his cane, and smiled at her. She didn't react. She just stared ahead, out at the traffic which was rushing by in front of her.

There were about ten cars. They would drive by, turn around in a circle outside of camera range, and drive back in the opposite direction. The extras in the background did the same thing. After Charlie had twirled and tipped and smiled a few times, he held his hand up toward the camera and said, "Cut." The megaphone man yelled, "Cut!" and everything stopped.

I told Austin Jewell that I thought the director always carried the megaphone and told everyone what to do. I also told him that D. W. Griffith directed every movie. Austin thought this was an interesting idea, so he passed it along to the assistant director. The assistant director laughed and told the cameraman. The story finally got to Chaplin and he came over and asked where I had learned this bit of information. I said my mother had told me and he said that on this picture they were making an exception and that Mr. Griffith was letting him direct it. He took the giant megaphone from the assistant director and pantomimed a movie director at work. He pretended to yell through it, first through the small end, then the big end. He put it on the ground and leaned his elbow on it, thinking. He sat on it, crossed his legs, took off his derby, scratched his head and thought some more, then he stood up, got the megaphone stuck on his foot, and limped around.

Everyone stopped work and watched the act, all laughing hysterically. When Chaplin had finished, he gave the megaphone back to the assistant director and told him to get the cars and extras ready for another "take." While this was being done, Chaplin explained that what my mother had probably told me was that D. W. Griffith was a great director, but he couldn't possibly direct every movie made. He also said that yelling through the megaphone wasn't always the best way to get people to do what you wanted them to do—that it was usually better to speak quietly or not at all. He said he found it best to show people rather than tell them. He then went on to explain that Austin Jewell and I were to be newsboys and we were supposed to shoot peas through a peashooter at him while he was helping the beautiful blind girl, Virginia Cherrill, across the street. Then, sometime later in the picture, when the tramp (Charlie) was released from jail, the girl (Virginia) would have recovered her sight and she would ignore the poor tramp (Chaplin always referred to the tramp in the third person). He said he would tip his hat and offer to guide her across the street. While he was doing this, I was to sneak up behind him and grab his cane. When he turned to recover the cane two men would grab him and try to pull him away. I was to hold on to the cane as long as I could. He asked if I could do this. I said yes and offered to show him. He said, "No. I'll show *you* when the time comes." He told us to go with the second assistant director to wardrobe and make-up, and he would show us our parts when we came back. He then went back to the set to repeat the scene he had just done. The megaphone man yelled, "QUIET!" As we tip-toed away, I took one last look over my shoulder for D. W. Griffith. I didn't see him. I never did.

The wardrobe department was a strange-looking warehouse-like room with hundreds of different kinds of clothes hanging on racks. There were uniforms for policemen, firemen, and soldiers. There was a gorilla suit. There were rows and rows of hats and shoes. And there was a wardrobe man who said to the assistant, "The clothes they're wearing look pretty crummy to me. We'll just give them each a cap."

The make-up department was something else again. I sat up in a barber's chair with a mirror in front of me and lights shining in my face. A man squeezed some brownish sticky-looking stuff out of a tube onto his hand. With the other hand he took little dabs of it and smeared it on my face. When my face (including my ears) was completely covered, he took a big dirty powder puff, dipped it in a can of pink powder marked "Max Factor No. 26," and started slapping me in the face with it the way I had seen the other man doing out on the street. When the powdering was finished, he took a pencil and painted my eyebrows. He then took two little tin boxes about the size of the ones we used to take to school full of "doo doo" for ringworm tests back in Georgia. One of these was filled with a bluish paste, which he put above my eyes. The other was filled with reddish-brown lipstick. He rubbed his finger into it and showed me how to purse my lips. I did and he rubbed the lipstick on my lips. When he finished, I looked in the mirror and wanted to throw up.

The assistant director took us back to the street where Charlie Chaplin was still doing what he had been doing two hours before. He saw us and told the assistant director to take us back and get the make-up taken off. Back to the barber chair, this time for a cold-cream face bath and the make-up man muttering, "I wish they'd make up their minds."

When we came back, Chaplin showed the cameraman, Rollie Totheroh, where to set up the stationary camera. He looked through the finder and told Rollie to lock it off. The camera seldom moved in Chaplin's films. He then did his part. He showed us how he would walk, how he would twirl his cane, how he would tip his hat, how he would smile at Virginia Cherrill, and so on. Then he became Virginia Cherrill, the beautiful blind girl, and the tramp at the same time, jumping from one position to the other, twirling his cane, holding his hands out in front of his "sightless" eyes, then smiling, first as the tramp and then as the blind girl.

As he passed in front of our corner, Austin Jewell and I raised our peashooters. Chaplin said, "No, wait!" and promptly stopped being the tramp and the blind girl and became two newsboys blowing peashooters. He would blow a pea and then run over and pretend to be hit by it, then back to blow another pea. He became a kind of dervish, playing all the parts, using all the props, seeing and cane-twirling as the tramp, not seeing and grateful as the blind girl, peashooting as the newsboys. Austin and I and Miss Cherrill watched while Charlie did his show. Finally, he had it all worked out and reluctantly gave us back our parts. I felt that he would much rather have played all of them himself.

We did the first bit and were kept on salary (five dollars per day) for several weeks, waiting for Charlie to get around to shooting the last scene. He was shooting in continuity because he made things up as he went along. Before we did the last scene, Harry Myers, who played the rich alcoholic, became ill and we weren't called back for three months. By this time, Austin Jewell and I had grown several inches, popped a few adolescent pimples, and I had cut my hair for a bellhop bit in another film. When Charlie saw us, he was angry because we didn't match the scene he had already shot. I thought we were going to be fired, but he finally decided to reshoot our first sequence before shooting the last.

I never worked for him again, but later I became a film editor and I got to know him quite well. He once asked me to look at some rushes of *Monsieur Verdoux*. There were five takes of a simple shot of Charlie doing a little dance at the foot of some stairs. Charlie was good in all the takes, but in take three the camera panned a little bit too far and you could see an electrician leaning on a lamp for about six frames (a quarter of a second). Charlie asked me which take I liked best. I told him take two or take five. He said, "Did you like my dance in take three?" I said, "Yes, but what about the electrician?" Charlie jumped out of his seat and said, "What are you looking at *him* for? You're supposed to be looking at *me*. If you noticed the electrician that means I wasn't holding your attention."

Thirty-five years after I worked in *City Lights*, I met Charlie in Waterville, on the west coast of Ireland. He couldn't wait to tell me, " 'Our' picture, *City Lights*, is playing a revival in New York and doing smashing business." He knew the seating capacity of the theater, the daily gross figures, and how much he would receive as his share (most of it). He reminded me that he would have made a bigger profit if I hadn't caused him to reshoot because of my pimples and my short haircut.

As we sat on the beach and watched his children run in and out of the surf, he reminded me of our first meeting and said he never forgot my telling him that D. W. Griffith directed every movie. He said he had seen *Birth of a Nation* on an average of once a week during its Los Angeles run. He also said he thought Griffith's *Birth of a Nation, Intolerance,* and *Hearts of the World* the best pictures ever made.

On another occasion, he asked me and my wife to his studio to hear the musical score he had written for *Limelight*. He hadn't actually shot the film yet, but he had written and recorded the music four times, this last time with a sixty-piece orchestra. As the music played, he acted out each scene as he proposed to do it when he shot the film. It was a wonderful performance, well over an hour. When it was over, I hesitatingly suggested that the usual form was to make the picture first and *then* record the music to the picture. "Don't be ridiculous," he said. "I wouldn't think of trusting any conductor with my performance."

He really wanted to do it all. I don't think he ever fully accepted the idea of not being able to be behind the camera and in front of it at the same time. He didn't even seem to like the idea of turning his film over to the laboratory for developing and printing. Movies are collaborative. No one can do it alone, but Charlie Chaplin came closer than anyone else I ever met.

After my experience on *City Lights*, I had but one permanent ambition—to be a movie director. There were, of course, other ambitions from time to time, but the longer I lived in Hollywood and worked around the studios, the more I wanted to be a part of the movies. When I knew I was going to work on a certain day, the night before was glorious with expectancy. I would go to bed wondering what the next day would bring in the way of costumes, sword fights, car chases, and beautiful girls. When I finished a job and had to go back to regular school, the day was dead, empty.

I suppose if I had lived in Scranton, Pennsylvania, I might have wanted to be a coal miner, or in Pittsburgh, a steelworker. As it was, I lived in a factory town and the factories produced movies, just as Detroit produced automobiles, and Hershey, Pennsylvania, produced chocolate. People went to work early, came home late, and the assembly line at each of the big studios turned out an average of one feature film per week, more than five hundred films per year. The country was about to plunge into the darkest depression in its history, but in Hollywood there was plenty of work for everyone, even kids.

7

Our Gang

T//HE CENTRAL CASTING agency was set up on the tenth floor of the Taft building at Hollywood and Vine to furnish extras to the studios. You would call Hollywood 3701, and when the casting switchboard answered, "Central," you gave your name. The operator would repeat it to the casting directors and then give you instructions for the next day's work. "Report to RKO studio at seven-thirty A.M. Summer school clothes. Panchromatic make-up. Five dollars and overtime. Director Seitz."

More often, there was no job for you, and the operator said, "Try later," usually in a nasal voice. For a long time, they just said, "Nothing," but the extras complained that it was too discouraging, so it was changed to "Try later." Either way, it meant "No work for you tomorrow." You always kept phoning until you got a job or Central Casting closed the switchboard. The phone was the lifeline. My mother insisted that we keep it covered at all times. The words "try later" became a joke password with Hollywood's extras. If you asked a girl for a date, she would say, "Try later." If you asked to borrow money, you were likely to be told to "try later." Some years afterward, Frankie Darro opened a bar called the Try Later, where the extras met to discuss their hopes and fears, exchange wardrobes, call Central Casting, and even drink.

There was also a classified album of screen children published quarterly. It was called the *Casting Directors' Album of Screen Children*, and it stated, "Every player listed in this book has had screen experience." The average age of the advertisers was about four.

The parents would take their hopefuls to a photographer named Evansmith at 6605 Hollywood Boulevard. He specialized in children's photographs and made "clear, sharp, natural portrait stills of kiddies so essential for casting. $35 per 100. $20 per 50. $12.50 per 25. Plenty of proofs to choose from. There is no 'pull' like a good photograph." My mother put our picture in the album. The casting director at Hal Roach Studio saw it and called. It was my turn to "watch the phone."

"Is Mrs. Parrish there?"

"No. Can I take a message? This is Robert Parrish, her son."

"Are you on page fifteen of the album? Above Jackie Condon and Pete the dog?"

Pete was a sort of bulldog with a white head and four white legs. His owner had painted a brown circle around his right eye and trained him to bark on cue, yawn, roll over, sit up, lie down, and do anything else the director wanted. In fact, the Pete on page 15 was Pete Number Three. The owner had cornered the "dogs for movies" market and kept breeding mongrels until he hit upon one approximately like Pete Number One, i.e., with a white head so that the circle around the eye would show. He had three or four reasonably good facsimiles in reserve, all properly trained and all waiting for the star, Pete Number One, to die or get drunk or temperamental. As it happened, Petes Numbers One and Two were killed in a kennel fire, and all the understudies moved up, in the best show-business tradition.

I didn't want the casting director to think I was a dummy about what was going around town, so I answered, "You mean above Pete Number Three?"

There was a long pause and the casting director finally said, "Are you Robert Parrish and are you on page fifteen in the album?" I said yes and he said, "OK, come to Hal Roach Studio in Culver City for an interview at five o'clock tomorrow. If you are selected you will work with director Robert McGowan in the *Our Gang* series."

I said, "Yes, sir. You can tell it's Pete Number Three because it has a white belly." He had hung up and missed this bit of information.

Aside from Pete and Jackie Condon, the *Our Gang* "regulars" were Joe Cobb (fat boy), Mickey Daniels (freckle-faced and glasses), Farina (black boy), Farina's sister (black girl), and Jean Darling (white girl). Then there were the "stand-bys" or "hopefuls"—five other kids who moved up if there was a vacancy or served as "the other side" in team games, fights, etc. I was chosen for the latter group.

Before actually working in front of the cameras, we were given a week's training course by Robert McGowan, the director. I remember him as a dour, pock-marked man who always wore a hat and vest and never smiled except when publicity pictures were being taken. The first thing we learned was the Do—pronounced "dough." In fact, it was a simple "single take"—i.e., an expression of surprise, but not as extreme as a "double take." That was a Double Do—pronounced "double dough."

McGowan started, completely expressionless, dead eyes (pickled?), in a monotone: "Kids, I'm gonna show you this once and if you don't get it, you're out. Savvy? Let's see you all open your mouths as though you were going to spit out a turkey egg. Good. Now nod your head a little bit. No, for chrissakes, not from side to side—up and down. OK. Now, open your mouths, nod your head once, and say 'dough' at the same time."

We all did our best, and McGowan said, "OK, except for that kid at the end. He's out." The kid's mother rushed forward like a protective hen. "Mr. McGowan, Philippe is the most experienced actor in this group. The rest are only extras. I think you should give him another chance." McGowan turned his fried-egg eyes on her like a turtle. "Forget it, lady. Your kid can't even do a Do. What the hell's he going to do when we get to the hard stuff? These kids are going to have to do Double Dos, Butterflies, Flipflops, Angel Wings—the works, and your kid can't even manage a simple Do. He's out." As he walked away, I heard him mutter out of the side of his mouth to his prop man, "Jesus Christ. The goddam kid's mother says he's an experienced actor and the little sonofabitch can't even do a simple Do."

We then got the full repertoire of the standard reactions expected of us. A Butterfly: "You stand up on your toes, flap your arms like a butterfly, roll your eyes around, and then fall on the ground." A Flip-flop: "The same as a Butterfly except that you spin around three times before you fall down." An Angel Wing: "Start with a Triple Do, then cross your arms, hands sticking out in the back like wings, fall over backwards flapping your hands." Hydraulic: "Bug out your eyes and shake your head up and down fast like a hydraulic drill." European: "Hold your hand to your crotch and put your knees together like you have to take a leak." (This was McGowan's favorite. He pronounced European "you're-a-peein'.")

After McGowan had given us the basics, we were turned over to his assistant, who drilled us to razor-edge perfection. When we finally arrived on the set, we found we were to be substitutes sitting on a bench while a football game was being played by the first-string Gang. Farina was to sneak up behind and hit each of us on the head with a rubber ball-peen hammer. We were supposed to react in various ways.

McGowan passed in front of us, pointing as he passed. With an absolutely deadpan expression, he said, "Do, Flipflop, Double Do, Butterfly, You're-a-peein'," and so on. And then, in the same monotone, lips hardly moving, he muttered, "Makeitlively, show-someexpression, keepitalive, don'tfallasleeponme, camera, action, goaheadFarina, giveitto'em. Hard."

Farina did, and when we felt the thud of the hammer (hard rubber, not sponge rubber), we rose to our feet and did our assigned bits. I was the new boy and given a simple Double Do. McGowan liked my work. He said to his assistant, "The new kid's OK. Change him with that dope who's fucking up the Butterfly." We made another take and McGowan said, "Cut. Fine. Print. Next set up." He came over to me and said, "That was a good Butterfly, kid. Keep up the good work and you'll be doing You're-a-peein's before you know it."

It was the first praise I had received from a director.

8

The Black Pirate Returns

U NITED ARTISTS was formed by artists to make and distribute quality movies. The artist-founders were D. W. Griffith, Mary Pickford, Charlie Chaplin, and Douglas Fairbanks. Griffith had made *Broken Blossoms* for United Artists, so I thought I might see him when I was called to United Artists studio on Santa Monica Boulevard to be interviewed for a page-boy job in *The Iron Mask,* starring Douglas Fairbanks. I hadn't kept up with Hollywood politics, so I didn't know that Griffith had long since left United Artists and was operating out of Mamaroneck, New York. United Artists was now being run by the three remaining artist-partners—Chaplin, Fairbanks, and Pickford.

Central Casting sent six twelve-year-olds to the interview. Allan Dwan, the director, chose the Barnett twins, two well-behaved redheaded kids who were the best students, the best actors, and the least trouble of any of the kids working around Hollywood. They were also a pain in the neck to the other kids. The rest of us were given carfare and told to go home. Instead, Dick Johnson and I sneaked into Douglas Fairbanks's private gymnasium and started to work out on the rings, parallel bars, and horizontal bars.

After a while, Douglas Fairbanks came in and watched us. He was a physical-culture enthusiast and worked out every day. He showed us how to do some stunts on the bars, then we all went outside and practiced broad jumping on the grass. He asked if we had thought about entering the Junior Olympics that were being run by the Los Angeles *Times*. We told him we'd like to but you needed a sponsor. He said, "I'll sponsor you."

He took us to Allan Dwan's office and said, "Allan, how about using these boys in the picture?" Dwan said, "I've already got my two page boys. They're being fitted now." Fairbanks said, "Don't you think we need four page boys?" Dwan said, "Yes, I think we do." That's when I first learned that a director quite often listens to a star.

Dwan later said in an interview, "My policy—I just let the actors tell me what to do and I get along very well."

The Iron Mask was a silent film and Fairbanks had three musicians on the set playing "mood" music. In the big scene where the man in the iron mask was brought before Louis XIV, they played "Pomp and Circumstance," the first time I had ever heard it. The pianist, accordionist, and violinist tried their best (loudest) to make it sound impressive, but it came out pretty thin in the cavernous stage. Marguerite de la Motte was in the picture, and I was told that Douglas Fairbanks, Jr., played the part of the man in the iron mask, but I wasn't sure as I never saw his face.

That's about all I remember about the actual shooting on the set because Douglas Fairbanks kept us working out in the gym whenever we weren't before the camera.

He told Mrs. Geddes, the welfare worker, that he was teaching us physical education. I asked him if D. W. Griffith had directed *The Black Pirate* and had shown him how to ride the knife down the sail. He said no, that Al Parker had directed *The Black Pirate* and that a stunt man named Dick Talmadge had worked out the stunt with the sail. He took us to the back lot where the pirate ship was still standing. The mainsail that had been filled with a strong wind when I had last seen it, at the Lyric in Columbus, was now hanging listlessly. Behind it was a complicated network of wires, pulleys, rope ladders, and platforms. The "ship" was in a dry tank about four feet deep and was mounted on hydraulic rockers. Around the dry tank were eight wave makers, machines that could dump thousands of gallons of water into the tank at the director's bidding. There were also five wind machines covered with sheets of canvas. They were actually wooden airplane propellers with a small engine attached.

Fairbanks got a special-effects man to rig the "knife" on the sail. A baseball bat (the "knife") was stuck through the sail with ten inches of the small end showing on the front or camera side. This ten-inch section had been carved to look like the handle of a knife. On the other side of the canvas, the large end of the bat was rigged with a pulley mechanism to slide up and down. Below the bat, on the camera side, was a platform to stand on. It was wired to move up and down in synchronization with the baseball bat. After showing us the complicated mechanics, the special-effects man strapped Fairbanks into the rig and lowered him to the deck of the ship. As the special-effects man unbuckled the harness around his right leg, Fairbanks explained that the audience would be shown something else while this was being done and when they saw him again he would have the real knife in his hand, his leg would be free and he would go about his business of rescuing ladies, stabbing extras and smiling.

He said I could try it if I wanted to. The special-effects man adjusted the rig and strapped me in. As they lowered me to the deck, I held on to the baseball bat for dear life. I looked down and pretended Douglas Fairbanks was Jack Dimon. When I got to the deck Fairbanks said, "Very good, except for one thing. You forgot to smile."

9

Always Say Yes

I F CENTRAL CASTING asks you *anything,* say yes." The golden rule from my mother to her four children: Gordon, Robert, Beverly, and Helen. "Can you sing?" "Can you dance?" "Are you tall?" "Are you short?" "Do you have a blue suit?" "Red?" "Green?" "Cerise?" The answer was always an emphatic, unhesitating YES! If we didn't have what was called for, my mother would make it that night. If we couldn't sing, dance, ride bareback, swim under water, walk a tightrope, speak Polish, or whatever, we said yes and reported for work, hoping we wouldn't actually be called upon to do what we had lied about. Or, if we were, that we could perform well enough to get by. The worst that could happen was that we would be sent home with a quarter-day's pay and a threat that we would never work again for that company . . . until they needed us.

So when Jimmy Townsend, assistant to director Frank Lloyd, asked for drummer boys to work in *The Divine Lady,* starring Corinne Griffith, Victor Varconi, and Montagu Love, I applied and said I could beat a drum.

This was the dream job of the year, especially for twelve-year-olds. Seven weeks at sea with Lord Nelson's fleet, which was based at the Isthmus on Catalina Island. A holiday with pay. As soon as I was selected and fitted at Western Costume, I went to Munchie Munson, the drummer in the school band, and paid him fifty cents to "teach me to drum in three days." He did his best, but it was hopeless. After hours of work and absolutely no progress, he threw up his hands and said, "Forget it. You've got to have *some* sense of rhythm and that's what you haven't got. Here's your four bits back."

He was right, of course. I couldn't beat time then and I can't beat time now. But I reported for work and was shipped off by water taxi to H.M.S. *Vanguard,* twelve miles off the California coast. If I hadn't been seasick and wasn't worried about being exposed as a nondrummer, it would have been great fun. As it was, I was miserable. I wound up on the main deck of the

Vanguard laced into a tight costume, with a large drum strapped across my narrow shoulders, two sticks in my hands, bile in my stomach, and fear in my heart.

In this version of the famous love story, Lord Nelson's crippled flagship, H.M.S. *Vanguard*, had been towed into Naples Bay, and Emma Hamilton was to come aboard to welcome the one-armed, one-eyed Nelson, now Rear Admiral of the Blue, Commander of the Bath, and Baron Nelson of the Nile. Frank Lloyd decided to shoot Corinne Griffith's scenes first and then get rid of her and the "wrecking crew," the affectionate name given to the scores of people who followed in the wake of female stars—the hairdressers, make-up men, wardrobe mistresses, relatives, etc.

The drummer boys were supposed to execute a drum roll, starting low and building in tempo and volume as Lady Hamilton was piped aboard. This was a silent film, but when Lloyd was halfway through shooting, the front office decided to dub sound effects in at some later date. The drumming had to look real.

Thornton Freeland, the first assistant director, was rehearsing the scene with Miss Griffith and two hundred extras, including two lifeguards from State Beach in Santa Monica (Joel McCrea and Andy Devine) and a nervous drummer boy (me). As Lady Hamilton was received by Captain Hardy (Montagu Love), Jimmy Townsend yelled, "Start the drum roll!" and I did the best I could, which wasn't good enough. In fact, it was terrible. My situation wasn't helped by the fact that the other two drummer boys were genuine drummers.

It took Frank Lloyd about fifteen seconds to discover that a serious casting mistake had been made. I was whisked off H.M.S. *Vanguard* to the base camp at the Isthmus, stripped of my splendid drummer's uniform, and told to stay out of sight. At the end of the day, Jimmy Townsend said, "I thought you told me you could beat a drum." I answered, "I can. You didn't ask me how *well* I could beat it." Townsend was a born con man who later became a theatrical agent. He appreciated this bit of dishonesty and said, "OK, kid, don't worry about it. We'll cut your pay in half and you can be a powder monkey. The drummer boys only work a few days, and we'll need the powder monkeys for the full seven weeks. Just stay out of sight until Mr. Lloyd stops foaming at the mouth."

At first I was bitterly disappointed. Aside from the disgrace

Douglas Fairbanks: *The Black Pirate*

(Top left) Author's mother. (Top right) Author's father. (Middle) Author, author's mother, author's brother Gordon. (Bottom) Parrish boys in photographer's buggy.

(Top) A new hero: D. W. Griffith directing *Intolerance*. (Bottom) Tears flowed freely.

(Top) Angelus Temple, where Aimee MacPherson preached the word.
(Bottom left) Aimee in action. (Bottom right) A genuine "Extra!"

(Top left) Jack Dempsey and Estelle Taylor. (Top right) Rudolph Valentino. (Bottom) A yellow rose from John Ford to Rudolph Valentino.

(Top) Rudy lying in state, June Mathis mourning. (Bottom left) Rudy arriving in Pasadena, California. (Bottom right) "Poor man," said Mother. "Nonsense," said Father.

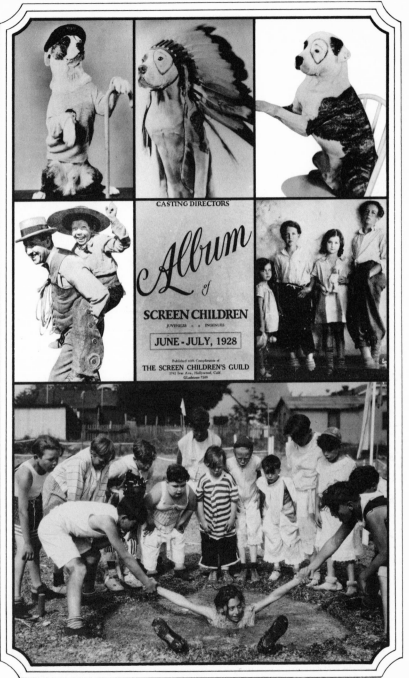

(Top) Petes No. 1, 2, and 3. (Middle, left to right) Robert McGowan, director of *Our Gang; Screen Children;* Parrish brood. (Bottom) "Makeitlively, showsomeexpression . . ." Author is at far left.

(Top) Austin Jewell, author, and Chaplin in *City Lights*. (Bottom) "Lord Nelson has been wounded!" Author's feet (mid-air) at left.

of being exposed as a nondrummer (and a liar), I was banished to the base camp, and all the action would be taking place at sea, where the director was. My disappointment was soon forgotten when I met Jose, the camp's Filipino cook. There was nothing else to do, so I helped him in the kitchen tent. At the beginning, he just let me collect garbage and carry it to the big hole a few hundred yards from the camp, where I buried it in a shallow grave. Jose told me to bury it deep so the wolves wouldn't get it. I wanted to see a wolf, so I barely covered it at all. In fact, there were no wolves on Catalina Island, but one day I surprised some wild goats at the garbage dump. I told Jose about it. He got his .22 rifle and we stalked a tough old billy goat. Jose shot him and I helped skin him and roast him for the unit. After that, Jose and I became hunting and fishing partners and he taught me some Spanish words.

I hung around Jose for a week, during which time we found the wreck of what I thought was an old pirate ship on the other side of the island. Jose said, "No, not a pirate ship. We built it for *Old Ironsides* last year." I knew he was telling the truth, but I decided not to believe him.

When I went back to H.M.S. *Vanguard,* it had been rerigged H.M.S. *Victory.* Since Lady Hamilton's visit at Naples, Nelson had scored a decisive victory at Copenhagen, impregnated Lady Hamilton, chased the French fleet to the West Indies and back again, and was now preparing for final victory and death at Trafalgar.

I was dressed in rags for my new role, and as our water taxi passed a beautiful high-powered speedboat headed for the mainland, I saw Corinne Griffith and her wrecking crew and the other two drummer boys. Miss Griffith (or was it her stand-in?) waved, and I waved back. The other drummer boys thumbed their noses at me and I gave them the old middle finger.

There were three powder monkeys on H.M.S. *Victory*— Howard Hickenlooper, thirteen, Godfrey Craig, twelve, and me. The ship was our home, school, and playground for the next six weeks. The State of California Child Labor Laws insisted that a teacher–welfare worker accompany each film company when kids were employed. By law, minors could work before the cameras for only three hours a day. The rest of the time, while the director was proceeding with the complicated tasks of maneuvering British and French ships into position, dealing with the stars, fighting the wind and sun, etc., we were supposed to go to school. Then, when all was ready, we were supposed to be liberated from the classroom and sent into action. In fact, we avoided the classroom like the plague whenever possible. The teacher's aim was to catch us and teach us. Our aim was to keep from being caught and, if we were caught, to keep from learning anything.

I tried to stay as close to Frank Lloyd as possible because everything seemed to stem from him. I remember him as a man of complete authority, with bushy eyebrows hovering over deep blue, penetrating eyes. Unlike Robert McGowan and Chaplin and some of the others, he actually *used* his megaphone, especially when he had to give instructions from one ship to another. After the drummer-boy fiasco, I didn't have much to do with him personally, which was understandable. He had two hundred Marines, six ships of the line (French or British, depending on which flag they were flying and which uniforms the Marines were wearing), and a film crew of over one hundred men to worry about. I worked in several scenes close to the main action, and when they were preparing Nelson's famous death scene, Frank Lloyd picked me to hold Lord Nelson's hat. An assistant said, "You can't use him, we just saw him being carried away wounded at the other end of the ship." Lloyd said, "That's OK, we only saw his feet." He didn't indicate that he knew I was the defrocked drummer boy.

Lloyd handed me Nelson's hat and then had the make-up man, Bert Such, put an ugly bullet wound on my shoulder. Lloyd looked at the wound, wasn't satisfied, and asked for a syringe of blood. As he squeezed a few drops onto my shoulder, he said, "Have you been practicing your drums?" I said, "No, sir," and he said, "Why not?" I told him I had too much schoolwork to do and he said, "Good lad. We'll get this shot done in a short time and you can get back to your books."

The assistant directors yelled, "Quiet!" Lloyd raised his megaphone and said, "Action." I picked up Nelson's hat and handed it to a young lieutenant (Ben Alexander). Lloyd said, "Cut." Then, to me, "You're picking it up with your wounded arm, lad. Use the other one." I said, "Yes, sir," and we repeated the action. This time it was OK and Lloyd sent for the teacher. "This lad's done a good job. How about excusing him from school for the rest of the day?" The teacher said he was glad to hear that I had done a good job but that I had been ducking school too much lately and that he was grateful to Lloyd for turning me in.

The teacher on *The Divine Lady* was Mr. Francis Slayton ("Mr. Slayton" to his face, "Teach" behind his back). He was a smart old codger who decided to take advantage of the fact that we were involved in an historical film. He concentrated on Lord Nelson, H.M.S. *Victory,* Admiral Villeneuve, and Trafalgar. If he could work in some extraneous education with other subjects he would shamelessly hook us with a reference to Lord Nelson because he knew we were interested in him. We saw Nelson every morning in the make-up department.

Mr. Slayton wanted to teach us something about Emerson, so he asked, "Who wrote the best book ever written about the English, and what did he say about Lord Nelson?"

His powder-monkey class came up with Shakespeare ("No, Howard. Shakespeare died in the seventeenth century and Nelson wasn't born until the eighteenth century. Guess again"), Lord Byron ("You're in the right century, Godfrey, but the wrong country. The man I'm thinking about is an American"), and Mark Twain ("Not bad, Robert. Mark Twain wrote about England during the reigns of King Arthur and Edward VI, but I don't remember anything he wrote about Nelson"). We tried the other American authors we had heard of (we had about eight among us) and Mr. Slayton said, "No, it's Emerson. Ralph Waldo Emerson. In *English Traits* he wrote 'and Nelson said of his sailors—they really mind shot no more than peas.' "

We were interested to hear that the man with the Hungarian accent whom we saw in make-up every morning had said that about his sailors, but when Mr. Slayton moved on to a lecture about Emerson and his "philosophy of self-reliance, the obligation of optimism and hope," etc., Howard Hickenlooper said, "Did he say all that about Nelson?" Mr. Slayton realized he was losing his audience, so he eased out of English literature and back into the history that we could see around us. When he told us about Nelson's death and "Kiss me, Hardy," which we had seen acted out (with Montagu *Love* playing Hardy!), we concluded that we were in with a bunch of fairies. We invented endless jokes about queers. The fact that our schoolroom was stuck away in a corner of the "poop" deck didn't escape our attention either. We changed "Teach" Slayton's name to "Frances," and when his back was turned we swished around with our hands on our hips, lips pursed, and our powder monkeys' rags flowing in the sea breeze.

On one occasion when he asked Howard Hickenlooper if he had finished his homework, Howard got up enough nerve to say, "No. But would you like a kiss, dear?" Patient old Mr. Slayton finally cracked. "Not from you, you stupid little bastard," he said. "You get your work done by tonight or I'll have your ass back on the mainland before you can say England expects that every powder monkey will do his goddam homework."

After that, our relations with Mr. Slayton improved. Any teacher who could say "bastard" and "ass" and "goddam" in what was officially a classroom couldn't be all bad. I told him this and he said, "OK, then let's cut out all this fag crap and see if we can learn something."

After six weeks at sea, we were put up in tents at the Isthmus. In those days, it was a primitive, idyllic spot with wild goats running up and down the scrubby hills and hundreds of fish in the lagoon waiting to be caught. Mr. Slayton taught us to cook barracuda in a rock-lined hole in the sand. He knew how to prepare the fish with sage and other herbs from the island, wrap it in a palm leaf, and bake it to a tender, succulent turn.

One night, a week before we finished shooting, Mr. Slayton barbecued a wild goat on a spit and treated us to a real feast. We sat around a fire on the beach and watched Lord Nelson's fleet lying quietly in the water a few hundred yards out in the bay. Mr. Slayton gave us each a book by Joseph Conrad as a "graduation present." Inserted in each book was a reproduction of the page from the log book of H.M.S. *Euryalus* recording Nelson's famous signal at the Battle of Trafalgar. As I look back on it, I guess Mr. Slayton was the best teacher I ever had. Howard Hickenlooper got *Lord Jim*, Godfrey Craig got *Victory*, and I got *Youth*, which I read in Lord Nelson's cabin the next day. I still have the book, and I often reread the passage where Conrad tells about his first command of a 14-foot lifeboat:

> . . . *and I remember my youth and the feeling*
> *that will never come back any more—the feeling that*
> *I could last forever, outlast the sea, the earth, and*
> *all men; the deceitful feeling that lures us on to joys,*
> *to perils, to love, to vain effort—to death; the*
> *triumphant conviction of strength, the heat of life in*

*the handful of dust, the glow in the heart that with
every year grows dim, grows cold, grows small, and
expires—and expires, too soon, too soon—before life
itself.*

I never had a better summer in my whole life. I think of Mr.
Slayton with affection every time I pass Trafalgar Square, and I
have never said no to a casting director.

PART

2

10

I Left My Love at Fractured Jaw

I N THE 1930's Raoul Walsh, Henry King, and John Ford were the three big "location directors" at Fox Studio. They made pictures on the stages too, but they preferred working on location, as far away as possible from front-office supervision. Walsh's *The Big Trail* was to be Fox's major effort in 1930. He was given a large budget, a top cast of Tully Marshall, Tyrone Power, Sr., Marguerite Churchill, David Rollins, Ian Keith, and El Brendel. He was also given a new process to try out. The picture was to be shot in normal 35mm and in "Grandeur," using for the latter a 70mm negative for greater depth and scope. In fact, *The Big Trail* was only successfully released in 35mm, and it was to be years before CimemaScope, Todd-AO, Panavision, and other wide-screen processes succeeded. I think Walsh was the first to try one on a big commercial feature.

Walsh was part Spanish, part Irish, a salty ex-prize fighter and ex-actor who wore a black patch over his right eye. The eye had been cut out when a jack rabbit jumped through the windshield of a car he was driving while directing and starring in *In Old Arizona*. He recast Warner Baxter as star of the picture but completed the direction himself. When asked how he lost his eye, he used to say, "A buzzard pecked it out."

Walsh needed a young man to play the scout for the covered-wagon train making its way across America on the "Big Trail" from St. Louis to Oregon. John Ford recommended Marion "Duke" Morrison, a USC football player who had worked for Ford in *Hangman's House, Salute,* and *Men Without Women.* Morrison had also worked as a prop man at Fox during his summer vacation. Most of the studios gave summer jobs to athletes from the local universities, and many of them remained in the industry. "Cotton" Warburton became a film editor, Aaron "Rosey" Rosenberg, Howard "Red" Christie, and Mike "Big Mike" Frankovich became producers, "Racehorse Russ" Saunders became an assistant director, and Marion "Duke" Morrison became

John Wayne. His name was changed when Walsh gave him the job in *The Big Trail*.

A six-year-old girl was needed to play Marguerite Churchill's sister, "Honey Girl." This part was given to Walsh's daughter, Marilyn, but Walsh wasn't sure she could do it so he hired my sister Helen as an understudy. A wise move, this, because in the first scene, involving thirty covered wagons, over two hundred horses, oxen, mules, and the full cast, Marilyn said, "I don't want to do it, Daddy." Marilyn's acting career thus ended at age six, and Helen's started. I was taken along as an extra, a coveted job —three months in Jackson Hole, Wyoming. Another paid vacation with no drums to play and no danger of seasickness.

A luxurious tent city was constructed on the shores of Jackson Lake in the Grand Teton Mountains. The wagons, cameras, lights, and wind machines were brought from Hollywood by train. Most of the actors and livestock were also brought from Hollywood, but in such a big western there was work for a number of local cowboys, Indians, and extra horses and mules. The head wrangler on *The Big Trail* was Jack Padjan, an ex-cowboy who had played Wild Bill Hickock in Ford's *The Iron Horse* and now had a ranch in the San Fernando Valley and supplied livestock and wagons to the studios. His number-one assistant was an Indian named Buck, a quiet, kind man who had graduated from the Colorado School of Mines on a scholarship given to "Reservation Indians." Some people said Buck couldn't find work as an engineer because he was an Indian, but Buck told me he worked for Jack Padjan because he liked horses and the pay was good. He was a vital part of Padjan's operation from 1928 until he joined the Army, just after Pearl Harbor. He became an officer in the Nisei Division and was killed in Italy in 1944. No one ever told me why he was in a Japanese-American outfit.

Buck had a daughter named Caroline. She was two years older than I was and she was the most beautiful girl I had ever seen. She was also the first girl I ever really fell in love with. Caroline came to Jackson Hole to help her father with the horses. I never met her mother and I never heard Buck or Caroline speak of her.

Although I was only an extra I was living in a "star's" cabin with my mother and my six-year-old "star" sister. At 6:00 A.M. the third assistant director knocked on the door and yelled, "Rise and shine!" I got up and built a fire in the wood-burning stove, and my mother cooked breakfast. When the cabin was warm and the breakfast ready, we woke Helen up. At 6:45 a make-up man with a falsetto voice arrived and spent over an hour and twenty minutes putting grease-paint make-up, false eyelashes, and Max Factor Panchromatic Lipstick No. 7 on a six-year-old child. It was usually hours before Helen was in a scene, so the make-up man patched her up from time to time during the day. She would also have to go to school four hours a day and have some rest. If she managed to do anything in front of the cameras, everyone would say, "What a trooper," or "That kid's going to be a star," or "It's too bad some of the grownups can't remember lines the way that kid does." Stuff like that.

Helen came on the picture as an understudy at $50 a week. When she succeeded Marilyn Walsh as Honey Girl, her salary was boosted to $250 a week. I was making $45 a week as an extra. The Depression was on and my father was earning just under $40 a week as a traveling salesman for the Coca-Cola Company.

Late one night, Helen and I were awakened by sounds of a fight outside our cabin. Cheyenne Flynn, one of the cowboys, was drunk and accusing Charlie Stevens, an actor playing a half-breed in the picture, of cheating at cards. Helen and I watched through the window until my mother hustled us back to bed. The fight went on, and I heard Cheyenne say, "I'm going to bite your ear off, you goddam half-breed." Poor Charlie was a gentle Irishman with straight black hair who only *looked* like a half-breed. I heard him make a weak protest, then scream in pain. There was a scuffle, running footsteps, and then a diminishing whine as Charlie made his way to the first-aid tent.

The next morning, I found a neat mouthful of Charlie's ear, covered with ants, outside our cabin. I cleaned it up and took it to Buck. He said it was too late to sew it back on Charlie, so I put a piece of rawhide through the lobe and hung it on our cabin door until my mother made me take it off.

Faced with a one-eared half-breed, Walsh wrote a scene in which a squaw bit Charlie's ear off in an Indian raid sequence.

The teacher–welfare worker lived in the next cabin and kept a close eye on the kids in the company. Too close from my point of view, so I asked Jack Padjan if I could bunk with his wrangling crew. He needed an extra hand to take care of the mules, so he arranged it with Sid Bowen, the assistant director. I moved out of the family cabin and fixed up a pad in the stable area.

My chores included feeding, watering, and saddling the horses at dawn. I also had to clean out the stalls and saddle-soap the harness and saddles. But my main responsibility was the mules. We had twenty of them. A mule wrangler was known as a "mule skinner," so Buck called me "Skinner" from then on.

I learned each mule's name, and it became a matter of pride to have them groomed, fed, and watered better than the horses and oxen for which the older wranglers were responsible. One day Walsh rode by and saw me currying Annabelle, a particular favorite of mine. He stopped his horse, rolled a cigarette with one hand, lit it, and watched me for quite a long time. Finally he said, "What's that hanging around Annabelle's neck?" I told him it was Charlie Stevens's ear, and he said, "Well it looks a hell of a lot better on Annabelle than it did on Charlie. You're doing a good job, kid," and he rode off. From then on I would have done anything in the world for him.

One of the added attractions of location shooting in those days was that almost everyone could arrange to indulge his or her sexual desires. As soon as the train pulled out of the station in Los Angeles the pairs started to form. A camera operator would pour a Prohibition drink from a flask for a wardrobe mistress; a stand-in would settle down with a stunt man. Quite often the assistant director or casting director would have a stable of young girls from which he could choose for himself or recommend to the male stars, the director, the producer, and other members of the unit. You might call these girls hookers today, but they were listed on the payroll as "stock girls." In fact, they were not all of easy virtue. Some were friends from the front office, some were relatives . . . and a few were hookers. All were extras on weekly salary instead of day checks.

As a boy just turned fourteen, I was aware that a lot was going on between people who were not married. I had to start getting my mules organized while it was still dark, so I often saw cowboys scurrying from the stock girls' tent to the bunkhouse (and vice versa) just before dawn. I never could figure out which actors were married to which actresses. They all appeared to be enjoying a movable feast. It seemed to me that everyone was in on it except the make-up man and me and my mules.

I particularly noticed that Ian Keith, who was playing the heavy in the picture, was seeing a lot of the director's wife, Lorraine. She was a magnificent redhead who had nothing to do for hours on end while Walsh was out on location, sometimes thirty miles from the main camp. I noticed that when Keith was not on call he would take Mrs. Walsh fishing or riding.

Once, when the company was shooting all night, I saw Lorraine coming from Keith's cabin. I somehow felt that my new hero, Walsh, was being treated badly, and I considered telling him of my suspicions. Then I thought better of it and decided to talk it over with Buck first. I hoped I'd catch him alone, but Caroline had just fixed his dinner, and they were sitting down to eat. I had already eaten with the other wranglers, so I sat with them while they ate two beautifully cooked trout that Caroline had caught that afternoon. She was so pretty that I just watched her and pretended she was my girl and that she was cooking for me instead of Buck. Buck said, "What's on your mind?" and I said, "Nothing," because I didn't want to talk about Walsh and Lorraine and Keith in front of Caroline.

Buck said, "Well, you must have been thinking about something." I felt trapped. I couldn't say that I was pretending Caroline was cooking for me instead of him so I said, "Fish. I was just thinking how good the fish looks and how I wish I hadn't already eaten."

Caroline said, "Tomorrow's Sunday and the company isn't shooting. There's more trout where these came from. Would you like to come fishing with me? We could have a fish fry by the lake."

I was so stunned to be invited by this beautiful older girl that I must have turned beet red. I literally couldn't answer. I looked to Buck for help. I hoped he would say something, anything. As usual, he didn't let me down.

"Sounds like a good offer to me. You'd better grab it before she changes her mind."

I said, "OK. I can go as soon as I finish my chores." So it was set, and now I wanted to get away as fast as I could. Buck came through again.

"Caroline, while you're doing the dishes, Skinner and I are going to check the horses. Come on, Skinner."

As we walked to the corral, I forgot all about Walsh's family problems. My mind was on the fish fry. I liked Buck a lot, but I hoped he wouldn't come with us tomorrow.

"So what is it? Something's eating you. You want to tell me about it?"

I told him what I had seen and what I suspected, and he said, "Yeah, I know. Everybody knows."

I said, "Then why doesn't somebody tell Mr. Walsh?"

Buck said, "He probably knows too. If he does, he'll handle it his own way. If he doesn't, it's not your place to tell him." Then he said one of the best things anyone ever said to me. "Jack and I are taking some wagons out to the new location tomorrow, so I won't be able to come to the fish fry."

Caroline and I fished from a little jetty in a remote part of the lake. Caroline caught two trout. I caught a trout and a small bass. We built a fire and fried the fish in butter. Then we ate and swam and I kissed her and she returned the kiss and we fell in love. We didn't *make* love or anything like that. We just *fell* in love.

From then on I forgot about Ian Keith and Lorraine. I only thought about Caroline and my mules. The picture was going well. At the end of two months we were well ahead of schedule. The main part of the shooting was finished. Most of the company was to be sent home and a skeleton crew (no women) was to accompany Walsh, Ian Keith, and John Wayne to another location in Utah for the final fight scene between Keith and Wayne. My mother and sister, Mrs. Walsh, Marilyn, and the other women were packed and ready to go. I brought my stuff over from the wrangler's cabin and was checking it with the assistant in charge of transportation when Walsh saw me. He said, "Where the hell are you going?" I said I had been told that I would not be going to Utah. He said, "I'm going to need some mules in Utah, and somebody's got to take care of them." He turned to the assistant and said, "Put Skinner's stuff with the Utah bunch," and he walked off.

I was torn, because Jack Padjan was handling the Utah livestock and Buck was returning to Hollywood with the main unit. And with Caroline. I ran over to Buck's cabin, burst in, and found him having a beer with Walsh. I apologized for not knocking. Buck said it was OK, and Walsh offered me a beer and invited me to sit down. We talked about the picture and about baseball and about Indians and horses. Walsh told Buck he had noticed that I was a good mule skinner, and Buck said, "He's learning pretty good." Then they shook hands and Walsh said, "OK, Buck. See you in Hollywood."

When we were alone I told Buck I wanted to go back with him and Caroline but that I also wanted to go to Utah with Walsh. Buck said he and Caroline would be at Jack Padjan's place when we got back and that I should stick close to Walsh and try to learn a few things about making pictures.

I said good-by to Caroline at the back of the wardrobe tent. We kissed and promised to meet as soon as I got back. I said I would write to her from Utah, and she promised to answer. We both kept our promises. My letter said, "Zion National Park is beautiful but not as beautiful as Jackson Lake. I miss you. I love you." Caroline's letter said, "I miss you too. I won't be here when you get back because I'm going to live with my mother in Klamath Falls, Oregon. I love you too."

I never saw her again.

On the last day of shooting, Walsh staged the fight scene in which John Wayne finally catches up with Ian Keith and thrashes him for the scoundrel that he is. The last shot was to be a close-up of Ian Keith. John Wayne was to throw a final punch from behind the camera, and Ian Keith was supposed to react like a man with a fractured jaw.

Walsh said, "I'll throw Duke's punch, Ian. You put your hand up to ward off the blow, but don't move your head. I'll feint with my left, then throw the right between you and the camera, and if you jerk your head back it will look like the blow connected."

Keith said, "Look, Raoul. I've been taking punches on the stage and in movies for years. You just throw your punch when you want. I'll get out of the way."

Walsh said, "OK. Camera." The assistant cameraman said, "Running." Then, a few seconds later, he said, "Speed." Walsh said, "OK, Ian. Action. Here it comes." Ian braced himself. Walsh feinted with his right, then threw his left. Ian was too slow. Walsh's left fist crashed into his jaw and fractured it in three places.

When I told Buck about it later, out at Jack Padjan's place, he said he was sorry to hear about it. I said it was lucky it happened on the last shot in the picture. Buck looked me straight in the eye for a long time, then said, "It sure was. Old Raoul is a lucky man. It would have been a problem if an accident like that happened early in the shooting."

The premiere of *The Big Trail* at Grauman's Chinese Theatre was the big event of the season. Lights, crowds, fancy gowns, tuxedos, etc. And it was the first time that a movie director was invited to sign his name in the cement blocks in the forecourt of the theater, an honor reserved until then for stars. Raoul Walsh was to have this unique distinction.

Jack Padjan brought one of the covered wagons from the

picture up to the forecourt of the theater in the morning. The Fox publicity people spent the day fussing about the wagon, setting up seats for the fans, and selecting an appropriate plot for Walsh's signature. They also came up with suggestions for something clever for him to write beside his name. This was important. The theater was owned by Sid Grauman, an old-time showman whom all the stars claimed to know intimately, so aside from making their footprints in the wet cement, they were expected to write something cute or sentimental, like:

> *DEAR SID, MY LITTLE TOOTSIES, DON'T STUMBLE OVER 'EM* — JACK OAKIE
> *MAY THIS CEMENT OUR FRIENDSHIP* — JOAN CRAWFORD
> *WITHOUT YOU, I WOULDN'T BE HERE* — MICKEY ROONEY
> *TO SID, OUR KING OF SHOWMEN* — BEBE DANIELS
> *TO SID, FOLLOWING IN MY FATHER'S FOOTSTEPS* — TYRONE POWER
> *TO SID, HAPPY LANDING* — DON AMECHE
> [*Happy Landing* was Don Ameche's latest picture]

If a star was identified with anything special, he tried to work that in. Tom Mix drew a picture of a cowboy hat and had Tony, his horse, stomp his hoofprints next to Tom's cowboy-boot prints. When William S. Hart heard about this, he went back with some fresh cement and added imprints of a Colt .45 on either side of his handprints. Sonja Henie wrote something in Norwegian (TIL-LYKKE) and added her skateprints. Jimmy Durante drew a picture of his nose and wrote DIS IS MY SCHNOZZLE. Eddie Cantor was famous for singing a song called "Barney Google, with His Goo, Goo, Googly Eyes." Cantor's own eyes kind of popped out of his face, so he drew two big popeyes and wrote HERE'S LOOKING AT YOU SID — EDDIE CANTOR.

In the middle of the "Forecourt of the Stars," surrounded by cement blocks signed by Judy Garland, Fred Astaire, Ginger Rogers, Bob Hope, George Raft, and the Marx Brothers, is one block that says IN ETERNAL MEMORY OF MY DEAR MOTHER, ROSA GRAUMAN — SID GRAUMAN. It's the only block with no handprints, footprints, hoofprints, or snappy greetings, so it's more like a tombstone. When you step from Groucho's slab onto Rosa Grauman's, you suddenly get the feeling that you are in a cemetery and that all the famous movie stars are buried there in a common grave with Rosa Grauman, Tom Mix's horse, William S. Hart's six-guns, Sonja Henie's skates, Jimmy Durante's schnozzle, and Eddie Cantor's goo, goo, googly eyes.

When Walsh arrived, he posed for a photograph in front of Jack Padjan's covered wagon with Emslie Emerson, Louise Carter, Helen Parrish (dressed in her *Big Trail* costume), Marguerite Churchill, and Tully Marshall from the *Big Trail* cast. The publicity department had also found an 87-year-old pioneer of the original wagon trails named Thomas C. Hull, so they pushed him in between Helen and Marguerite Churchill and told him not to blink when the photo bulb flashed. They needn't have bothered, because the old fellow was stone blind. They tried to get him to look at the camera or down at the cement block, but Mr. Hull's sightless eyes could only look straight ahead.

After the photo session, the cement mixer said the block was ready. The publicity man gave Walsh a piece of paper with several suggestions: "To Sid, On *The Big Trail* to Happiness," "To Sid, *The Big Trail* Blazer of Showmanship," etc. Walsh glanced at the paper, crumpled it up, and put it in his pocket.

"Where's the wet cement?" he said.

"Over here, Mr. Walsh. Beside Colleen Moore, just above Joan Crawford and Ann Harding."

Walsh followed him over to where a movie gossip columnist was waiting with the traditional wooden stick used for signing names in the cement. He signed his name and wrote in the date —November 14, 1930. Then he put his left fist into the wet cement. Harry Brand, the Fox publicity director said, "What's that, Raoul?" Walsh looked at him for a moment, then wrote above the imprint of his fist—HIS MARK.

11

Dragnet

MAE WEST was being blackmailed. The special investigator from the Los Angeles district attorney's office didn't seem to be able to catch the blackmailer. One of the reasons for this was that he was the blackmailer. His name was Jack Chris and he wore a Panama hat every day, indoors and out, until he went to jail. He may have even worn it there. It wouldn't surprise me.

My connection with Chris was Jack McHugh, a friend who worked extra with me. When we weren't working, McHugh and I went to Fairfax High School on Melrose Avenue. Franklin D. Roosevelt had been elected president of the United States, but the Depression was still on and money was scarce. My father had left my mother and didn't do much about supporting the family. My mother continued calling Central Casting but the "try laters" came more often than jobs, so she went back to making hats.

McHugh and I had morning and afternoon paper routes. I also made twenty-five cents each Saturday morning taking care of six Japanese children, aged two to nine. They were the sons and daughters of the Fukuda family, who lived on Romaine Street in back of the Luciano Barbershop. Mr. Fukuda was a gardener at Harold Lloyd's mansion in Beverly Hills, and Mrs. Fukuda was a maid at Leatrice Joy's house. She also helped my mother with her millinery work.

On Saturday afternoons, McHugh and I usually went to the movies, especially if there was a good movie at the Melrose Theater, where my brother worked as an usher. Gordon would leave the fire-exit door open, and McHugh and I would sneak in and slump down in the front row to keep from being discovered by the assistant manager. We saw the first half of *All Quiet on the Western Front* five times just to catch a glimpse of ourselves as extras in the schoolroom scene, when Lew Ayres returns from the front to visit his old schoolmaster. As soon as our bit in the movie was over, we sneaked back out through the fire exit and went to Alex's malt shop for a "too thick for a straw" malted milk.

"How would you like to make five bucks a night just for riding around in a car?" McHugh said. I said I would like it. He told me about this guy he knew in the district attorney's office who was looking for two "bright young men" to do some work for him. I said I was a bright young man and McHugh said he had suspected as much. He also confessed that he too was a bright young man. After a while, we decided that we added up to just what Special Investigator Chris wanted, so we went to see him in the Hall of Justice in downtown Los Angeles.

Jack Chris turned out to be a distant relative of McHugh's on the sleazy, cheap-politician side of the family. We were ushered into Chris's office by a uniformed policeman. So far, so good. All very official, Jack Chris's name on the glass door under "District Attorney, Special Investigator." Chris was fat and short of breath. He sat behind a table with nothing on it except an ashtray and a copy of the racing form. He wore his Panama hat and dark glasses and reminded me of a sinister Guy Kibbee. McHugh and I later decided he was probably bald, but we were never able to confirm this. We also speculated about his eyes, which neither of us ever actually saw. McHugh said they were blue and I said they were crossed.

When the policeman left, McHugh said, "This is the guy I told you about."

Chris said, "How old are you?" I told him I was sixteen and he said, "Let me see your driver's license." I showed it to him and he said, "OK. Wait here." He left the room and McHugh said, "I think he likes you." I said, "How could you tell?" McHugh said, "Chris never says 'OK' to anyone unless he likes them." I said, "Does he like you?" and McHugh said it didn't matter because he was related and nobody had to like relatives.

Chris came back and put three photographs on the table. He said, "Can you pick out the photograph of Mae West?" The other photos were of two plug-ugly prize fighters, one black and one white, so it wasn't a very difficult test, especially since the photo of Mae West was autographed. However, I didn't want Chris to think I was a fresh kid with a quick answer, so I said, "It can't be this one because that's Chalky Wright, the featherweight contender. He's also black and has a broken nose. Everyone knows Mae West hasn't got a broken nose, so it's one of the other two."

Chris sat there a long time, not saying a word. He finally turned to McHugh and said, "You got a smart friend here." He picked up the third photo. "This is Johnny Indrisano, Mae

West's bodyguard. The other one is her chauffeur. I want you two guys to follow them every night after they drop her at the Ravenswood Apartments on Rossmore Avenue. Find out what they do, where they go, anything you can about them, and give me a weekly report. Here's a credit card for a car-rental place opposite the Vine Street Brown Derby. Take a different car each night and park outside the Ravenswood Apartments until they drop Miss West off, then follow them. Meet me every Friday night at seven o'clock at the big pepper tree in front of the American Legion fight stadium on El Centro. When you give me your report, I'll give you your money. You each get five bucks a night." He reached in his pocket and took out two ten-dollar bills. "Here's a couple of nights in advance."

McHugh picked up the bills, nodded to me, and started for the door. Before we got out, Chris said, "Don't tell anyone who you're working for and don't ever come back to this office. Always meet me at the pepper tree."

When we got outside, McHugh gave me my ten dollars and said he would meet me at the car-rental place at eight o'clock that night. He said he had to go back and get the details from Chris. I wanted to ask him why Chris didn't want us to work out of the district attorney's office like the other special investigators instead of from a pepper tree, but he was gone before I had a chance. The whole thing smelled slightly fishy to me. On the other hand, Chris had actually been in the district attorney's office, with his name on the door. I looked up at the sign on the building—HALL OF JUSTICE. I took out the ten-dollar bill, held it up to the light and couldn't see through it, so I guessed everything was all right.

I walked down Main Street, the skid row of Los Angeles, to the big public market. I bought two bunches of sweet peas for my mother for five cents a bunch, and some shelled lima beans, and twelve ears of corn. When I got home I told my mother that I had a night-shift job in the district attorney's office at the Hall of Justice. She said, "Can you get off if you get a call from Central Casting?" I told her I could, so she thought everything was all right. She related everything to working in the movies. If I had suddenly become secretary of state she would have approved the job, but only if I could get off when Central Casting offered me a job.

McHugh and I presented our credit card at the car-rental place. The man asked for our driver's licenses. McHugh said,

"Show him yours." The man said, "Who's driving the car?" and McHugh said, "He is." The man took my license, went in his office, picked up the phone, and closed the door. I said to Mc-Hugh, "Don't you have a driver's license?" and he said, "Hell, no. If I had a driver's license I wouldn't need you."

The man came out and said, "What kind of car do you want?" We chose a black Chevrolet two-door sedan because we had seen a lot of Warner Brothers gangster movies and that's what Humphrey Bogart, Edward G. Robinson, and James Cagney always drove. I didn't find out until years later that they drove Chevies because Jack Warner had made a deal with General Motors. They furnished all the cars Warner needed and he showed them in his movies. We worked for Jack Chris for two weeks and we always chose a black Chevrolet two-door sedan, a different one each night, but all looking exactly the same.

On the first night we parked outside the Ravenswood Apartments and waited for Mae West's black Cadillac (license plate 3W5). We arrived at eight-thirty and spent the next three hours speculating about why Jack Chris would hire two pimply-faced high-school students to shadow Chalky Wright and Johnny Indrisano when the district attorney must have a number of experienced investigators ready, willing, and able (and paid) to do this kind of work. McHugh said Chris wanted some fresh blood. I said mine wasn't all that fresh and that, in any event, I wasn't anxious to give it to Jack Chris and/or Mae West. Mc-Hugh said, "Tomorrow night we should get a car with a radio." I agreed and got out to pee.

About halfway through, McHugh hissed, "Hey, shithead. Here they come." I scrambled into the car. We watched as the procession approached the Ravenswood. The big Cadillac drove south on Rossmore. Chalky Wright was at the wheel in a chauffeur's uniform. Mae West and her manager-companion, Jim Timony, sat in the back seat. Following at a discreet distance was Johnny Indrisano in a two-door Chevrolet sedan! Mc-Hugh said, "Come on, write!" I got out my pad and pencil and peed a little more. McHugh looked at his watch. "Eleven-twenty-six—3W5 approaches Ravenswood driving south on Rossmore at—how fast is the sonofabitch going?" I was nervous, so I looked at my watch and said, "Eleven-twenty-seven." McHugh said, "No, you asshole. I know what time it is. How fast are they going?" I said, "About twenty miles an hour."

"Make it twenty-seven. Never give 'em an even number." He didn't explain why, and I was too excited to ask him, so I wrote, "Victim turned into Ravenswood underground garage at 11:27 P.M. after driving 27 mph on Rossmore. She was wearing a silver-spangled . . ." That's as far as I got when McHugh hissed, "Start up! Hurry, start up! They're not going in. They're driving past! Step on it!"

I dropped the pad and pencil and reached frantically in my pocket for the car key. By the time I discovered that it was already in the ignition, the two cars had passed and turned left on Beverly Boulevard. I jammed my foot on the starter and prayed for a good, fast, clean, Warner Brothers getaway. The starter whined and nothing happened. McHugh's voice had graduated from wild hysteria to ominous threat. He was now repeating over and over, "You're fucking it up, you're fucking it up. . . ." He broke the rhythm to scream, "You haven't turned on the goddam key!" Then, as I turned on the key, crunched into low gear, and lurched away from the curb, he started his disconcerting chant again, "You're fucking it up, you're fucking it up. . . ."

We screeched into Beverly Boulevard, and the two cars were nowhere to be seen. We raced down to Larchmont, did a wild U-turn, and went back as far as Highland Avenue. We looked up and down every street in the neighborhood and finally went back to our spot opposite the Ravenswood. We waited and watched until two-thirty, but there was no sign of Johnny Indrisano's Chevy or Mae West's 3W5. I finally got tired of hearing McHugh saying "You fucked it up" and persuaded him to go to the Pick-a-Rib Barbecue Pit on Melrose Avenue. As we chewed on the ribs, we debated about what to write in our report. McHugh said, "Let me see what you wrote before you fucked it up." I showed him my pad and he said, "She's not a 'victim,' you silly jerk, and Jack Chris doesn't care what kind of dress she's wearing. He only wants to know about Indrisano and Chalky Wright."

"So what can we report? That they turned left on Beverly Boulevard while I was trying to start the car. The End. At least let's give Chris something for his money. Let's put in that Jim Timony was wearing a bow tie and that Chalky Wright was smoking a Chesterfield or a Lucky Strike or something, and then we could put in something about the weather and the traffic and stuff like that."

McHugh said, "Nah, he'll never buy that. Let's wait until

tomorrow night. We'll start over. We'll keep the engine running all the time, even if we have to wait three hours. We'll follow the two guys, find out what they do, then we'll make up a slightly different story for tonight's report. We've got four days before we have to see Chris."

The next night was the same, except that we got a Chevy with a radio and listened to the Ink Spots singing "If I Didn't Care." We also heard Ted Fiorito's band playing "I Wanna Go Back to My Little Grass Shack in Kaala Kalua Hawaii," with Muzzy Marcellino singing the vocal. At nine o'clock KFI ("the Earl C. Anthony station") told us some news about Pretty Boy Floyd holding up a bank in Kansas. McHugh said, "Turn on the engine." I told him they hadn't come by until after eleven-thirty the night before, and he said, "I don't want you to fuck it up again. Turn it on." I turned it on.

The midnight news told us how they still hadn't caught Pretty Boy Floyd, and the gas gauge on the dashboard told us we had used up most of our gas. Earl Burtnett was playing "Just One More Chance" when McHugh said, "Here they come."

Sure enough, the old 3W5 came creeping along, followed by Indrisano in his Chevy. Again they drove right by the Ravens-wood. This time I glided out from the curb and fell in behind the Chevy. We all turned left on Beverly Boulevard. Then left again on Arden, two blocks to Clinton Street, left again to Ross-more, and this time, as they approached the Ravenswood, Chalky Wright put out his hand for a left turn. Johnny In-drisano did the same, so I put my hand out too. McHugh said, "No, jerk. Just park across the street and keep the engine running."

After fifteen minutes, the Chevy drove out, with Chalky Wright at the wheel. McHugh made a lewd remark about why Johnny Indrisano had stayed in Mae West's apartment. I reminded him that fat Jim Timony and his bow tie had also stayed and that it must be pretty crowded up there, and McHugh made another lewd remark, this time including fat Jim Timony and his bow tie.

We followed Chalky Wright across town to Jefferson Boulevard, where he turned East to Central Avenue, downtown Los Angeles, the heart of the black section. He parked the car and went into the Club Alabam, a predominantly black night club that welcomed heavy-spending whites. Wright went over and sat at the bar. McHugh and I lurked in the back, watching.

"Hey, Bob. Whatchall doing down here?"

I turned around and saw Mush Morris, one of the few blacks who went to Fairfax High. He was on the track team and was also a drummer in the school band. I soon discovered that he worked nights as a drummer at the Club Alabam. I told him we had come down to see Chalky Wright, the guy over at the bar. Mush took one look and pulled me out into the street. McHugh followed. Mush said, "Now look here. That's a very rough boy. You stay away from him. He's already involved in a knifing down here. I don't know what you guys have to do with him, but whatever it is, it can only give you trouble."

I looked over at McHugh and back to Mush Morris's serious black face. McHugh said, "What kind of trouble?" Before Mush could answer, Chalky Wright came out, stopped in front of the door, and asked Mush for a match. He lit a small black cigarillo, and the flame of the match showed us, in startling close-up, the battered face. The scar tissue over his left eye gave him a perpetual wink, and when he looked at me I had to fight back an almost uncontrollable impulse to return the wink the way I had done with poor old Mr. True at Aimee's church. He gave the matches back to Mush and said, "Thanks, drummer man. You seen Mildred?" Mush said, "Not tonight, Chalky." The fighter walked to the corner, leaned against the building, and waited. Several passers-by said, "Hi, champ," or "How ya doin', Chalky?" when they saw him.

Mush pulled us back into the club and ordered us each a Coke at the bar. McHugh said, "I'll have a shot of rum in mine," and the black barkeeper said, "Sure, kid. You'll shit too, if you eat enough. Let me see your driver's license." McHugh said, "Let me see yours. I'm from the district attorney's office." The barkeeper studied McHugh's acne-covered face for a moment, then said, "You're the first D.A. I ever saw with jerk blossoms." He turned to Mush and said, "Get these punk kids out of here, Mush, before the cops come in for their free drink." McHugh squeaked, "I'm over eighteen," and the barkeeper said, "Then you're old enough to stop pulling your pud. Out, both of you, or show me your driver's licenses." I reached in my pocket to get mine out, but McHugh said, "We don't have to show this guy anything. Let's go." He took my arm and started toward the door. Mush grabbed us and ushered us to a side fire-exit door behind the orchestra. It was between sets, so the musicians were hanging around smoking and drinking. A white pianist with dark glasses was playing "When It's Sleepy Time Down South."

Mush said, "Go this way. I don't want Chalky to see you. You can get to your car through the alley." McHugh said, "Why?" But Mush had closed the door and we were alone. That is, we were still together, but we were so scared that it seemed alone. We heard Mush's muffled drums pick up the tune from inside— "Dear old southland with its dreamy song, takes me back there where I belong." The pianist was now singing. He had obviously heard Louis Armstrong sing "Sleepy Time Down South."

I said, "Let's go home." McHugh said, "OK, but I'm going to get that blackass barkeeper one day." When we got to our car, Chalky Wright was still standing on the corner across the street talking to four or five blacks. I started the car, and McHugh said, "Wait a minute." I looked over and saw a pretty black girl walk up to Chalky. She said a few words to him, and the men Chalky had been talking to drifted away. The girl and Chalky were now talking excitedly, arguing. We couldn't hear what they were saying. Finally, Chalky slapped the girl and walked over to his car. The girl ran after him and managed to get in the front seat beside him as he drove off.

"Follow him," McHugh said, trying to sound like Edward G. Robinson. I tried to think of what Cagney would say, but all I could come up with was "Nuts to you. I'm not following anybody. I'm going home."

McHugh said, "For chrissakes, you took the job, didn't you? You're getting paid, ain't you? What kind of crap-out guy are you?"

I said, "Did you see the way he slapped that girl?"

"She probably insulted him, called him a nigger or something. Come on, let's go. We'll just follow him long enough to find out what general direction he's headed in, then we'll have something for our report. I promise you we won't even get out of the car. No matter what happens."

I reluctantly pulled out from the curb and fell in behind the other black Chevy. McHugh started making notes furiously. I couldn't imagine what he was writing. We were just following a two-door Chevy sedan down Central Avenue. "What are you writing?" I said. "Last night's report," he said. "I'm saying that most of this stuff happened last night. Up until when he slapped the girl. Then I'm picking it up with a different beginning for to-night. I'm saying, 'Suspect went straight from Ravenswood to . . .'" He looked up and saw that we were crossing 107th Street.

He went back to his pad, muttering the words as he wrote. "'Suspect turned east on 107th Street to heart of Watts area, where he arrived and stopped his car at 1:55 A.M.'" He looked up and realized that we had stopped, but that the "suspect" was disappearing in the distance. I was desperately trying to start the car, which had sputtered to a standstill the way cars do when they're out of gas. "Follow the sonofabitch!" McHugh screamed. "He's getting away." I kept my foot on the starter but all I got was a rhythmic "r-r-r-clunk, r-r-r-clunk." This was soon supplemented by McHugh's dreaded "you're fucking it up, you're fucking it up." He'd come in on the offbeat, so it went "r-r-r-clunk, you're fucking it up, r-r-r-clunk, you're fucking it up, r-r-r-clunk . . ."

I finally turned off the key and said, "We're out of gas. It's your fault for making me keep the engine running for three hours in front of the Ravenswood." McHugh sat in silence for about a minute, then put his hand on his forehead and drew it slowly down over his face in his best imitation of Edgar Kennedy's slow-burn act. He had done a bit as an elevator boy in an Edgar Kennedy comedy at RKO a few months before and had picked up the annoying habit of impersonating Kennedy whenever the opportunity presented itself.

We sat there in silence, McHugh with his eyes closed waiting for me to absorb the full impact of his slow burn. I looked straight ahead down the dark, run-down street, wishing I had never gotten involved in the special investigator business. Finally, I looked over at McHugh and saw that he was now doing his Humphrey Bogart twitch, his eyes still closed. A deep bass voice came from nowhere. "You boys want some tea?" I looked around and saw, just outside my window, the blackest face and the whitest teeth I'd ever seen. I said, "Huh?" and the black face said, "Tea. You boys want some tea?" While I was wondering what he was talking about and trying to decide whether or not to roll my window up, another, even deeper, voice said, "Tea, weed, marijuana. You boys looking for tea?" I turned and saw another black face at McHugh's window.

McHugh now seemed to be imitating a pimpled sixteen-year-old high-school student, scared out of his wits. He quickly recovered and said, "How much?" Deep Voice Number One said, "How much you got?" McHugh turned to me and said, "Tell him how much you got." I said, "I've got a dollar and thirty-five cents." Deep Voice Number Two said, "Shee-it. You couldn't buy

shit with that." I asked if they knew where we could buy some
gas instead, and Deep Voice Number One told us about an all-
night gas station around the corner, at 109th Street and Comp-
ton Boulevard. Deep Voice Number Two said, "You better get
your white asses outa here and don't come back until you got
more'n a dollar thirty-five." I said, "Yessir," and McHugh didn't
say anything.

That is, he didn't say anything until after we had our gas
and were driving home. Then he said, "Why did you kiss his
ass?" I said "Whose ass?" and McHugh said, "That dope hustler.
You called him 'yessir.' Anybody who says 'yessir' to anyone is
an ass-kisser. You're even worse. You're a black ass-kisser." I
thought about this for a while but decided nothing could be
gained by arguing, so I didn't answer him until I dropped him
in front of his house. He lived with his mother in two rooms
over a garage in back of a stucco house on Willoughby Avenue,
near the Goldwyn Studio. As he got out and slammed the door,
I yelled, "Nuts to you!" after him and drove away.

On Friday night, McHugh and I arrived at the pepper tree in
front of the American Legion Stadium an hour early to watch
the movie crowd. We saw Lupe Velez go in with Johnny Weissmuller; we also saw Lynne Overman, Jack Oakie, Ruby Keeler,
and Al Jolson. I told McHugh that I knew Al Jolson because I
had worked as a chorus boy in *Harold Teen* and had taken Ruby
Keeler's sister out. McHugh said, "Why don't you say hello to
him if he's such a big pal of yours?" I was just about to say "Hi,
Al," when Jack Chris came up behind us. "Gimme the reports
and don't look at me," he said. We both turned around, slack-
jawed and surprised, and stared at his fat profile. He had his
back to the pepper tree and was looking straight ahead, not at
us. The top part of his face was quite sinister, the Panama hat
pulled low over the dark glasses, the red nose, the cigar. But the
bottom half, the Guy Kibbee part, was soft and powdered white,
like an uncooked loaf of bread.

"I said don't look at me," he said. "Just lean against the tree,
fix your eyes on some object, and look ahead. Pretend you're
waiting for somebody." We followed his instructions, one of us
on each side of him. I fixed my eyes on a poster for the fight that
night—Baby Arizmendi versus Bert Colima.

We had been on the assignment four nights with varying
degrees of success. Some nights we followed Chalky Wright,
some nights Johnny Indrisano. Wright always went to the black

section of town (McHugh: "He's going to coon-hollow again"), and Indrisano to an Italian restaurant called the Napoli on North Broadway (McHugh: "Doesn't that wop bastard ever get tired of spaghetti?").

After the experience with the dope peddlers, we decided to stay in our car, get a rough idea of where the two bodyguards went, and make up the rest. McHugh would make notes in his own inimitable style, telling the facts, exactly what happened. I would then type up the actual report. I went to a typing class at Hollywood High night school so, every night before picking up the Chevy I took McHugh's notes in and typed the actual report, cleaning up McHugh's language and adding anything that I thought would interest Jack Chris.

McHugh version, first night:	*Arrived Ravenswood 8:30. M. West, etc., arrived at 11:30 P.M. while Parrish taking a piss. Parrish fucked up mission because: (a) he had to pee, (b) he's a lousy driver and couldn't start the car until Mae West, her fat friend, and the coon and the wop disappeared.*
Parrish version, same night:	*McHugh and Parrish arrived Ravenswood as scheduled.*

Subject A (Mae West) arrived 11:27 riding in back seat of large black Cadillac, California license no. 3W5.
Subject B (Chalky Wright) driving.
Subject C (Jim Timony) riding in back with Subject A.
Subject D (Johnny Indrisano) following in black Chevrolet, California license no. 4Z9026.

Both cars passed Ravenswood, turned left on Beverly Boulevard, left on Arden Boulevard, left on Clinton Street, left on Rossmore, and then left into Ravenswood underground parking basement.
11:42. Black Chevrolet (4Z9026) left Ravenswood with Subject B (C. W.) driving. McH. and P. followed Subject B to Central Avenue but lost him in traffic due to accident between fire engine and milk truck at Central Avenue and 11th Street.

Chris said, "Now, don't look at me, but when I light my cigar put the report in my right coat pocket." I was on his left. As I was thinking how to get over to his other side without looking at him, McHugh pulled out some papers and stuffed them in Chris's pocket. Chris walked away and was lost in the crowd.

When I felt it was safe to stop staring at Baby Arizmendi's poster, I turned to McHugh and said, "What did you give him?" McHugh looked at me patiently and said, "I gave him the reports, jerk. What do you think I gave him, dirty pictures?"

"Did he give you our money?" I said.

McHugh paled visibly. He was so nervous he had forgotten about the money. "Don't worry about it," he said. "He'll pay us next time."

"I don't think he will," I said.

"Why not?" His voice was an octave higher.

"Because you gave him your notes. I've got the typed reports here."

I suggested we work out some explanation and go see Chris at the Hall of Justice the next day—say it was a joke or something, give him my typed report, and get the money that Chris owed us. McHugh was against this. "Chris told us not to come back to his office," he said. "He gets nasty when you cross him." I said he might get even nastier when he realized he was paying ten dollars a night for a report in McHugh's handwriting (I emphasized that) on me peeing. I pointed out that *he* would eventually have to see Chris at family gatherings or church socials or funerals or something, but that *I* could just forget the whole thing, cut my losses (I would have made two-fifty a night instead of five dollars) and not be a special investigator any more. McHugh finally saw my point and agreed to go to Chris's office.

We got out of the elevator and walked down the long marble corridor. Chris's name was still on the glass door, but he wasn't there. The policeman on duty said he was out of town for two weeks. We asked the policeman if he had left anything for us, an envelope with twenty dollars in it or anything like that? The policeman looked at us as though we were crazy and said, "Chris? You must be kidding." We weren't, but we smiled dismally as though we were, and I handed him the envelope with my typed reports. "Please give him this when he comes in." The policeman said OK and I said thanks and we left. When we were in the elevator McHugh said, "What did you suck around *him* for? You didn't have to say please or thanks. All you had to do was give him the goddam envelope." I told him nuts to him again. That was now my standard retort when he criticized my behavior. I found that it didn't make him angry like "fuck you" or "kiss my ass" but still showed that I wasn't taking his criticism lying down.

It was Saturday and we didn't have to go to school, so we took a streetcar to the Coliseum at Exposition Park and saw Cotton Warburton lead the University of Southern California to a 21-to-6 victory over Stanford. We decided we would keep on being special investigators for another week as though nothing had happened, and then, if Chris didn't show up at the pepper tree on Friday night, we would prorate our earnings and quit. We figured we would each have made ninety cents a night for eleven nights.

We also talked vaguely about driving the rental Chevy to Tijuana and leaving it there to get even with Chris. We abandoned this idea because it would have cost more than the ten dollars Chris had given us to get home, and besides, I had signed for the car personally. McHugh said I could change my name to Charley Sucker and nobody could ever trace me. "Except you," I said. "Let's forget it."

McHugh said, "OK, we'll give the sonofabitch another week. If he doesn't come through next Friday, we'll write him off. I'm not going to be pushed around by some fat distant relative of my old man, who's been dead for thirteen years anyway." I reminded him that the policeman had said Chris would be away for two weeks. McHugh said, "He's full of shit. Never trust anybody in a uniform. Especially a cop."

Chris was waiting for us at the pepper tree the following Friday night. He seemed much friendlier, so I looked at him instead of at the fight poster (Jimmy "Killer" Meehan versus "Handy" Evans). He looked at me too, and said, "I liked your report, kid. Here's your money." He handed me some bills and said, "Count it later." He turned to McHugh and said, "I didn't like your report as much as I liked your partner's." He handed him some bills and walked away. We went around to the other side of the tree and sat down on the curb to count our money. We figured Chris owed us fifty-five dollars each. When we straightened out the bills, we discovered he had given me sixteen dollars (a ten-dollar bill and six ones), and McHugh (his relative) unfolded four crumpled one-dollar bills.

"Hello, Bobby. You'll never see the fight from here." I looked up and saw Al Jolson and his piano player and close friend,

Harry Akst. I stuffed the sixteen dollars in my pocket and stood up and shook Jolson's hand. He said, "Ruby and Gertrude" (Ruby's other sister, not the one I had taken out) "couldn't come tonight. I've got two extra tickets. Would you kids like to use them?"

McHugh was staring at his four one-dollar bills, still in shock from the meeting with Chris. I said, "How about it, Jack. Mr. Jolson has offered to take us to the fight." McHugh looked up and went into one of his imitations. This time he was a syco-phantic teen-ager who couldn't believe he was being introduced to one of the greatest entertainers in the world. He jumped to his feet, held out his hand, and said, "Pleased to meetcha, Mr. Jolson. Bob has told me a lot about you." I said, "This is my friend Jack McHugh." Jolson said, "Any friend of Bobby's is a friend of mine," and shook McHugh's hand. When he felt the four crumpled-up dollar bills he said, "No, you can't pay. The fight's on me."

As we entered the stadium and went to our ringside seats, all eyes turned, and practically everybody said, "Hi, Al," or "Good evening, Mr. Jolson." Carole Lombard yelled, "Hi, Jolie!" from across the ring.

Jack Chris was sitting in the third row, to the left of us. McHugh and I waved to him, but he showed no sign of recognition. "That's Jack Chris, the guy we work for," McHugh blabbed. Jolson said, "What do you mean, you work for him? I thought you were still in school, Bobby."

I said, "Well, I am, but I'm doing some work for the district attorney's office too, on the side."

He said, "And you're doing it for Jack Chris?"

I said, "Yes. He hired us, but he hasn't paid us."

Dan Tobey, the tuxedoed announcer, jumped into the ring and said, "LAADIEES AND GENTLEMEN—YOUR ATTENTION, PLEASE!" The stadium erupted in applause and boos. Jolson leaned over to me and said, "Have supper with me after. I want to talk to you."

"Handy" Evans split "Killer" Meehan's eye in the second round and won on a TKO. Jolson paid Harry Akst twenty dollars (he had given two-to-one odds on a ten-dollar bet) and said, "Let's eat." He took us to Henry's, on Hollywood Boulevard near Vine. He asked more about our special investigator jobs. I told him everything, and McHugh wound up the story with, "I'm related to him and he only paid me four lousy dollars."

Jolson said, "How much does he still owe you?" I told him ninety dollars, forty-five dollars each, and he said, "Now lemme tell you what you're gonna do and what you're *not* gonna do. First of all, you're not gonna follow anybody any more. Forget being special investigators. You're high-school students again. OK?" We both stopped chewing on our club sandwiches and nodded. "Then, next week, I want you, Bobby, to come to Warner Brothers Studio and have a chat with Blayney Matthews."

Matthews was head of the Warner Brothers Studio police department. The year before he had been the chief investigator for the district attorney's office and assigned to a drunk driving, hit-and-run manslaughter case. A famous, talented and, at that point, irreplaceable dance director was the driver of the death car. He was also in the middle of shooting one of Warner Brothers' most expensive musicals. When the case came up, the special investigator, Blayney Matthews, said it wasn't the dance director's fault after all. The dance director was acquitted and went back to directing the Warner Brothers musical. Shortly after, Matthews resigned as chief investigator for the district attorney's office and was appointed head of the Warner Brothers Studio police department. It was well known that the appointment was in recognition of the good sense and high integrity that he had shown in the matter of the dance director.

Matthews was a big, red-faced man with kind blue eyes. He listened to my story with great interest. When I finished, he said, "OK. Go to the pepper tree next Friday night and if Jack Chris doesn't show up and pay you what he owes you, let me know, OK?" I said, "OK." He said "OK" again, but I felt that we had had enough OKs, so I said, "Thank you, Mr. Matthews," and was glad McHugh wasn't there to accuse me of kissing his ass.

The following Friday night, Speedy Dado was fighting Buddy Cohen, a local favorite from Boyle Heights. Every seat was sold, and scalpers were hawking tickets at a premium. When McHugh and I arrived at seven o'clock, Chris was already standing at the pepper tree. He walked over to meet us, gave us each an envelope, and said, "The job's over. Here's your final pay." McHugh said, "Do you mind if we count it?" Chris said, "Kiss my ass," and walked away. There was a one-hundred-dollar bill in each envelope, the first ones I had ever seen.

I called Blayney Matthews and told him we had been paid in full with a bonus. He said he was glad to hear it. I thanked him and asked him how he had arranged it. He ignored my question and told me to be sure and tell Al Jolson how it all came out. I said I would.

Jolson was shooting *Wonder Bar*. When I finally got him on the phone, he asked me to have lunch with him at the studio. "I've got a little story to tell you," he said.

"Once upon a time, there was a very nice lady named Mae West," he began. "She was quite well known and made quite a bit of money—so someone wrote a note threatening to kill her if she didn't pay the writer a large amount. She took the note to the district attorney's office and the case was assigned to Jack Chris, one of their top investigators. Chris took one look at the note, recognized the handwriting and the style of the black-mailer, and had him locked up within forty-eight hours. He then went to Miss West and said he thought her two bodyguards should be thoroughly investigated in case they had anything to do with the blackmail attempt. He said he could personally handle the investigation for one hundred dollars a day, cash, that it wouldn't interfere with his regular work at the district attorney's office.

"Then, Bobby, guess what he did? He hired two high-school kids to do the job for ten bucks a day and he pocketed the other ninety.

"But that wasn't enough for him. He was a smalltime crook who couldn't stand to see a corner uncut, so he shortchanged the kids. He could have milked out his little racket indefinitely if he hadn't been so greedy. But those guys always slip up, and once they slip, they keep sliding until they bump into somebody smarter and tougher, somebody like Blayney Matthews, for example. When that happens, the smarter and tougher guy says to the smalltimer, 'I think you made a mistake when you paid those kids last Friday night. It might be a good idea to pay them all you owe them and give them a little extra for good luck.' The smalltimer usually says, 'Thank you for pointing that out to me,' and does as the smarter and tougher guy suggests. And you know somethin', Bobby, that's exactly what Jack Chris did. Not only that, he was so grateful to Blayney Matthews that he sent him a case of champagne, which Blayney exchanged for a case of bourbon."

Jolson finished his smoked salmon and scrambled eggs and continued, "I talked to Mae West this morning and she said that a nice fellow named Jack Chris had now completed a thorough checkup on her two bodyguards and that they are both clean as hound's teeth." (I pictured Johnny Indrisano and Chalky Wright in a hound's mouth, sparkling with innocence.)

Jolson finished his coffee just as an assistant director came to our table and said, "They're ready for you on the set, Mr. Jolson."

Al said, "Be right with you." When the assistant director had gone, he turned his head slightly away from me but kept his eyes on me. It was an effective way he had of looking at people when he was serious or suspicious or kindly. I had seen him use it on three thousand people at the Winter Garden Theater in New York, as he sat on the stage apron and said, "You ain't heard nothin' yet," before singing "Mammy." I had seen him use it on Ruby Keeler, whom he loved very much, and I had seen him use it on a Warner Brothers lawyer, whom he didn't love very much. So when he gave you that sideways look, out of the corners of his eyes, you never knew exactly what was coming.

"Bobby," he said. "You told me and Ruby you want to be a director. The Hall of Justice is the worst place in the world to learn that kind of work."

The waitress brought the check and I said, "Let me take it, Al." He looked at me for a moment, smiled and said, "I don't think she can break a hundred-dollar bill." Then he turned to the waitress and said, "Put it on the production account, honey."

12

C. B.

C ECIL B. DeMILLE probably gave work to more extras than any other single director. I worked for him many times in large crowd scenes. Sometimes I'd be so far back in a crowd of Israelites or Crusaders that I wouldn't actually see DeMille's face, only a figure in riding pants and puttees, with a large megaphone hiding him from the shoulders up. Ominous sounds would come out from behind the megaphone, and "Hezzy" Tate, Eddie Selvern or one of the other assistant directors would assure us that it was DeMille yelling abuse at us. We accepted the assistant's word and we accepted the abuse, because if we didn't we wouldn't get our three dollars (later five dollars) at the end of the day.

Along with Erich von Stroheim and a very few others, DeMille was considered a bona fide member of the Royal Family of Hollywood. He was also a caricature of the tyrannical movie director. Crowds (and seas) parted when he approached. He carried a riding crop, which I never saw him use on a star; but I did see him use it on the man whose sole job was to carry a chair around and slip it under the royal bottom whenever DeMille chose to sit. The occasion on which he failed was witnessed by several hundred extras and some visitors from the Southern Baptist Convention.

DeMille was carrying his engraved leather-bound, spring-back script and a copy of the Old Testament in one hand. His riding crop hung around his wrist. He decided to sit down next to a wind machine to add some text from the Bible to the script (or vice versa—no one ever found out which) and the chair-carrier was caught off guard. As he thrust the chair forward, a fraction of a second late, he caught DeMille on the back of his bald head. The script binder flew open and script pages went sailing over the children of Israel (us) like large pink, blue, and white snowflakes. DeMille managed to hang on to the Bible and his riding crop.

It was probably a reflex action and he probably didn't mean it, but he struck out at the chair-carrier and caught him across the seat of his pants, not a hard blow, but enough to keep the man on his toes and the chair under DeMille for the rest of the picture. Even so, from that day on, DeMille always glanced back before he sat down.

DeMille started his professional life as an actor and remained an actor throughout his directing career. On his productions, he was always the star, and the publicity department was kept well aware of this. DeMille permitted the other actors to perform in front of the motion-picture camera, and he did his bits in front of the still camera.

I finally met the great man in person at Paramount, where he was preparing a contemporary picture called *Rough on Rats* (later changed to *This Day and Age*). Charles Bickford was the star, supported by Judith Allen, Richard Cromwell, Eddie Nugent, and Harry Green. As I remember the story, Bickford played a crooked mayor. A bunch of teen-agers, led by Richard Cromwell, decide to take over the city and rid the government of corruption and dishonest politicians. The climax to the picture was a scene in which the teen-agers abduct Bickford and tie him to a long eucalyptus pole. They march him through the town to the fairgrounds, where they have dug a pit fifteen feet square and ten feet deep. The bottom of the pit is full of large rats. The teen-agers dangle Bickford over the rats until he agrees to reform.

I was chosen by DeMille to play one of the leaders of the revolutionary teen-agers. On the day of the big finale he hired several hundred boys and girls from the local schools to fill up the fairgrounds. After we had dangled Bickford over the rats to DeMille's satisfaction and the scene was "in the can," it was announced to the four hundred hungry teen-agers that we would now make a still picture. It was one-fifteen and union rules said we had to go to lunch at one o'clock, but none of us had the guts to buck "the old man."

Still photos of the action in a picture were a necessary part of every production—necessary for the sales and distribution of the picture. Most directors paid little attention to this, but De-Mille was a salesman first and a director second, so he usually "directed" his own stills. As a matter of fact, he often seemed to spend as much time and energy on the stills as he did on the actual scenes.

He would get in front of the whole company and act out the scene for the stars. Then they would mimic him, and when he saw the action or the expression he wanted, he would yell,

"Still!" and everyone would freeze. If he saw anyone moving after he said "Still!" he would make life very uncomfortable for the culprit.

DeMille and the camera crew were on a twenty-foot platform at one end of the stage. The cast and four hundred extras were sweating under the hot lights at the other end. DeMille's megaphone-muffled voice boomed out from the tower, "Raise Mr. Bickford!" We hoisted Bickford over the rats. DeMille screamed, "Action!" Bickford grimaced in horror. The four hundred raised their fists and yelled, "Down! Down!" We lowered Bickford closer to the rats. DeMille yelled, "Don't anyone look at the camera! Hold it! STILL!" We all froze like statues, and the still photographer snapped his picture.

In fact, we didn't *all* freeze like statues. One of the boys holding the end of the eucalyptus pole apparently moved his head just as the picture was snapped. DeMille saw the movement and yelled through his megaphone, "That boy in the sweater moved. Hold up your hand. No, not you. The boy at the other end. Yes, you, in the *green* sweater. Hold up your hand." If the boy had held up his hand poor old Charles Bickford would have been dumped into the pit on his head, so he just shook his head and said, "I didn't move, Mr. DeMille."

DeMille turned to his assistant and said, "Bring him up here."

The assistant ran down and helped put Mr. Bickford into a safe position on the side of the pit, away from the dreaded rats. He said to the unfortunate pole-holder, "Mr. DeMille wants you to come to the camera."

When the boy arrived at DeMille's side, DeMille addressed the whole company through his megaphone. "This young man says he didn't move and spoil the shot when I said 'Still!' I think he did. I've sent the picture to be developed. As soon as it's back from the lab, we'll know who was right. In the meantime, you can all sit down where you are and wait."

After about fifteen minutes the sweating photographer came back with a wet print of the still. The boy's face was a blur. DeMille was right. He thanked the still man and picked up the megaphone. "The still was spoiled because this young man didn't listen to directions. When I say 'Still!' I expect everyone to remain perfectly still. Now we'll try it again." He turned to the unfortunate pole-holder. "All right, son, you can go home. We won't need you any more."

The boy climbed down from the platform and DeMille

started to lecture the crowd about giving a full day's work for a full day's pay. As he talked he noticed two men far in the back muttering to each other. DeMille stopped his lecture and said, "That man in the back in the gray coat—hold up your hand." The man held up his hand. DeMille said, "Yes, you. Come up to the camera, please."

The man made his way through the crowd to the platform and climbed up to DeMille's side. DeMille said through his megaphone, "This man was talking while I was talking, so he must have something terribly important to say. I'm going to let him say it to all of us." He handed the megaphone to the man. "Go ahead. Tell us all exactly what you think is more important than what I was saying."

The man said, "I'd rather not, Mr. DeMille."

DeMille said, "Nobody's going to hold it against you." The man still refused.

DeMille said, "All right, you can go home too. We'll ask your friend." He turned to the crowd and said, "Will the other man involved in this urgent conversation please come to the camera." The man worked his way through the crowd and climbed up to the platform. It was now almost two o'clock.

"There are four hundred people waiting for lunch because of you. Will you kindly tell them what you had to say that was so important?"

The man, Eddie Boyle, a tough little seasoned extra, took the megaphone and said in a loud, clear voice, "I said, 'I wonder when he's going to call lunch.' "

The crowd burst into cheers. DeMille muttered something to his assistant and started to climb down from the platform. Amazingly, there was a trace of a smile on his lips. The assistant announced, "Lunch. One hour."

There is a legend, according to which, what Eddie Boyle said was "I wonder when that bald-headed old sonofabitch is going to call lunch." Eddie Boyle was tough and seasoned, but he was not as tough and seasoned as all that, though some of us at the time wished he had been.

13

Soap Gets in Your Eyes

DIRECTORS were "typed" the same as actors. Lewis Milestone was a "war" director because he directed *All Quiet on the Western Front*. After *The Iron Horse* and *Stagecoach*, John Ford was known as a western director. *The Dawn Patrol* made Howard Hawks an airplane man. After *Trader Horn*, W. S. (Woody) Van Dyke was typed as an outdoor-location (adventure) director.

In fact, there were only two kinds of directors, good and bad. The good directors directed all kinds of good pictures, and the second-raters directed all kinds of second-rate pictures. Milestone directed *Of Mice and Men* and *The Front Page* as well as *All Quiet on the Western Front*. Ford directed *The Grapes of Wrath, Arrowsmith, The Informer*, and *How Green Was My Valley*. Howard Hawks didn't need airplanes to make *Red River* and *Bringing Up Baby*, and Woody Van Dyke was just as good with *The Thin Man* as he was with *Trader Horn*. King Vidor made *The Big Parade*, one of the great war pictures—he also made *The Crowd* and *Street Scene*.

Be that as it may, the one director guaranteed to bring tears to your eyes was Frank Borzage. *Secrets*, starring Mary Pickford, *Man's Castle, Seventh Heaven*—all tender, beautiful pictures. Who better to direct Charles Boyer and Jean Arthur in *History Is Made at Night?*

This was a love story involving, among other things, the sinking of the *Titanic*. The passengers were lined up at the rail, waiting for the lifeboats to be lowered. We were supposed to sing "Nearer My God to Thee" as the camera, mounted on a platform suspended from the ceiling of Stage 3 at Goldwyn Studio, moved in front of us. Our base pay was seven-fifty per day, but if we sang, we were raised to ten dollars per day. Then Borzage decided he wanted six of the doomed passengers to cry. Another two-fifty adjustment for the lucky half-dozen.

This was "special business," and Borzage turned it over to Arthur Ripley, the second-unit director, and Joshua Logan, the dialogue coach. In those early days of sound, it was an accepted fact that motion-picture makers couldn't talk and couldn't direct others to talk. Consequently, a "dialogue expert" was often brought out from the "speaking stage" in New York to help with the words, or, in this case, with the crying. Joshua Logan was our coach. Ripley would select the criers and Logan would coach the tears at the proper time.

Ripley said, "How many of you can cry?" We all held our hands up and he said he would try us out, one at a time. He started testing at the opposite end of the line. I was so nervous I ran out to the toilet. While I was there, I noticed the bar of Lux soap which was furnished to all studios in exchange for publicity photos of the stars using Lux. I scraped my fingernails across the soap, lodging enough Lux under my nails to keep me crying for a week. When I got back to the set, Ripley and Logan were having a rough time. They had found only three genuine criers. The rest were poking themselves in the eyes and thinking about their dead mothers, the Depression, the loss of the two-fifty adjustment, and any other sad thoughts that might bring on tears. When my turn came, I squeezed some soap into my eyes and burst into song—*"E'n tho' it be a cross, near-er to thee—near-er my God to Thee, near-er to Thee. . . ."* The tears flowed, the cameras rolled, and Frank Borzage's reputation as a sentimental director was intact.

14

Having a Wonderful Time

RKO bought *Having Wonderful Time*, Arthur Kober's stage hit, and decided to make it with Ginger Rogers, Douglas Fairbanks, Jr., Lee Bowman, Lucille Ball, and Red Skelton playing parts created on the stage by Jewish actors, among them Henriette Kaye, Jules (later John) Garfield, Shimin Ruskin, and Irving Israel. Stillwell's Camp at Big Bear Lake, a mountain resort a hundred miles from Hollywood, would serve as the location, which had been a camp in the Catskills in the stage version. There were serious discussions as to whether or not the Jewish accents, which provided much of the humor in New York, should be retained in the film. It was finally decided that Ginger, Douglas Fairbanks Jr., Lee Bowman, and Lucille Ball didn't look Jewish, so they settled on gentile accents for the stars but compromised by assigning a Jewish director.

For the rest of us, cast and crew, it was a happy holiday. Nine weeks surrounded by some of the most beautiful mountains and girls in the world. The casting directors had raided the Connover and Powers modeling agencies in New York, signed twenty sensational-looking girls, and given them stock contracts for the picture. Along with nineteen other boys, I was hired as a stock actor. Being young and innocent, I thought the twenty girls were for the twenty boys, one for each. Of course, it didn't work out that way. Each beauty was on the picture for a specific reason.

The reasons were the president of the bank which financed RKO, the producer, the director, the leading actors, the cameraman, the assistant directors, and other key personnel, right down to, but not including, the lowly stock actors. The model I picked before I learned this devastating news was a charming, full-bosomed blonde named Betty. She wasn't fat, but she leaned toward an attractive plumpness.

We reported to RKO on Gower Street at 6:00 A.M. An assistant director herded us onto the bus. He checked the boys in first and told us to go to the back of the bus. Then he checked the girls in and told them to sit in the front section, where he was sitting. I was one of the last of the boys, so I sat in the middle. Betty was one of the first of the girls, so she sat in the seat next to me.

The assistant director went to the production office for ten minutes. When he came back, all the boys and girls, except Betty and me, had changed seats, and the bus was completely integrated. The assistant director told me to move to another seat, and he sat down with Betty. I wound up next to a six-foot brunette named Kay who treated me like a turd all the way to San Bernardino. It turned out that she was the friend of the president of the bank that backed RKO and felt she should have been driven to the location in a private car. I had seen her picture on the cover of *Vogue* and *Harper's Bazaar* many times, every time they needed a cold-looking girl with hot eyes, a perfect nose to look down at you from, and no tits.

After our pee stop at San Bernardino, Betty sat down next to me in Kay's seat and said, "I'd rather sit with you." Being a sophisticated man of the world and a goddam fool, I said, "Won't your boy friend mind?" She said, "He's not my boy friend, but if you'd rather I didn't . . ." I quickly recovered my *savoir-faire* and said, "No, please. I'd rather sit with you too." She said, "What's the matter, don't you like Kay?" I said, "She's all right, I guess, but we didn't have much to talk about what with my not being the president of the bank backing the studio and all." Betty said, "I don't like bankers, they're all so old." I didn't remember ever actually having met a banker, but I said, "I feel the same way. I can't stand old bankers."

I looked over my shoulder and saw that the assistant director and Kay were talking animatedly. She wasn't treating *him* like a turd. She was looking down her perfect nose at him (he was much shorter, even sitting down) and smiling as though he were the director instead of the fourth assistant. He was smiling up at her too. If he had been sitting on her lap, he would have looked like Charlie McCarthy. As it was, he reminded me of a duck grinning up at the Statue of Liberty. Neither of them was looking at me, so I put my hand on Betty's. When we arrived at Stillwell's Camp, I had known Betty four hours, held her hand for two, and thought I was in love. The clear smell of no city had a lot to do with it, but the fact that she squeezed a note saying "Please come see me tonight" into my palm influenced me too. No question about it, this was the high point of my eighteen-year-old life. All signals were go.

The stock girls were put in individual cabins around the lake shore. The stock boys were quartered in a large dormitory-like bunkhouse with the lower-echelon members of the crew. Dinner was served in the camp dining room at seven o'clock. Everyone was there to get instructions for the next day. That is, practically everyone was there. Most of the pretty girls, including Betty, and most of the top production brass were missing. The fourth assistant director was missing too. I asked one of the girls where Betty was and she said Betty was tired and went to bed early. After dinner I went to her cabin and knocked on the door. There was no answer.

Being a stock actor seemed like a dumb job to me. We put on thick grease-paint make-up and stood reacting in the background. We were herded around like sheep, yelled at like cattle, and regarded as necessary evils. We weren't really actors. We were extras on weekly salary. I hated it. We couldn't even get a tan through the make-up.

In southern California in those days, it was considered obscene to have normal-colored skin. You always had to look as though you were a playboy with nothing to do but sit in the sun. It's different now, I guess, what with a blanket of smog hanging over the Los Angeles basin most of the time, but in those days a tanned face was a status symbol and very important to anyone working in the movie business.

During the second week of shooting, one of the canoes tipped over and dumped two of the stock girls in the lake. One of them couldn't swim, and I helped pull her out. My wardrobe white flannels and sweater were soaked, so I stayed in the water and helped the prop men with the canoes for the rest of the day. I liked it a lot better than "acting," so I asked Jane Loring, the associate producer, if I could continue on that job for the next few days, while we were shooting on the lake. She said OK and I became a temporary prop man.

Jane Loring was a thin, sharp-faced woman of about forty. She had been a script girl, then a film editor, and was now the assistant to the head of the studio. He had sent her on this location as his representative. She was the front-office boss, and a very capable one.

When we finished the work with the canoes, I went to see Miss Loring in her room at the lodge. She was talking on the phone to the head of the studio as I came in. ". . . drunk, Pan. He's drunk all the time. I've got enough problems without a drunken fourth assistant."

She motioned me to sit down and continued on the phone. "The models were a mistake too. It's always a mistake to have too many pretty stock girls on a location picture. We should know that by now. They're all jumping in and out of bed like fun-loving otters. . . . What? . . . I *know* that, Pan. I know that's part of their job. I know the head of the bank wants to get laid. I know the director needs comfort after a long day in the hot sun. I know these things, Pan, and I can handle the situation if I can get a decent assistant instead of a lush."

She motioned for me to pour myself a drink while she listened to the studio boss. I shook my head and started to leave, indicating that I would be back later. I didn't want to hear any more details about the activities of the pretty models. After all, Betty was one of them and I knew from personal experience that she wasn't any fun-loving otter—at least not with me. Since the bus ride, our relationship had leveled off to friendly politeness, not at all what I had anticipated. If she was jumping in and out of somebody's bed, it certainly wasn't mine, and I didn't want to hear Jane Loring tell the head of the studio whose it was. Before I could get out, she motioned for me to sit down and wait.

"Surely we can find a sober assistant director," she said into the phone. "I tell you I've got to have some help." A pause, then she said, "OK. Get him up here as soon as you can." She hung up, lit a cigarette, and turned to me. "You sure you wouldn't like a drink?"

I said, "No, ma'm."

She said, "Don't you drink?"

I said, "No, ma'm."

She said, "Why not?" and I almost said, "Because I want that job," the truth. Instead I said, "I don't like the taste of it," which was true too.

She said, "What's on your mind? Why did you want to see me?"

I said, "I was going to ask you if I could keep on doing some other work on the picture besides acting. We're finished with the canoes and the prop man doesn't need me any more. I couldn't help hearing what you said on the phone. Could I fill in until you get a new fourth assistant director?"

She said, "Well, we only call him a fourth assistant director. I actually want an assistant to me. I want someone who will get up at four in the morning, make fires in all the cabins, wake up the cast and crew, and then report to me so I can tell him

his next duties. On some days he'll be in charge of transportation, and on others he'll clean up the set or help with the
wardrobe. From time to time he'll be asked to make hot coffee
and chocolate or drive the prop truck. He'll have to do anything
that someone else isn't doing, including acting when he's asked
to. Do you still want the job?"

I said yes, and she said my salary would be cut ten dollars
a week except when I was acting, then it would be raised again
for the days I acted. I agreed, and she called the studio and told
them not to send a new fourth assistant.

I had dinner with her that night, and when I left her I
rushed to Betty's cabin to tell her the good news. Still no answer
when I knocked.

The next morning, when I knocked again in my official capacity as new fourth assistant, Betty's door was answered by
the man I had replaced. I told him I was supposed to build a
fire and wake Miss Stone and he said not to bother, he would
take care of it. As he closed the door, I felt terrible, but my depression didn't last long. After I had lit a few fires and seen
what some of the models looked like when rustled out of bed
at the crack of dawn, I didn't feel so bad. Besides, when I
thought about it, it seemed like a pretty fair deal. He had my
girl and I had his job. He and Betty left the next day and were
married by a justice of the peace in San Bernardino. He stopped
drinking, and several years later he was second assistant on a
picture I directed at RKO.

During the next few weeks, I learned a lot about location
shooting and a lot about fun-loving otters. On more than one
occasion, an otter would be alone when I arrived to pass along a
late-night change of call or to wake them up at dawn. They
often wanted to talk to someone they trusted, like a fourth
assistant director who knew where all the other girls spent
each night. On some very cold mornings, I would take coffee
or tea to certain ones in bed and listen to their problems. I had
keys to all the cabins, and I found that if I speeded up my
fire-building and carefully rationed my time, I could hear more
and more problems every day. In special cases, I sometimes
skipped the fire-building altogether and went right into the prob-
lem-hearings. Even old Kay stopped treating me like a turd as
soon as her banker went back to New York.

I got to know her pretty well, as a matter of fact. I asked
her why her banker went back to New York and she said he
had to go back on urgent family business. She also said that

whenever he was around she had a spastic colon and had to rest most of the time. I said I was sorry to hear that and could I get her a hot-water bottle and she said no thanks, that she felt fine now, that it was the damnedest thing, she only had this spastic colon when the banker was around, but it would be nice if I could just stay with her awhile, talking and getting her more tea and things like that.

I told her I thought she didn't like me that day on the bus and she said she thought I was just one of the stock actors and that her banker had told her to keep away from actors. However, now that I was an assistant director he couldn't complain, could he?

I said, "No, especially when he must be almost to Chicago by now."

She turned the full power of her *Vogue–Harper's Bazaar* eyes on me and said, "Why don't you come to bed?"

I stayed with her for over an hour and then suggested she should take the day off in case the spastic colon returned in the middle of a shot.

As I came out of Kay's cabin, Jane Loring met me and said, "Bob, you're looking tired. I'm worried about you. I think you're spending too much time waking the cast up. From now on I'll get one of the older boys to handle that job. I want you to take charge of all the transportation on the picture. It's more responsibility, but you'll get more sleep and you won't have to waste so much time listening to the boring problems of the stock girls."

I said, "Anything you say, Jane. You're the boss. However, it might be a waste of manpower. After all, I know all the stock girls now, and I'll have to start fresh with the truck drivers. Do you want to waste what I've learned about waking up the cast and getting them on the set?"

She looked straight at me through her glasses. "It won't be a waste, Bob," she said. "You can remember what you've learned and use it on the next picture. I want you to handle the transportation."

I paused a moment and thought to myself that she was, after all, right. It was time to go on, to learn about truck drivers and transportation. "OK, Jane," I said. "My aim is to become a director, and the more I learn, the better."

When the location work was finished and we returned to the studio, Jane Loring said, "If you really like the business so much and want to stay in it, you should go to work in the cutting room. That's the best place to learn." Very good advice, because in those days many directors were former cutters. The trouble was that it was practically impossible to get a job in the cutting department. Every executive had a relative who wanted to be a director, and they knew about the cutting-room route too.

Jane Loring finally used her influence and got the man in charge of the negative vaults to take me on as a "dupe-negative measurer." Duplicate negatives of all of the old F.B.O. and RKO pictures were filed away in vaults. Despite the efforts of the experts, the negatives of these films would shrink after a few years. My job was to measure each foot of dupe negative and record shrinkage by the year, month, week—to say nothing of by the reel, foot, frame, and sprocket hole.

I reported for work, and the first thing I was asked was "Are you in the union?" When I said no, I was told I couldn't go to work until I had a union card. I went to the editors' union and said I wanted to join. The executive secretary, a Mr. Sharpe, asked if I had a job. I told him I would have a job as soon as I had a union card. He said the membership was closed, and in any event, I couldn't join the union until I had a job. Stalemate. I started to leave, and he said, "The initiation fee is one thousand dollars." I said I didn't have a thousand dollars and couldn't possibly raise it. He said, "Well, if you can raise five hundred dollars and agree to pay me ten dollars per week in cash until you've made up the other five hundred, I'll see what I can do."

I told him that what he could do was forget the whole thing. I went back and told Jane Loring what had happened. She said, "Go home and sit by your phone."

Mr. Sharpe phoned two hours later and asked if I could come in and see him. When I arrived, he was most cordial. He said that he had been thinking about our meeting that morning and had suddenly remembered a rule in the bylaws that permitted taking in new members where they saw exceptional possibilities. He said I looked like a young man with exceptional possibilities, and he handed me a card with my name on it. The initiation fee (including the first year's dues) was one dollar. I paid the dollar and became RKO's first card-carrying dupe-negative measurer.

The RKO studio management changed quite often in those days. Joseph Kennedy, Charles Koerner, Howard Hughes, David O. Selznick, and Pandro Berman were some of the names that were periodically painted in and out on the doors of the executive suites. At this time, the current management suddenly became aware of the cost of keeping old dupe negatives, so they decided to make a survey and find out which ones to keep and which ones to throw out—as is done, from time to time, with old bank statements, old clothes, and old friends who have proved disappointing. The doomed films were to be sent to the lab and melted down for silver nitrate salvage.

I sat at a little bench at the end of the vault with two film rewinders, a negative-measuring machine, and some loose-leaf binders in which to write down my findings: "*Cimarron*, 1931, Reel 6, three hundred feet into reel: negative has shrunk .006 milligrams per 100 feet. This is .0003 milligrams more than Reel 6 of *King Kong*, 1932. This could be because of lack of camphor in *King Kong* vault or because of difference between Bell and Howell and Eastman perforations."

On my first day on the job, I heard two grizzled old cutters talking outside my window: "What's the new kid doing?"

"Measuring negatives of the old pictures."

"What for?"

"Beats the hell out of me. They ought to burn all that crap anyway. Not worth a dime."

I didn't care. I was in the union and I was actually working with film. Good film, too. Those two guys were cutting Leon Errol comedies and I was measuring *King Kong*.

When I finished measuring a complete film, I was supposed to recommend whether or not to scrap the negative, depending strictly on the degree of shrinkage. When I measured a picture I liked, I would fake the figures, hoping to save it from destruction. I added their silver nitrate salvage potential to the films I didn't like and justified my actions by telling myself that I had preserved something good and saved some vague, future audience from being bored by something bad. I was playing God-critic and I was only making fifty-four cents an hour!

A month after I started work, Mr. Sharpe was arrested for fraud and was subsequently sent to prison for six years. I remember being glad that they didn't catch him until after I had gotten my union card.

I measured negative until I thought my eyes would pop. I filled three thick volumes with data about old pictures that would remain unloved until years later, when they were sold to television for millions of dollars. After that, the 16mm rights were sold for additional millions. The last I heard about that vault full of old film was that the successors to RKO were negotiating a deal for the 8mm rights. It shouldn't be too difficult because the original 35mm negative has probably shrunk to 8mm by now.

As far as I know, there has never been another "dupe-negative measurer" in the film editors' union.

15

Billy Hamilton, Positive Cutter

AFTER my tenure at that post, I helped out as an apprentice and assistant music cutter and as a sound-effects cutter on many of the pictures being made at RKO. Among the other assistants were Theron Warth, Bob Wise, Mark Robson, Bob Belcher, John Sturges, and Henry Berman. They were all extremely helpful to the new boy, especially Bob Wise and Mark Robson. They taught me to splice, clean reels, carry cans, file trims, and keep my mouth shut in the projection room. Then they taught me to "bloop" sound tracks (paint out extraneous noises), to do synchronization (work the numbering machine that put matching code numbers on each foot of sound track and picture), to lie to producers, and, finally, to begin to edit sequences.

There were also two top music editors, George Emick and Walter Hannemann, who patiently tried to teach me to edit music. After a short time they found out, as Frank Lloyd had years before, that my sense of rhythm was deficient. Instead of firing me, as they might have done, they covered for me and gave me nonrhythmic chores like carrying reels to the dubbing room, cutting sound effects, and cleaning up the cutting room. Besides *Having Wonderful Time,* we worked on *Gunga Din, The Informer, Winterset,* the Astaire-Rogers musicals, *Bringing Up Baby*, and *Mary Queen of Scots.*

Our boss was a wide-eyed little man named Billy Hamilton. He was considered one of the best cutters in Hollywood. He had been a boxer and then a stunt man and was now a permanent RKO fixture who had survived four or five studio administrations. His cutting room was decorated with Petty-Girl cutouts from *Esquire* magazine and a sign that said, "In this room ART is spelled with an F."

Billy drank. He wasn't a drunk, but he would sometimes come into the cutting room in the morning in a very shaky condition, assign work to us, and then make his way out of the back gate to the Melrose Grotto, where he would drink steadily until noon and then return to the cutting room ready for three or four hours of sobering work.

Quite often, he would let assistants actually edit sequences and then he would sit patiently with them and correct their mistakes. One day, after I had shown him one of my sequences, I asked him if he wasn't afraid we would learn too much and become editors and take his job.

"Editors, my ass," he said. "You don't edit film, you cut it, the same as you cut cloth or sheet metal or cheese. So we're cutters, not editors. And when you guys learn to cut better than me, you can have the goddam job. From what you've just shown me, I'm not worried. Put it on the moviola and we'll recut it. I'll be back in ten minutes." And off he went again to his oasis, the Melrose Grotto.

The moviola is an editing machine through which you run the picture and sound on two separate pieces of film. The picture is projected on a miniature screen on the right and the sound is amplified (or was then) by means of a photoelectric cell on the left.

When Billy came back, we worked on the sequence for three hours before he turned the reel over to me for splicing (patching). In those days, we stuck the pieces of film together with an acetone-base film cement instead of with Scotch tape as they do today. We used a heated Bell & Howell splicing machine that we worked with our hands and feet. A piece of positive film would be put in place, emulsion side up. We'd scrape the emulsion off, down to the celluloid base, apply some cement with a little brush, and then clamp the next piece onto it, celluloid to celluloid. These two pieces were held firmly between two hot metal plates for a few seconds and then the spliced-together film was rolled onto a metal reel. Each splice took about fifteen seconds to make, and one frame was lost each time, two sprocket holes on each side of the splice.

"After you finish splicing the reel, come over to the Grotto and we'll have a drink," Billy said. This was the first time I'd been honored with an invitation. He didn't particularly like his protégés to see him boozing. When I joined him at the bar, he asked me what I wanted and I said, "I'd like a glass of milk."

Billy and the bartender stared at each other for a full twenty seconds, and then Billy said, "Don't you drink?" I said, "No," and he said, "No wonder you couldn't cut the goddam sequence."

We drank silently for a while. He put three double bourbons away while I had another glass of milk and a hamburger. Finally, he said, "We didn't 'edit' that sequence"—he said the word as though he were squeezing a turd through his teeth— "we *cut* it. And then we recut it. And then we cut it again. And again. And about ten times after that. And now we're going back to have another whack at it because I've just had an idea about the end. But we're not going to 'edit' it. We're just going to keep cutting it until we get it right. That's what's fun about this business, getting it right, correcting all the mistakes, especially our own. The cutting room is the court of last appeal. It's the last chance to put out the best possible movie." He swallowed the last of his drink. "You can't take something that's basically bad and make it good, but you can usually make it less bad. And what you *can* do if you're not careful is take a good picture and louse it up."

He asked the bartender for four quarters, which he inserted in the illegal one-arm bandit slot machine on the other side of the bar. He drew blanks on the four tries and kicked the machine as the last lemon fell into place. "Let's get back to work," he said.

As we walked back to the cutting room, he said, "You can make film do anything you want it to do. It will lie for you or tell you the truth. It can make you cry or laugh or inspire you or confuse you. You just have to learn how to work with it so that it says the things you want it to say."

When we finished cutting a picture, we added sound effects and music and took it out to a "sneak preview" before cutting the negative. The sneak previews were exciting affairs, a picture's first test in front of an impartial audience. A number of theaters in southern California were equipped with "doublehead projection." That meant they could run the separate sound and picture strips in synchronization. If the sneak preview went well, we would cut the negative and "marry" the two strips into one—the "answer print." If it didn't, we'd recut and preview again.

When a preview location was chosen, we would pile into big black studio limousines and drive to the theater about an hour before our film was scheduled to start. It could be a Hollywood theater near the studio, or one as far away as Santa Barbara or San Francisco. If it was an important picture, we'd have a large group of hangers-on and executives from the front office. If it was a less expensive "program picture," we could all fit in one or two cars—usually the contract producer, the head sound mixer, Billy Hamilton, and one or two assistants. Sometimes the director was invited, sometimes not. The head of the studio usually came or sent a stooge to report the results to him. The name of the picture was not announced, but the theater manager put out a sign saying MAJOR STUDIO FEATURE PREVIEW TONIGHT. They rolled this sign out whether the picture was *Gone with the Wind* or a Roy Rogers western.

After the preview, stamped cards were handed out to the audience as they left the theater. They were asked to answer certain questions—age, occupation, sex, nationality, etc. And then they were asked to judge the picture they had just seen ("excellent," "good," "fair"—they never put "poor" on the cards) and to add comments about the stars. Pencils were provided in the lobby, and you could either fill the card in then and there or mail it in later. Mel Frank, a writer, claimed to have invented a card that blew up in your face if you wrote "stinks" on it.

We would collect the cards and stand around on the sidewalk in front of the theater sorting them out and discussing the picture. If it had been a successful running, everybody always had a lot to say. If it was an obvious disaster, most of the people from the studio would slink away or stand around waiting for the studio head to say something so they could agree with him. Not Billy Hamilton, though. He had seen more pictures, good and bad, than any of them, so he was the acknowledged expert. Sooner or later, someone would say, "What do you think, Billy?" and he would tell them, cold turkey, exactly what he thought.

"It's OK. I think we should ship it." Or, "It dragged a bit after the opening. I think we'd better take out some footage." Or, "Ginger's song is too long. Let's drop a chorus and get back to the story" (*Flying Down to Rio*). Or, "This audience didn't understand it. Let's take it out again tomorrow without making any changes. We'll go to some highbrow neighborhood" (*Winterset*).

As we drove to my first sneak preview, Billy said, "Take the film to the projection booth and stay in there to see that the dumb sonofabitch puts on the right reels." (He firmly believed that all projectionists were out to sabotage our efforts.) "Then, when the picture's over, you personally pack the reels in the cans and bring them back to the car. Don't let the bastard touch the film except when he's actually threading it up. Watch him all the time and cough or fart or drop a film can from time to time to keep him awake. After the film is locked in the car, you can hang around and listen to the big brains tell us how to fix the picture. They'll tell us this whether it needs fixing or not. Sooner or later, somebody will say it's too long and somebody else, usually the producer's wife, will say, 'Yes, I think you could lose about eight minutes.' Now you'll notice that the less experienced they are or the dumber they are, the more likely they are to know exactly how many minutes should come out of the picture. After they've talked for a while, I'll agree to everything and then we'll go back to the studio and go to work."

By the time I had absorbed these instructions and was ready to acknowledge them, he had dozed off.

The preview went just about the way Billy told me it would. The projectionist threaded up the first reel, dimmed the lights in the theater, and threw the switch that started the machine. I held my breath as I watched the film "leader" (the twelve feet of blank film that lead up to the first frame of picture) snake over and around the several sprockets until it finally passed in front of the bright carbon-projection lamp. When the first splice went through the gate it made a loud click. I had heard that click many times in the studio, but somehow here, with our film on show to a live audience, it seemed much louder. I looked around and saw the projectionist opening the door to the fire escape to light a cigarette. Smoking was not allowed in the booth because the nitrate film used in those days was highly inflammable. I knew he was supposed to watch the film through the little window into the auditorium and keep an eye on the projection machine in case it went out of focus or the film broke or the sound was too low or too high. I reminded him of his obligation, and he said, "Look, kid, relax. If the picture's any good they won't notice whether it's in focus or not, and if it's a stinker they'll start to applaud or walk out."

As the preview title ("This is a pre-view of an RKO-Radio Picture. Kindly fill out the preview cards in the lobby as you leave the theater") faded out and the RKO trademark faded in (a radio tower that sent out animated, lightning-shaped Morse code signals), I was proud as could be, because my first two splices had held.

The main title came on:

RKO-RADIO PICTURES PRESENTS

Ginger	Douglas
ROGERS	FAIRBANKS, JR.
(loud applause)	(applause)

in

Having Wonderful Time

with

PEGGY CONKLIN (no applause)

LUCILLE BALL (loud applause)

LEE BOWMAN (no applause)

RICHARD (RED) SKELTON ("Who's he?")

ANN MILLER ("Who's she?")

DONALD MEEK (polite applause)

The title lasted ninety feet (one minute), so I had a breather. It was all one piece of film, no splices. After that I sweated out the splice clicks for the first reel (about eight minutes), and then after the projectionist switched over to the second reel, I put the first reel in the proper cans and watched the screen. The picture seemed to go well for the first half hour (three reels), and I began to relax. The projectionist read a magazine the whole time, except when he had to stand by the machines to change reels.

About six minutes into reel 4, the comedian (Red Skelton) in charge of the bus to "Camp Carefree" started one of his routines, and the audience wasn't amused. The harder Skelton tried, the more restless the audience became. Finally, two or three people got up and walked out. From then on the preview was a shambles, but not just because of Red Skelton.

I was now used to the rhythmic click of my well-made splices going through the projection machine and stood with my face pressed to the window to the auditorium, watching Red Skelton lose customers. Suddenly, the rhythmic clicking was cut off by a terrible metallic sound, and the screen went white and silent—no picture, no film through which the carbon light could project its larger-than-life-size image of Red Skelton overacting. Somebody (me?) had left a paper clip in the reel, and it had jammed the machine. I watched in horror as the film piled up, crunching and ripping as the wheels ground irrevocably on. The projectionist put his magazine down and stopped the machine. I fought back a wild impulse to run out on the fire escape and dive off, head first. Billy Hamilton came in, took one look at the mess, and said, "Start the other machine." The projectionist did as he was told and the next reel started just as the audience's derisive applause reached alarming proportions. Fortunately, the new reel started with music, so Billy said, "Turn it up louder." The projectionist did as he was told again, and the audience settled down to watch Ginger Rogers in a bathing suit.

I will say this for Billy's self-control. He didn't hit me. He didn't even kick me as he had the one-arm bandit. He just said, "Clean it up," and went back to the auditorium. I sorted out the bits and pieces and wished I were back in Columbus, Georgia. People continued to drift out during the rest of the running. In another particularly embarrassing Red Skelton number, there was some slow applause again, and it brought the projectionist in from the fire escape. He looked through the window to the auditorium and said, "See what I mean, kid? Perfect focus, perfect sound, perfect splices—but crappy picture." He was not my favorite person. We had worked like hell on every foot of that picture.

On the sidewalk outside, it all worked out just about the way Billy said it would, except for the paper clip. Nobody had counted on that, not even Billy. The producer said, "What the hell happened?" and Billy said, "Probably the goddam projectionist." The producer said, "It was going great until the break." Billy said, "Yeah, except that people were walking out." Red Skelton's agent came up and said, "The cards are sensational. Here's a whole batch saying that Red Skelton is a great discovery." Billy said, "Let me see them." He shuffled through a few cards and said, "They're all written by the same person."

Finally, the producer himself (not his wife) said, "Look Billy, I think we should take out about seven or eight minutes and preview again. How soon could you be ready?" Billy said, "We'll go back and work all night and tomorrow and be ready tomorrow night." We piled into the cars and headed back to the studio. Billy never mentioned the paper clip, but every time I went to a preview with him after that, he slipped a paper clip into the palm of my hand.

When we got back to the studio, Billy said, "Just stick the main title on reel two and meet me over at the Grotto. Nobody pays much attention to the first eight or ten minutes of a picture anyway." We followed his instructions and previewed in another theater the next night, with the same disastrous results. After that it was decided to "shelve" the picture, i.e., hide it away and pretend that it hadn't been made. It rested in a vault unwanted and unloved for six months before George Stevens was persuaded to take it over. He replaced Red Skelton with Jack Carson, reshot some old scenes, invented new ones, and the picture was finally released about two years later. The results were unspectacular.

After the New York reviews came out, I sat with Billy in the Grotto and said, "What went wrong, Billy? Everybody tried hard on that picture."

He finished his third bourbon and said, "It went wrong in an office. It always starts there. Some guy says, 'Let's make this Broadway hit into a movie.' Another guy says, 'What's it about?' The first guy says, 'Well, there are these Jewish kids, with accents and Jewish humor and . . .' The second guy says, 'It sounds great. We'll get Ginger Rogers and Douglas Fairbanks, Jr., and a new comic named Red Skelton.' The first guy says, 'Is he Jewish?' and the second guy says, 'Not necessarily,' and the first guy says, 'OK, let's go.' "

Out of respect for Billy, I ordered a Cuba libre instead of a glass of milk. He started on his fourth bourbon.

"So they shot the picture and we cut it and it's a flop. But let's not slit our wrists. We're starting another picture tomorrow. It's called *Bringing Up Baby*. Maybe it'll be better."

"Who wrote it?" I said.

"Who wrote what?"

"*Bringing Up Baby*. Who is the writer on the picture?"

"How the hell do I know? I never know a writer's name until I see it misspelled on the main title."

"What about the script? Don't you read the scripts?"

"Of course I do, but not until after I've cut the negative. I read 'em then just to see if they're anything like the picture. I used to read 'em before that but they always confused me."

I soon found out that many cutters felt that way about writers. The cutters were a realistic lot whose main concern was the film that arrived from the lab, not the pages that were given to the director. Billy once told me he tried to run a script through the projection machine and it looked terrible. Some years later, I began to meet writers and discovered that they often felt the same way about cutters and that there was something to be said for both sides.

16

The Ice Age Comes
to Hollywood

S ONJA HENIE was a Norwegian Olympic ice-skating champion. She was hired by Twentieth Century-Fox to make the first American ice-skating musical film at about the time I was laid off as a sound-effects editor by the same studio. The assistant casting director was a friend of mine and suggested I work as an ice-skating chorus boy on the film until work picked up in the sound-effects department. Several hundred hopefuls were herded into one of the large sound stages. The assistant dance director said, "How many of you are expert ice skaters?" Most of us lived by the "Always Say Yes" policy, so most of the hands went up. The assistant dance director and the head casting director, Lew Schreiber, selected thirty of the prettiest girls and thirty of the prettiest (and tallest) boys. The rest were dismissed.

Schreiber addressed the lucky sixty, "Now listen you kids. We're building a new stage with an eighty-thousand-dollar ice rink. It won't be completed for three weeks, so we can't test your ice skating." We all breathed a silent sigh of relief. Schreiber walked down the line, looking at each of us like a drill sergeant. "I'm taking your word that you're all skaters. If I find out that any one of you is lying, I'll throw you right off the picture. Is that understood?" We all nodded and tried to look like ice skaters. Most of us had never seen a pair of ice skates, but we felt we could somehow learn to skate before our perfidy was discovered.

Schreiber said, "We'll give you contracts for forty-five dollars a week. You'll be measured for costumes today, and when the rink is frozen and ready to skate on we'll call you and you'll start rehearsing. Any questions?"

A soft-spoken girl said, "I have a question." She was Virginia Ray, the prettiest of the nonskaters. She would have been a beauty in any company—not very tall, she had delicate, beautiful legs, strong hands, perfect features. Her complexion, though, was what made her stand out from the other pretty girls. Pure peaches and cream, and a smile that made you think she was smiling at you for the first and last time in her life, and yours. There was something secret about it that only you could possibly know. She was intelligent too. In later years, she married Budd Schulberg, divorced him, and married Peter Viertel. At Salka Viertel's openhearted house on Maybery Road above Santa Monica Canyon, I have seen her more than hold up her end of the conversation with Aldous Huxley, Irwin Shaw, Bertholt Brecht, and Christopher Isherwood, though not all at the same time. She crossed the Atlantic on the Ile de France with Ernest Hemingway, and he called her "Daughter." She had a full life and a tragic death. But that day she was just an extremely attractive young girl questioning a remarkably unattractive older man. She flashed her secret smile and he melted.

"OK, what's on your mind?" Schreiber said in his softest, gentlest voice. His softest, gentlest voice was not unlike a donkey braying.

Virginia (or "Jigee," as she was later known) said, "How much will we be paid while we're waiting for the rink?"

Schreiber unmelted and snapped back to real life. "What's your name?"

Jigee said, "Virginia Ray."

Schreiber said, "You get paid nothing until you start rehearsing."

"What if we are offered another job?" Jigee said, not smiling now.

"That's your business," Schreiber said, also not smiling. "But if you want this job you'll keep yourself available until we call you. Any other questions?" There were none. We signed our contracts and were measured for the costumes. I spent the intervening three weeks at State Beach surfing and getting a tan.

This was the ideal situation in southern California at that time. A guaranteed steady salary at a definite future date and no necessity to look for work in the meantime. Even if jobs were offered, you could decide to work or not work, according to the weather. If the weather was good—'Sorry, I'm not available." If it was bad—"Yes, what time do I report?" And you could tell the other beach bums, "I'm starting at Fox next week on a ten-week run. I'm getting a tan so I won't have to wear make-up." The other bums would say, "Gee, too bad. I'm glad I don't have to work in this weather," and you would say, "Yeah, I guess you're right, but they're paying ninety bucks a week"—you usually lied, doubling your salary—"I can't afford to pass it up," and both of you would wish you were in the other's position.

When the ice rink was ready, I reported to Twentieth Century-Fox along with the other fifty-nine boys and girls. We were fitted with skates and told to "just get out there and skate around a bit. Test the ice."

Out of the sixty, only three could make it across the rink. The three who made it were professional hockey players from Canada, who looked like hockey players, not chorus boys—flat noses, cauliflower ears, and a paucity of front teeth. The rest of us flopped around like the nonskating fakes that we were. Ice skating was not as popular in southern California as getting a tan, so it would have been difficult to find replacements. Besides, we had all been costumed at great expense. The studio was stuck with three hockey players and fifty-seven non-skating liars.

I was slightly embarrassed, but not too much. The whole movie business was an illusion, dreams on inflammable nitrate celluloid that disappeared immediately after they were flashed on a blank screen. Fakery was the name of the game and I thought we were no worse than the very able head of Twentieth Century-Fox who had had some copies of an otherwise possibly unpublishable novel printed at his own expense so that he could pass himself off as a writer. Besides, I had gotten away with posing as a drummer boy, a mule skinner, and a special investigator, so I really thought I could somehow make it as an ice skater if they would just give me a bit of ice and time to practice.

Darryl Zanuck, the self-published writer, and his hatchet man, Schreiber, came down to view the sorry spectacle. After watching us flail around like wounded ducks for a few minutes, Zanuck and his cigar went back to his office without saying a word, and Schreiber called us together at one end of the stage. He was angry. He pointed out that we were the worst bunch of crooks it had been his misfortune to come across during his entire ten years as casting director for Mr. Zanuck, and unless we got out there and skated properly and stopped all this kidding around he would have to call the producer down to deal with us.

This was not a very serious threat because the producer was a gentle man named Raymond Griffith, an ex-comedian who had lost his voice and could not work as an actor after sound came in. His last acting job had been in Lewis Milestone's *All Quiet on the Western Front.* He had played the dying French soldier in the shell hole with Lew Ayres. He could only speak in a hoarse whisper now, so he would actually be a welcome change from the screeching, hysterical Schreiber, who finished with, "Mr. Zanuck is disgusted with you. Now how about it? Whadda ya gonna do? Ya gonna skate, or do I call Mr. Griffith?"

Jigee said, "Mr. Schreiber, most of us can't skate. We can't skate for you, we can't skate for Mr. Zanuck, and I seriously doubt if we could even skate for Mr. Griffith. We would like to skate, but we can't. And one of the reasons is . . ."

"Who the hell are you?" Schreiber said.

Jigee said, "I'm still Virginia Ray."

"Well, Miss Still Virginia Ray," Schreiber said. "You're in with a bunch of liars and con men who are costing this company thousands of dollars. I've a good mind to replace all of you except those three guys out there." He pointed his cigar at the three plug-uglies who were skimming around the rink.

Jigee turned on the old secret smile and said, "And what would you do with the extra fifty-seven costumes?" She kept smiling, and before Schreiber could answer she said, "Before you replace us and start fitting the replacements and finding out if *they* can skate, wouldn't you like to hear *why* our skating is a bit rusty?" She knew (and Schreiber now knew) that there weren't more than five or six ice-skating members of the Screen Actors Guild.

"Rusty!" Schreiber exploded, "Who the hell do you people think you're kidding? I should have you all arrested for fraud. I mean you should be ashamed of yourselves. Have you got any idea of what Mr. Zanuck is going to say to this?" He walked over and put his beet-red face six inches from Jigee's peaches-and-cream face. "Have you?"

Jigee came through like the champion that she was. "He's probably going to say, 'Those kids have got us by the balls, Lew. Henie goes on salary in six weeks. The sets are being built. Commitments are made. And we don't have any skaters. Why not, Lew?' And you're going to say, 'Because they double-crossed me.' And he's going to say, 'Yes, I know, Lew, but isn't this a bit late to find that out?' And you're going to say, 'They'll never work for Twentieth Century-Fox again.' And he's going to say, 'That doesn't help, you dumb shithead. When can we start the picture?' "

Schreiber turned away and leaned on the rail around the

rink, staring at the hockey players. Jigee went on, "What I was trying to tell you was that the reason our skating is rusty is that most of us have never skated before in our lives and up until today there's been no ice to learn on. Now that we have some ice we could probably learn to skate in a very short time. Wouldn't that be cheaper than importing skaters from Canada or the East, finding places for them to live, trying to get them into the Guild, remaking the costumes for them, and teaching them to perform in front of a camera?"

Schreiber said nothing. He just kept staring at the three hockey players, wishing there were sixty of them.

Jigee said, "Well, how about it, Mr. Schreiber? What do you think?"

Schreiber said, "It's blackmail, that's what I think. You're all fired. You took the job under false pretenses. I'm reporting you to the Guild." He got up and walked off the stage.

I went back to State Beach and worked on my tan. Two days later I was called back to Twentieth Century-Fox. The assistant dance director said, "The starting date of the picture has been postponed, we have six weeks to learn to skate and work out the routines. We'll do nothing but skate for the first three weeks, eight hours a day. Then we'll work out the routines. Everyone starts on full salary today. But week to week only. If you can't learn to skate, we'll have to let you go. There will be coffee and hot chocolate available for everyone all the time. Now get your skates on and start falling down."

We did. And at the end of three weeks there were a lot of sore ankles and some fairly good skaters. If you do anything exclusively eight hours a day, you can't help learning something about it. We were not ice skaters. We were extras who were learning to skate and who had been fitted with expensive costumes. The assistant dance director said, "OK, kids. That's the end of the free skating lessons. Tomorrow we start to work. So, get to bed early—and then get up and go home early." He winked at one of the "rough-trade" hockey players. "We want to give our all for Twentieth Century-Fox." He pursed his lips, turned his head, closed his eyes, raised his shoulder to his chin in the classic mock-fairy position, and minced away. When he got to the door, he turned back and said, "I love *all* of you!" We all gave him the bird. He waved his limp wrist at us and disappeared like Peter Pan. Our affectionate name for him was "Rubberwrist."

The next day we started working out dance routines on the ice, first to *Tales from the Vienna Woods,* then *Die Fledermaus* and finally, of course, *The Skaters' Waltz.* We skated our fool heads off all day and sometimes overtime into the night. We finally got so that we could manage without falling down or tripping each other. On the Sunday before the start of shooting, we had a dress rehearsal in costumes, with lights, props, etc. Zanuck, Schreiber, and Griffith came down to watch us. They brought with them Sonja Henie and her entourage and Sidney Lanfield, the director. This was the first time we had seen him. They all sat on a raised platform at one end of the rink. Zanuck and Schreiber smoked cigars. Lanfield chewed gum. Sonja Henie sparkled like a frozen Shirley Temple.

The house lights went off, the spotlights went on, the music started, and Miss Henie's skating stand-in (her skate-in?) flashed out of the shadows to the middle of the rink. A lot of us thought she was a better skater than Sonja, but she wasn't as pretty and she wasn't an Olympic champion. She did one spectacular spin and started toward the side to lead us on, sixty strong. We were in the form of a triangle, led by Jigee. As the skate-in zoomed toward us on one skate, we moved forward into the light. The skate-in was to come as close as possible to Jigee on a collision course, then at the last moment she was to stop, spraying ice in our direction, and skate happily away. Our glutinous mass was supposed to plod along after her in a flying wedge, singing "One in a Million," the title song, written especially for the picture by Lou Pollack and Sidney D. Mitchell.

It all went well for the first eight bars, then, just before the skate-in was supposed to stop and spray ice, she fell flat on her surprised plain face and slid into Jigee. Jigee went down and the next fifteen or twenty skaters in line followed like tenpins. It was a mess. The assistant dance director came running out on the ice, forgetting to turn the playback record off so the music continued on its noisy way as though nothing had happened. Wardrobe mistresses, make-up men, prop men, and all kinds of other people swarmed across the ice, some slipping and falling in the process. The dance director, sitting up in the Royal Box with Zanuck and Schreiber, kept screaming, "Stop the music!" but nobody heard, and "One in a Million" blared relentlessly on. Schreiber yelled at the dance director. Lanfield chewed his gum faster and tried to explain the situation to Miss Henie. She understood a little English, but not Brooklyn English, so she turned to her five Norwegians and said something in Norwegian.

No one was badly hurt, and it wouldn't have seemed so hysterical if someone had only turned off the goddam music. Finally the dance director climbed down and stopped it. Miss Henie came on to the ice and picked up the hairpin that had tripped the skate-in. She took it up to the Royal Box and gave it to Zanuck. He said something to Schreiber and started back to his office, preceded by his cigar and followed by Griffith and seven or eight assorted aides, including his barber, his masseur, his secretary, and Fidel La Barba, the former flyweight boxing champion whom I had first seen with Jack Dempsey at the "Breakfast with Champions." Nick Janois, who ran the studio commissary, brought up the rear.

Miss Henie told Schreiber she wouldn't skate until new hairdos were devised that guaranteed no hairpins on the ice. The assistant dance director was in disgrace for failing to turn the music off. One of the sixty skaters had sprained his ankle in the pile-up, so ominous rumblings about "danger money" started. The start of shooting was postponed a week to sort things out. At the end of the week we finally had a good dress rehearsal and were sent home early to rest for tomorrow, the first day of shooting.

When I arrived the next day, all the skaters were outside the studio gates and Lew Schreiber was having a shouting match with a man from the Screen Actors Guild. "It's no goddam good, Lew," the man was saying. "These are not extras, they are highly skilled specialty artistes. They're trained ice skaters. I'm not going to have them working for forty-five dollars a week. We have a minimum for specialty work. Swimmers and other athletes get sixty dollars, stunt riders get a hundred dollars. Even tap dancers get seventy-five dollars." He pointed to the sixty "specialty artistes." "And a lot of these kids are damned good tap dancers."

I thought Schreiber would explode. He was kind of a pink-red man to start with, short sandy-pink hair, pink eyes and lashes, pink face and teeth. All pink. And on this day he was wearing a pink tailored shirt with pink cuff links and a pink tie. Suddenly everything that was really his—the hair, the skin, the eyes, the lashes, the teeth—turned pinkish-green. The other things—the shirt, the tie, the cuff links—remained their original shocking pink. The effect was startling. "Bullshit," he said. "We

(Top left) Raoul Walsh. (Top right) Helen Parrish and Raoul Walsh at *The Big Trail* premiere. (Bottom) *The Big Trail* premiere. Thomas Hull, a real pioneer, is at center.

(Top) Raoul Walsh—his mark. (Bottom) *The Big Trail* cast. John Wayne is behind Helen Parrish.

(Top) Helen Parrish, Marguerite Churchill, David Rollins, and John Wayne. (Bottom) *The Big Trail:* the graveyard scene.

(Top) Johnny Indrisano, Chalky Wright: "clean as hound's teeth."
(Bottom) American Legion Stadium, Los Angeles.

JACK McHUGH

Talking Lines in "Flight"—Columbia Production
"Chinatown Nights"—Paramount   Featured in Educational Comedies

HOllywood 5797
Personal Management of Dixie McCoy—GLadstone 4226

(Top) Jack McHugh, author's "Dragnet" pal (casting photo). (Bottom) *Harold Teen:* at left, author and Marjorie Keeler.

(Top left) Cecil B. DeMille. (Right) *Having Wonderful Time.* (Bottom left) RKO Tower. (Right) Sonja Henie.

(Top) Billy Hamilton, one of the best cutters in Hollywood. (Bottom) *One in a Million* chorus. Author and Jigee are in front row.

(Top) Santa Monica State Beach when author first saw it. (Bottom) Santa Monica State Beach in 1940.

didn't *hire* them as tap dancers! We hired them because they told us they were ice skaters! They lied. None of them could skate." His pink-green eyes drifted over our way, and he spotted the three hockey players. "Except those three hockey players. They're the only honest ones in the bunch. The rest we had to teach how to skate. They were all bums who came in here under false pretenses and now you're giving me this "specialty artiste" crap. I'll pay the hockey players seventy-five a week just to show them that I respect honesty, and the rest of 'em can work for forty-five as agreed or I'll cancel the picture and these people will never work at Twentieth Century-Fox again."

The Guild man said, "Calm down, Lew. You only have to pay the hockey players sixty. *If* you want 'em to play hockey. That's the athlete's fee. But if you want them to act as specialty artistes in a dance number on ice, you'll pay them seventy-five dollars a week along with everybody else."

Schreiber said, "You heard me, Jerry. Seventy-five for the honest hockey players, forty-five for the crooks we taught how to ice skate. Take it or leave it. You got a half hour to decide." He turned and went back into the studio.

The Guild man took us over to the studio parking lot about two hundred yards from Schreiber's office, outside the studio gates. Twentieth Century-Fox had two giant parking lots, one for the lower-echelon "permanent" studio employees (lot A) and one for even lower-echelon "temporary" studio employees, i.e., extras (lot B). Each parking lot had places for one thousand cars. The studio executives, stars, directors, producers, and department heads parked inside the studio in parking spaces with their names painted on the asphalt. When a star finished a picture or a producer, director, executive, or department head was fired, his name was painted off the asphalt as soon as his car pulled out of the parking space. When a firing was imminent, the studio management notified the payroll department and the sign-painting department. When these departments were poised and ready to strike, the unlucky employee was notified. On D day a signal was flashed from the front office (Zanuck? Koenig? Goetz? Schreiber? Somewhere up there), and the departments sprang into action. A final check was sent to the now ex-employee's agent, and as the ex-employee drove off the lot, the sign painter rushed out and blotted his name off the asphalt forever.

The Guild man said we were being exploited, but he reminded us that we had signed contracts. The three hockey players suggested accepting the offer and splitting the extra ninety dollars they would be paid with the rest of us. Jigee pointed out that would only give us a $1.58 increase each, so we thanked the hockey players and looked for another solution. Jigee then said, "We've only signed *weekly* contracts. Why don't we tell Lew we'll work a week as per contract and then, if they like our work, renegotiate for the extra nine weeks that it will take to shoot the numbers?"

One skater, Jeremy Carroll, fought against this. He was all for sticking by the original terms. As the half-hour deadline approached, it was pointed out by several of the group that Carroll was the boy friend of the assistant dance director and consequently his objectivity was questionable. The way they expressed this was by yelling, "Fag fink! Fag fink! Fag fink!" every time he started to speak. We finally voted and decided (59 to 1) to follow the Jigee plan. We would skate as per the contract and then, at the end of the week, we would be free to leave if the management didn't come up with a better deal, and they would be free to fire us if our skating wasn't up to "specialty artiste" standard.

We waited in parking lot A and told each other how right we were while the Guild man went in to present our proposition to Schreiber. Jeremy Carroll sat by himself and pouted. The three hockey players started to deal a hand of three-handed poker, and the rest of us settled down to await Schreiber's decision. Encouraged by Jigee, we soon assured ourselves that we had been too easy on Schreiber: "Why should expert ice skaters only be paid seventy-five dollars a week, we should get at least a hundred like the stunt men!" "Yeah, this is dangerous work, don't forget the hairpin on the ice and Jimmy's sprained ankle!" "Yeah! we shoulda asked for at least one-fifty!" "Or two!" "Yeah, plus overtime and full insurance."

One especially militant young man named Jay Chandler stood up on the hood of a parked car and yelled, "All for one and one for all!" He had worked as an extra in the Ritz Brothers version of *The Three Musketeers* and remembered the electrifying effect this phrase had when D'Artagnan (Jimmy Ritz) yelled it in the picture. Jay yelled it again and everybody quieted down. I failed to see how this applied to our situation, so I said, "What in the hell does that mean, Jay?"

He yelled it again and added, "Two-fifty or nothing! All for one and one for all!" He was one of the few who had been able to pick up absolutely nothing about ice skating during the previous six weeks. He just couldn't do it and he would never be able to do it, something to do with his inner ear. He knew he would be fired at the end of the week if Schreiber accepted our proposition, so he had nothing to lose.

One of the hockey players looked up from the poker game and said, "We'll look like jerks if we try to raise the ante now." Having said his piece, he lost interest. He returned to the poker game and said, "One card." He was trying to fill an inside straight.

Jay yelled, "We'll look like bigger jerks if we give in to the capitalists. There's always a few who are willing to sell out. I SAY UNITED WE STAND, DIVIDED WE FALL. IT'S ONE FOR ALL AND ALL FOR ONE!" Jay couldn't skate, but he could sure come up with a cliché when he needed one, or, in this case, two. He got so excited that he raised his fist in what he thought was a Communist salute and came down hard on the hood of the car with his foot, yelling, "YOU'VE NOTHING TO LOSE BUT YOUR CHAINS!"

The hockey player filled his inside straight and said, "Bullshit, Jay," without looking up. At that point the owner of the car arrived. He worked on the night shift in the studio's accounting department. That gave him most of the day to work out with bar bells and learn judo. It didn't take his accountant's mind long to figure that Jay's scratchy footprints on the hood of his new gunmetal-blue Pontiac were worth about fifty dollars.

As he frog-marched Jay off to discuss this with the police, our Guild representative came back from Schreiber's office. He had been gone less than five minutes, and as he approached, my spirits rose. He walked like a man with good news. He was jaunty. He was smiling. He looked like a winner.

"The picture's off," he said. "They've canceled the picture." He was still smiling that nutty smile, so I thought he was teasing us and would next say something like "—but I talked them out of it." Instead he just kept smiling. I learned later that it wasn't a smile at all, it was a nervous grimace. When he got nervous the muscles under his eyes and around his nose tightened, pulling his upper lip up off his teeth.

Jigee said, "What did he say when you gave him our proposition?"

The Guild man said, "I didn't even have a chance to give him our proposition. As soon as I walked in the office, Schreiber said, 'The half hour's up, Jerry. Are those specialty artistes of yours going to go to work for forty-five dollars a week or do I cancel the picture?' I said, 'Lew, let me tell you how the kids feel about it," and before I could say any more, he said, 'Fuck the kids. Yes or no?' I told him we were not going to be bulldozed. He opened the door to his office and said, 'Get your ass out of here. The picture's off.' I told him he'd never get away with it, and he slammed the door in my face. As I walked down the hall, he opened his door and yelled after me, 'And get those goddam kids off our parking lot or I'll have 'em thrown off.' He was plenty mad, but so am I. And I'll tell you one thing right now. We're not going to take this lying down."

He paused, and I heard one of the hockey players say, "Gimme three cards."

I wanted to ask the Guild man why he was smiling so much when he came out of the office, but by now I was fed up with the whole thing and worried that last week's forty-five-dollar check was probably the last one I would see for a while. I have since discovered that union negotiators are quite often happiest when friction between labor and management is at its height. It puts them in the spotlight, though it also often puts the workers in the unemployment line and employers in the bankruptcy court. I remember feeling terribly depressed and wondering how Lew Schreiber felt—and what color he had turned. Pinker than ever, I guessed.

Was the whole thing a plot, with the union representative in on it? I thought of Mr. Sharpe up in San Quentin. And what about the director, the gum-chewing Mr. Lanfield? Where was he in all this? I particularly cared about his position, because I still wanted to be a director one day. I hadn't seen Lanfield since the day the skate-in fell on the hairpin. If the picture really was canceled, that would be one less picture to cut sound effects on, so it could even mean a longer layoff in the cutting department.

Jigee and the Guild representative started discussing strategy. The hockey players changed from poker to shooting crap and were now surrounded by most of the male specialty artistes, all waiting for a chance to lose last week's forty-five dollars. Jeremy Carroll had stopped pouting and was now smirking. He looked like a man about to say "I told you so." It was the last thing I wanted to hear, so I drifted away, hoping no one would notice.

Jigee saw me and said, "Where are you going?" I didn't really know where I was going, but I said, "To the beach." She said, "What, now? We've got to get this thing straightened out. Aren't you going to stay and vote?" I said, "For what?" She said, "For a course of action." I said, "I voted for a course of action once today. I'm going swimming."

I felt that we had all acted like jerks—Schreiber, Jigee, the guy from the Guild, the sixty "specialty artistes," all of us, with the possible exception of the three hockey players.

Twentieth Century-Fox Studio was between Pico Boulevard and Santa Monica Boulevard, halfway from my house to the beach. I put the top down on my black Dodge convertible and drove west toward the ocean. As soon as I was in my car, with Dick Powell singing "When Did You Leave Heaven?" on the radio, I felt better. The prospect of a day at the beach was much more promising than fruitlessly trying to argue my way back onto a dank sound stage. As I turned right on San Vicente Boulevard, Dick was just starting the part I liked best ("Do they miss you? Can you get back in? . . .") when he was interrupted by a news flash about Adolf Hitler's return to Vienna after the *Anschluss* and how there was no resistance from Britain and France and how Hitler said Germany's relations with Czechoslovakia would not be affected. When the news flash was over, Dick Powell had finished his song and I had missed the best part.

I turned the radio off and thought about Hitler and the Austrians until I turned right on Seventh Street and down through Santa Monica Canyon to the beach. I tried to picture the map of Europe and I remember thinking that whatever Hitler was doing, he was doing it a long way from Santa Monica Canyon, and besides, if England and France were not resisting, it must be OK because they were usually more or less on our side. By the time I had parked, put the top up, changed into my swimming trunks on the back seat (the front seat was too public), and plunged into the surf, I had forgotten about Adolf Hitler, Lew Schreiber, Jigee, and Czechoslovakia. In fact, I had forgotten about everything except the clear blue-green water and whether I should dive under the next wave or ride over it.

I swam all the way down to the Santa Monica pier, over a mile. I climbed up on the pier and had a hamburger and a chocolate malt at Eddie's. I then wandered over to Muscle Beach and watched the "body boys" working out and comparing muscles. When the hamburger and malt had digested, I dived back into the Pacific. As I swam north, I thought about not having forty-five dollars a week coming in. My mother was counting on my income and I felt guilty that I had stood passively and let Jigee and the Screen Actors Guild lead me into no income. When I was opposite Louis B. Mayer's beach house, I changed from the crawl to the breast stroke and thought about Hitler and the *Anschluss* for two hundred yards. As I approached the Santa Monica Swimming Club, I thought briefly that I should have joined Jeremy Carroll and tried to sway my colleagues into accepting Schreiber's deal. I also thought of what Schreiber said about not working again at Twentieth Century-Fox. He was a powerful man at the studio and his influence didn't stop at the casting office. He could probably keep me from working in the cutting room when work picked up there.

The water was so clean, the air so fresh, the sun so bright, that as I made my way north against the tide I soon forgot about Schreiber and the future and thought only about the sheer joy of swimming in clear salt water. I was far out beyond the breaker line, and as I passed Marion Davies's palatial beach house and came opposite State Beach where I would have to ride a wave in to shore, I seriously considered swimming on— past State Beach, past Malibu and Trancas, on and on and on— Ventura, Santa Barbara, San Francisco . . . I really felt I could swim forever.

Deep down, of course, I knew I'd better get back to the phone and find some work. The thought of dialing Central Casting and being told "Try later" was depressing, but life is real and I had now had my "get-away-from-it-all" swim, so I treaded water, waiting for a wave big enough to take me into shore. I cleared my mind of relatively unimportant matters and concentrated on catching the right wave. I mistimed the first two, but I caught the third. I saw it coming about fifty yards out and got set. The backwash from the previous wave swept me out to meet it. As it swelled under me I swam as hard as I could— flutter kick with the feet, arms flailing. I timed it just right and felt it pick me up. I arched my head and shoulders forward and down so the wave would catch under me and take me with it to the shore. My arms were held tight to my sides to cut down resistance. I remember knowing the exact moment when it all worked, when I knew the wave wasn't going to betray me, tumbling me over and over and then depositing me on the beach gasping and out of breath. I was swept along at tremendous speed, always just ahead of the crest, and finally, after what seemed a very long, wonderful time, found myself in shallow, safe water. My wave swirled around me for a moment and then disappeared forever. I stood up in the soft wet sand and thought, "That was a perfect ride." There was a completeness in it, something quite unique that no one would ever know about except me. It was like a charm, like a promise that everything was going to be all right.

When I arrived home, my mother looked at my wet hair and said bitterly, "You've been to the beach. Foxes have been calling all day." (It was always "Foxes" to her, never "Twentieth Century-Fox"—she never accepted Zanuck and Goetz's takeover from William Fox and Winfield Sheehan.) She was terribly upset. "Son, you must never leave the phone uncovered, you know that. Foxes called three times and said to call casting as soon as you come in. It's urgent."

I called and got some nasal-voiced girl in the casting office. She said, "Bob, can you come out this afternoon and sign a new contract for the Lanfield picture? The salary is seventy-five dollars a week plus overtime."

I said I would be right out, and she said, "OK, you start work tomorrow for a minimum of ten weeks."

PART

3

17

Producer-Director Relations

I WORKED as an actor and as an apprentice film editor on *The Informer* for John Ford at RKO in 1935. I had first worked for him as an extra several years earlier in *Mother Machree, Four Sons, Riley the Cop, Judge Priest, Steamboat Round the Bend,* and other pictures. Whenever he needed kids he called the Watson family (seven children of assorted sexes, sizes and ages), the Johnson family (six), or the Parrish family (four). This way he could fill a schoolroom scene and still only have to contend with three "movie mothers." In fact, with these three families, the kids became so film-wise that we were not always accompanied by a parent. One of the older kids in any one or all of the families could get the required number to the studio on the bus and see that they were costumed, fed, paid, etc. Or sometimes one of the six parents would come along by mutual agreement to keep an eye on all the kids.

Our three families became more or less Ford's kid stock company. He depended on us to give him no trouble, and we depended on him for work during the hard times of the Depression.

By the time *The Informer* came along I knew I wanted to be a director, so I hung around the set watching Ford as much as I could. He saw me on the set one day when I wasn't called as an actor and said, "Why aren't you in the cutting room?" I said I wanted to be a director and thought I could learn more on the set watching him. He stared at me for a while, chewing his handkerchief. I began to fidget. He then put his handkerchief in his hip pocket and pulled out a pipe. He filled it with tobacco from a pouch he had bought at Pesterres, the most exclusive men's store in Beverly Hills. I fidgeted some more. Finally, he lit his pipe and said, "Get back to the cutting room. That's where you learn about directing."

On the first day of shooting *The Informer* he asked Eddie Donahue, the first assistant director, to assemble the cast and crew on the set, and he introduced the associate producer of the film, a short, pudgy, red-faced man who had also served as Ford's associate producer on *The Lost Patrol* the year before.

"This is an associate producer," Ford told us. He put his hand on the associate producer's chin and gently turned his head so that we could see his profile. "Take a good look at him, because you will not see him again on the set until the picture is finished shooting." He shook the associate producer's hand and said, "Thank you, Cliff. I'll see you at the rushes."

The associate producer left, and we didn't see him until three weeks later. We were halfway through the last day's shooting when he walked on the set to congratulate Ford for finishing under schedule. At first Ford pretended not to see him. He sat in his chair chewing the end of his handkerchief. The people who worked intimately with Ford knew better than to approach him when he was chewing on his handkerchief. That was usually the sign that he was thinking or conniving or dreaming. In any event, it was considered dangerous to interrupt him. The associate producer should have known this, but he was so excited about being under schedule that he recklessly walked to the side of Ford's chair and said, "The stuff looks great, Jack."

The "stuff" was the rushes from the previous day's work. At RKO the front office viewed the rushes as soon as they arrived from the laboratory at 11:00 A.M. The director and crew usually viewed them with the editor after the day's shooting. I have read that Ford claimed he never looked at rushes. This may have been true on some of his films, but on the ones I worked on, he usually ran the rushes alone or with the cutter and the assistant cutter. If anyone else walked into the projection room, he would stop the screening and ask the intruder to leave. On the set the next day he would often pretend he hadn't seen the rushes.

From time to time, after viewing the rushes, an overeager associate producer would lose his head and become afflicted with the disease known in the trade as "rushes fever." When stricken, the victim would change from a normal (albeit quite often uncreative) administrator into a deluded bundle of nerves who, thinking that he had actually created the rushes, would dash about the studio telling everyone within earshot that "the rushes are sensational!" or "the stuff looks great!"

Quite often an associate producer would fake it. He wouldn't actually have rushes fever, he would only pretend to have it so that the director would not want to make retakes. Most directors could tell immediately whether or not an associate producer was sincere. Ford was the best diagnostician in the business.

He gave no indication that he had heard the associate producer. He just continued chewing on the handkerchief and staring ahead through his slightly smoked glasses. After a moment, the associate producer said tentatively, "Jack, I just saw the rushes. You're going to love them." Ford stopped chewing, turned slowly, and looked at the associate producer's stomach, which was just at his eye level. He then raised his eyes to the associate producer's face. He looked at him for a moment, then called his first assistant. "Eddie!" Eddie Donahue was off the set, so Ford's brother, Eddie O'Fearna, the second assistant, appeared. Ford ignored the associate producer and said to O'Fearna, "Have we finished shooting yet?"

O'Fearna said, "Not yet, Jack. We still have half a day to go."

"Then what's this front-office sonofabitch doing on the set?"

O'Fearna looked at his feet. Ford resumed chewing his handkerchief. The associate producer's face changed from normal beet-red to puce. Deathly silence from everyone else on the set. Finally, Ford called Joe August, the cameraman.

"Joe, the front office likes the rushes, so there must be something wrong. We'll have to keep shooting until we find out what it is. We won't finish tonight after all."

He turned to the associate producer and said, "What rushes did you see, Cliff?"

The associate producer said, "The Donald Meek interrogation scene, and believe me, Jack, he's sensational. When Preston Foster asks him . . ."

Ford cut in. He said to Eddie O'Fearna, "Call Donald in. We'll reshoot his interrogation scene this afternoon."

And we did. And we shot for two more days. Ford made extra close-ups, he reshot another sequence with Wallace Ford and Una O'Connor, and he spent almost a full day shooting main title backgrounds (shadows of British Black and Tans silhouetted against a process screen). The associate producer's premature congratulations cost RKO about $25,000.

The Informer swept the Academy Awards and is considered one of the classics of the American cinema. It is said that it only came into profit years later, when it was sold to television. I don't believe that, because, like all Ford's other films, it was economically shot and brought in well under budget. Still, it would have come into profit $25,000 earlier if the associate producer had stayed in his office.

18

Director-Cast Relations
(Female)

SOME of the actors and actresses in *The Informer* were from the Abbey Theatre in Dublin, but Ford selected Margot Grahame from the London Theatre to play Kay Madden, the prostitute.

The call sheet said "Ready on the set at 8:00," and Ford took it literally. The assistant director told Ford that Miss Grahame was still in the make-up department but that everybody was hurrying as fast as they could. Ford said, "For chrissakes, Eddie, it's her first day. Let's not panic just because an actress is a bit late. Let's give her some time." He sat down and put his pipe in his mouth. "What time is it now?"

The assistant said, "Two minutes after eight."

Ford said, "Well, let's give her until seven minutes after. There's no reason to make her nervous on her first day." He lit his pipe and the assistant rushed off to the make-up department.

At 8:07 Ford called Joe August and said, "Joe, it looks like we've run out of actresses. Let's do Victor McLaglen's scene." He went to another set on the same stage and started to rehearse with Victor McLaglen (Gypo Nolan) and Preston Foster (Dan Gallagher). McLaglen read his opening line and Ford stopped him. "Is that the way you're going to play it?"

McLaglen said, "Well this is only the first rehearsal, Jack. I thought you were going to shoot the girl's scene first."

Ford looked to the stage door. Still no Miss Grahame. He turned back to McLaglen. "You mean you really plan to play Gypo Nolan like that?"

McLaglen started to say, "Well, Jack, if you have any . . ." Ford said, "For chrissakes." He looked disgusted, as though he had just swallowed a bad oyster. McLaglen was devastated. Dead silence on the set. Ford said to no one in particular, "Well, we can't do this one either. What *can* we do? Is there any one actor around here who has done his homework?" He turned to J. M. Kerrigan (Terry) and said, "Will you take Victor over to the Grotto" (the Melrose Grotto, Billy Hamilton's hangout) "and get him a drink. Teach him his lines, and when he knows them, bring him back." He turned to his assistant and said, "Get Joe Sawyer and Gaylord Pendleton, we'll try them."

McLaglen had worked in several Ford films since they first met on *The Fighting Heart* in 1925. Ford treated him like an oversized child and McLaglen reacted like an oversized actor who recognized a good director when he saw one. McLaglen disappeared with J. M. Kerrigan, and Ford kept him off balance with this kind of treatment for the rest of the picture. He kept it up until McLaglen picked up his Academy Award as best actor for his work as the bewildered, sometimes drunken Gypo Nolan.

It was now 8:45, and Ford was making a close-up of Joe Sawyer (Bartley Mulholland). When he finished, he saw Margot Grahame and her make-up man and her hairdresser and her wardrobe mistress and several other ladies entering the stage. He looked at the group for a minute and then proceeded to make a shot of Gaylord Pendleton (Daley). When he finished, he went over and greeted the group of ladies cordially. He complimented them on the clothes, the make-up, and the hair. Then he said, "I wish you had been here at eight o'clock. We were scheduled to shoot your scene then, but we had to go on to something else. Now we won't have time for your scene. We'll just eliminate it from the script." And he did. The scene was never shot. As Miss Grahame and her party left the stage, Ford said, "It's a very pretty dress, though." The hairdresser burst into tears, and Ford said, "The hair's pretty too."

All actors (male and female) were punctual for the rest of the picture.

19

The First Lesson

WHEN I arrived on the set of *The Grapes of Wrath*, the cast and crew were sitting around waiting for John Ford to decide where he wanted to put the camera. He was standing alone in the middle of the set looking through the finder that had been removed from the Mitchell camera.

The finder was an optical device designed to match the characteristics of the camera's own lenses. Attached to the camera, it was normally used by the operator as a monitor. In those days the director often took it off the camera to find the right spot to shoot from—to find his "setup." It was about fourteen inches long, five inches wide, three inches deep, metal-encased, and quite heavy.

Ford was holding the finder in front of his eyes with both hands to block out the light and the rest of the world. Gregg Toland, the cameraman, stood a few feet away, quietly smoking a cigarette—waiting, patiently waiting. There wasn't a sound on the set.

I saw Eddie O'Fearna and started to speak. He held his finger to his lips, led me to Ford's side, and drifted back into the shadows.

After what seemed like an eternity, and without taking the finder from in front of his face, Ford said, "Is that you, Bob?"

I never quite knew what to call him. Henry Fonda called him Pappy. John Wayne called him Coach. Nunnally Johnson, the producer-screenwriter of *The Grapes of Wrath*, called him John. Jimmy Stewart called him Boss. Darryl Zanuck called him Jack. To some he was the Admiral or the Skipper or the Old Man. To Meta Sterne, his loyal script girl, he was Himself. I've often heard him called That Old Sonofabitch, but that was always behind his back. Even Wayne and Ward Bond and Henry Fonda and the rest started out addressing him as Mr. Ford.

I knew him for over forty years and I can't remember calling him anything but Sir. I tried to call him Pappy once, when he was best man at my wedding, but the word got stuck in my throat and I couldn't quite bring it up. For me "Sir" was, and remains, appropriate. He was the most honored American film director. The Motion Picture Academy of Arts and Sciences awarded him more Oscars than any other director. He also received top awards from the New York film critics, the British Film Institute, the American Film Institute, and the president of the United States.

So when he said, "Is that you, Bob?" I said, "Yes, sir. Did you want to see me?"

"Didn't you say you wanted to learn to be a director?" he muttered from behind the finder.

"Yes, sir." I had told him this five years before, and he hadn't referred to the fact until now.

"Well, here's your first lesson. Stand close to me and listen carefully." I moved up right next to him. I didn't want to miss a word. He still held the finder in front of his face. "From time to time, when you come on the set in the morning, you'll find that you haven't got an idea in your head, that you just can't figure out how to stage a scene. When this happens you call for the finder immediately. Go to the center of the set as though you know exactly what you are doing. Put the finder to your eyes the way I'm doing and close your eyes. That's important. Don't keep them open or you'll see something distracting. Now you're in a good position to think out how to stage the scene. Your cast and crew won't disturb you because they think you're looking for a setup. After you've held this position for about fifteen minutes and have just about got your problems worked out, a spy from the front office will arrive on the set. The jungle telegraph will have passed the word to the production office that it is nine-thirty and you haven't made a shot. This guy from the front office is usually a son-in-law or some prick like that and he's usually called 'associate producer,' so it's a ten-to-one shot that he's yellow. He won't come right up to you and tell you to get off your ass. He'll sneak in some side door and question his spies first. Then he'll slink up to you like a sidewinder to a position just about where you are now and say, 'How's it going Jack?' or 'Darryl likes the rushes,' or some such crap. Now listen carefully, Bob. This is the important part. As soon as the sonofabitch speaks, and you're sure he's in the right spot, you swing the finder around hard, like this."

With that, he turned his head and the finder sharply to the

left and cracked me on the forehead. Blood flowed and Ford kept on talking. He never took the finder from his eyes. "After you've been at it for a few years, you'll discover that your aim will improve and you can knock off two or three associate producers a week. With your eyes closed. That's the end of the first lesson. You can go back to the cutting room now. I think I've got my setup."

20

Director-Cast Relations
(Male)

I ALSO worked for Ford on *Stagecoach* and *The Long Voyage Home*. John Wayne gave superb performances in both pictures. In between Ford's two pictures, he gave less than superb performances in other pictures for different directors. One day, when I was working as sound-effects cutter on *The Long Voyage Home*, I got up enough nerve to go on the set and ask Ford how he managed to get such good performances out of Wayne while other directors weren't so lucky. I reminded him that I wanted to be a director and I thought he might give me some words of wisdom about working with actors. For example, "What do you say to John Wayne?"

I must have caught him at a bad time, because he just kept chewing on his dirty handkerchief and filling his pipe. After a while, I said, "Am I disturbing you, sir?" He lit the pipe and called his assistant director. This time it was his brother-in-law, Wingate Smith, known affectionately as "Unk."

"Unk, for chrissakes, can't you do something about keeping the goddam cutters off the set?" When he said that, I suddenly felt sorry for the associate producer on *The Informer*. Unk gave me the sign and I slunk back to the cutting room.

Three years later, I was a sailor in the United States Navy, assigned to the Field Photographic Branch of the Office of Strategic Services. My commanding officer was Lieutenant Commander John Ford, but I seldom saw him. The bridge between lieutenant commander and second-class petty officer was even greater than between director and sound-effects cutter.

Shortly after Pearl Harbor, I was mobilized and sent to Washington, D.C., for basic training and, after that, assigned to a new government agency called the Office of Strategic Services (OSS). President Roosevelt appointed Colonel William "Wild Bill" Donovan director of the new agency. Donovan selected Ford to head the Field Photographic Branch. Our first job was to make special photographic reports, *outside the con-*

tinental United States, for the president. The FBI, the OWI (Office of War Information), the ONI (Office of Naval Intelligence), and a number of other agencies, new and old, were falling all over each other in Washington and throughout America gathering information about suspected subversives, homosexuals, alcoholics, Fascists, Communists, "premature anti-Fascists," and other enemies of the people. Roosevelt wisely decided to limit Donovan's group to foreign activity. The spy-counterspy traffic was already too heavy on the domestic front.

Donovan made a pitch to be allowed to operate anywhere he wanted to, but Roosevelt was adamant. Donovan sent the order down from Twenty-fifth and E Street, where he had his headquarters, to the South Agriculture building, where Ford's Field Photo group was based.

SPECIAL ORDER

FROM :   *Commanding Officer, OSS*

TO :   *All Branch Officers*

*It is hereby ordered that no member of the
Office of Strategic Services will carry on any
activity within the continental limits of the
United States of America.*

This restriction annoyed Ford even more than it did Donovan. He sent for me and Bill Faralla. Faralla was a first-class petty officer. Ford didn't bother to read Donovan's special order to us. He said he had an assignment for us on the following Sunday. We were to take the new Cunningham Combat Camera and give it a thorough testing. The Cunningham Combat Camera was modeled after a captured German camera. The 35mm Eyemo-like mechanism was mounted with a two-hundred-foot magazine on a .30-.30 rifle stock. The camera started when you pulled the trigger. It was a dangerous-looking piece of equipment, more like a futuristic ray gun than a camera. It was named after Ray Cunningham, a brilliant technician in the RKO camera department, who had developed the camera for Ford's unit.

Ford got up from his desk and walked over to a box of sand he kept in the corner of his office. He spat in the box, lit his pipe, and turned to Faralla, the senior petty officer. "I want a complete photographic report on the old State Department building next to the White House. Cover it from all angles, from the street and from the tops of the surrounding buildings. If anyone asks you what you are doing, show them your OSS cards and keep shooting. Don't take any crap from anybody. Just do your job."

We checked out one of the two Cunningham cameras and went to the top of the hospital across the street from the old State Department. We were in our sailor suits and had no trouble with the hospital staff. One head nurse on the top floor challenged us as we started through the fire exit to the roof, and Faralla showed her his OSS card. I don't think she knew what the OSS was, but Faralla flashed his card with such style and assurance that she said, "Oh, yes, OSS. OK."

We set up our camera on a tripod, which made it look like a machine gun instead of a rifle. Faralla outranked me, but I knew more about the camera, so I actually operated and he became a kind of combination director, assistant cameraman, clapper boy, and script girl, or, in this case, script first-class petty officer. I told him to put on the telescopic lens so that we could get close-up details of the State Department roof. The long, heavy telescopic lens made the camera look even more like a Buck Rogers ray gun. As Faralla focused it, I took my position as operator. I adjusted the eyepiece to fit my eye and looked through. The first thing I saw was a United States Marine sergeant standing at the top of the fire-exit stairs on the roof of the State Department. He looked straight at us, then turned and waved frantically to someone down the stairs. I shot a few feet of this for comic relief and then panned over to the far corner of the roof, on the White House side. This was less than a month after Pearl Harbor, and the defense of public buildings was far from well organized. A .30-caliber World War I vintage machine gun was set up overlooking the White House. Two Marine privates were sitting casually in folding office chairs beside it, playing cards on a box between them. I shot fifteen feet of this tranquil scene and said to Faralla, the focus-puller, "Panning back to the nervous sergeant." As I panned back to the top of the stairs, a blur went by the camera, running in the opposite direction. When my camera got to the top of the fire-exit stairs, the Marine sergeant was gone, but a Marine captain had taken his place. He too was motioning hysterically down the stairs. Faralla said, "You better pan back to the machine gun. I think they're doing something interesting." "OK," I said, "As soon as I see what happens here."

What happened was that six Marine privates with rifles ran onto the roof, flopped down in prone position, and aimed their rifles straight at my telescopic lens. Faralla said, "You're missing the action with the machine gun." I panned back to the corner overlooking the White House. The Marine sergeant had taken over and swung the machine gun in our direction. One of the Marine card players was fixing a magazine belt onto the gun. The other was chasing the cards, which were now blowing all over the roof like fifty-two butterflies. Through my long-focus lens it all looked like *Shoulder Arms* or some other old silent war comedy. We were too far away to hear anything, but it was quite clear that the Marine sergeant was angry and the other two Marines were confused. The sergeant was screaming at the top of his voice and finally left his post at the machine gun long enough to run over and kick the card chaser and drag him, protesting, back to the machine gun. The cards floated gaily down to the west lawn of the White House, and I was panning with them when the Cunningham Combat Camera started to make a different sound, the sound it made when it had run out of film.

I said, "Ohshit," which is a word camera operators use when they run out of film during some interesting action, and took my eye from the eyepiece. Faralla said, "It's just as well. I think we've got all the cover we're going to get on this, anyway." I looked over the camera and got a comprehensive view of the top of the old State Department building.

The Marine sergeant and the two card players were still trying to load the machine gun and aim it in our direction. As they swung it around, the tripod collapsed and the Marine sergeant got even angrier. I thought he was angry at the card players, but Faralla said it was because the machine gun had crunched onto his foot. He was holding his foot and howling and dancing around like a wounded kangaroo.

The Marine captain and the six Marine riflemen had now been joined by four uniformed State Department policemen and two civilians. The six Marine riflemen were still zeroed in on us, but the other men were gesturing wildly to us and yelling. We couldn't hear them.

Faralla said, "They probably don't want us to take any more pictures."

I said "Gimme the other magazine. You heard Ford. He said to keep shooting and show our OSS cards." Faralla said he had been holding his card up from time to time while my eye was glued to the finder, but they probably couldn't read it from three hundred yards away. He suggested we now hold up both our hands instead so as not to get shot by the six Marine riflemen. He wasn't worried about the machine gun, because, with that crew, it was unlikely that it would become operational in the present war.

In 1942, the old State Department building had two "detention chambers" in the subbasement. Faralla and I were escorted to the "chambers" on Sunday afternoon at 4:30 P.M. and kept incommunicado until Tuesday morning at 11:00 A.M. We were stripped of our OSS cards, our Cunningham Combat Camera with its telescopic lens, and all of our personal belongings. We told the Marine captain that we were acting on orders from Commander John Ford of the OSS. The Captain listened and nodded and said we would be detained until our "camera-gun" (he kept calling it that) was checked out by ballistics experts and our film developed and examined by proper authorities. In the meantime, our Navy credentials would be checked. They said we couldn't be working for the OSS because the OSS only functioned outside the continental limits of the United States.

After forty-two hours, we were visited by Mr. Tom Early. He was one of Colonel Donovan's top aides. He was also a brother of Stephen Early, President Roosevelt's secretary. He said we were in rather serious trouble. He said that the Marine Corps captain wanted us court-martialed through regular U.S. Navy channels, but that he, Early, had talked to Commander Ford, and Ford had promised that we would be tried within the Field Photographic Branch of the OSS.

Ford presided over his version of a court-martial in the projection room at our South Agriculture building headquarters. The Marine Corps captain told his story. The Marine Corps sergeant, his foot still bandaged, corroborated it. Faralla and I told our tale—"Our commanding officer ordered us to photograph the State Department . . ." etc.

Ford said, "You mean you were arrested for following orders issued by the OSS?"

Faralla and Parrish: "Yes, sir."

Marine Corps captain: "The OSS is not allowed to operate within the continental limits of the United States."

Ford: "Maybe they *will* be when the results of this court-martial reach the president. I've seen the footage shot by Parrish and Faralla. I think it's an excellent record of how our important buildings are being protected, especially the part where that Marine sergeant takes over the machine gun." He paused for a minute to let this sink in, then said: "Faralla and Parrish were not aware of the new order. They were just doing their jobs. I think we should lock their film in our vault and dismiss the charges. Do you agree, Captain?"

The captain hesitated long enough to look at the Marine sergeant's bandaged foot and then said, "I agree, Commander."

Ford said, "Case dismissed." He sounded like a cross between Will Rogers and Irvin S. Cobb.

He turned to his secretary, who was now acting as court stenographer. "Have the records of the court-martial typed up and sent to Colonel Donovan. Make an additional note from me as officer commanding the Field Photographic Branch. 'It should be clear from this unfortunate episode that we cannot carry out our directives from the president if we are restricted geographically in our field of operations.' "

The report was sent through all conceivable channels, but to no avail. The "foreign-only" order remained throughout the war and is still in effect with the CIA, the successor to the OSS.

Ford congratulated Faralla and me on a job well done. We both saluted and turned to go. As I walked away, he said, "Just a minute, Parrish," I came back and he said, "That was good footage. Do you still want to learn to be a director?" I said I did and he said to be back in the projection room at 7:00 P.M. I thanked him, saluted, and took off. He called me back again and said, "Bring a pad and pencil."

Ford often ran his pictures for the Navy brass and other distinguished guests. When he enlisted in the Navy he had been a top Hollywood director, but in Washington government circles he was not so well known. He had a stock speech for the screenings: "I've been wanting to see this picture myself. I never saw it after it was all put together." This of course, was not true in every case, but it kept alive the image of the talented, Irish, free-spirited artist who could knock off *Young Mr. Lincoln* or *The Iron Horse* or *How Green Was My Valley* and not even bother to look at the finished product. When the screenings were over, he would shamelessly wipe away a tear and say, to whomever happened to be present, "I'm glad I waited until I could see it with you." Experienced Ford watchers would look at their feet in embarrassment, but first-timers were quite often taken in.

At seven o'clock the projection room was packed with admirals, captains, generals, and colonels (Marine Corps, not

Army). I was the only enlisted man. Ford asked me to sit next to him and to make a little mark on my pad each time John Wayne spoke. He was running *Stagecoach* and *The Long Voyage Home*. When the lights went up three hours later, Ford said, "How many speeches did Duke have?"

I had become interested in watching the films, so I had lost count after John Wayne's first two or three lines in each picture. I took a wild guess. "Seven in *Stagecoach* and five in *The Long Voyage Home*. Twelve altogether."

Ford said, "You missed a few in each picture, but, anyway, there's your second lesson. Don't let them talk unless they have something to say."

21

The Battle of Midway

THE OSS discovered that the Japanese fleet was planning an attack on Midway Island in May 1942. Ford asked to go there and film the attack. The defenses on Midway were negligible compared with the attacking forces, and heavy casualties were anticipated. Ford's request was approved, and he and Jack McKenzie, a cameraman from our unit, flew off to Midway.

The Japanese fleet attacked and was defeated by the combined efforts of the U.S. Navy, Air Force, Army, and Marines. It was the first major victory for the U.S. forces and a turning point in the war in the Pacific. Ford was wounded and was awarded the Legion of Merit, the Air Medal, and the Purple Heart.

He brought eight cans of 16mm color film to our headquarters in Washington. His left arm was still bandaged, he needed a shave, and he looked as though he hadn't slept for a week. He had come directly from Midway via Honolulu and Hollywood, stopping in Hollywood to have a rush print made of his film. He summoned me to the projection room, locked the door, and put an armed guard outside while we viewed the film. When we finished he said, "Do you think we can make a twenty-minute record of the attack on Midway from that?"

It was the first real combat film I had seen. There were some exciting shots, but I didn't know exactly what kind of film Ford had in mind. Our unit had made some technical films—*How to Operate Behind Enemy Lines, How to Interrogate Enemy Prisoners, Living off the Land, Nazi Industrial Manpower*, etc.—but they were for internal use, within the OSS. We had not made any films for the public.

I said, "Do you want a factual account for the record, or do you want a propaganda film?" Ford said, "What's a 'propaganda' film?"

I realized from the way he asked the question that he hated the word, so I said, "Well, I mean is it for the public or for the OSS?"

He said, "It's for the mothers of America. It's to let them know that we're in a war and that we've been getting the shit kicked out of us for five months, and now we're starting to hit back. Do you think we can make a movie that the mothers of America will be interested in?"

There were impressive shots of American boys being buried at sea. The flag-covered caskets were slid off the stern of PT boats while the officers and men saluted. There were close-ups of young American pilots in Torpedo Squadron 8 taking off from the carrier *Hornet* (only one man survived), and Air Force B-17s taking off from Midway to bomb the Japanese fleet. There were more shots of a bombed-out hospital and a dramatic rescue at sea. I told him I thought we could make a very moving twenty-minute film that would interest not only the mothers of America but also the fathers. He said the fathers already knew about the war because a lot of them were fighting it. He wanted the mothers to see how brave their sons were.

I said, "OK. I'll start to work right away."

Ford said, "No, I don't want you to work here. As soon as it's discovered in Honolulu that I've smuggled the film past the Navy censors they'll come snooping around with enough brass to take it away from us. They'll assign seven or eight high-ranking associate producers and public relations officers to the project. The four services will start bickering over it and the whole thing will get so bogged down in red tape that *we'll* never see it again, let alone the mothers of America. You get on a plane and take the film to Hollywood. Don't report to anyone. Go to your mother's house and hide until you hear from me."

I was wearing dungarees, so I said, "OK. I'll get changed and leave as soon as my orders are ready."

He said, "Never mind the orders. I'll send them to you later. And don't bother to change your clothes. Just pick up the film and get out to the airport. The Navy censor will be around looking for our film. I want to be able to tell him that I don't have any film."

This kind of red-tape cutting was often used in making movies. Ford had made it standard procedure. But we were now in the Navy. I reminded him of this fact and told him that when our caper was exposed, as it eventually must be, his superiors might not look too kindly on him.

He said, "It will be too late then. We'll already have our picture made. Besides, I'll tell them that it's not my fault if an enlisted man steals eight cans of top-secret film and runs home to his mother."

My mother was delighted to see me. I told her I didn't want anyone to know I was there, especially anyone from the Navy. She said, "You're not in trouble, are you, son?"

I said, "Of course not." I must not have said it very convincingly, because she said, "Then where is your luggage and why are you traveling in dungarees?" I told her I was on a secret mission for the Navy.

She said, "Then why don't you want them to know you are here? They must have sent you here if you're on a secret mission for them."

I explained that although I was actually *in* the Navy, I had been assigned to work with the OSS. She said, "What's the SOS, some kind of dungaree unit? I would feel much better if you went back to the plain Navy." I was in the OSS for four years and she always called it the SOS. She still does.

I finally told her the whole story. I think she was a bit disappointed to learn that she wouldn't be harboring a deserter, but when she heard that Ford was involved she was quite happy. As far as she was concerned the director was always right, and he was still a director.

The next day Dudley Nichols, the writer, phoned and said Ford wanted him to see the film. Nichols was on location and deeply involved in a big picture (*This Land Is Mine*), but he said if I would get a projection room, he would drop everything and return to Hollywood. He said Ford wouldn't have called him if it weren't important.

Nichols was a dedicated liberal and dedicated to Ford, a firm believer in both causes. He had written the screenplays for *The Informer, Stagecoach, The Long Voyage Home,* and other Ford successes, so he knew Ford well.

I found a projection room in a small laboratory in the San Fernando valley and screened the film for Nichols. He asked me what Ford had in mind and I said, "He says he wants to make a film for the mothers of America."

We discussed the possibilities and Nichols said Ford would arrive the next day. He said he really should go back to his location in northern California but he didn't want to let Ford down.

When Ford arrived I asked him about my orders. He said my orders would arrive in due course and that the only important thing was to get on with the work.

Nichols, Ford, and I ran the film, and Ford said things like "This really happened" and "A council of war was held" to describe specific shots. He also identified officers and enlisted men in the action—Logan Ramsay, Captain Simard, Colonel Shannon, "Junior" Johnson, etc. When the film was over, Nichols and Ford exchanged ideas and I listened. Finally Ford turned to me and said, "Have you got enough film for this?" I said, "I think so." Ford turned to Nichols and said, "What do you think?" Nichols said, "I can't wait to get started. I think it's great." Ford said, "Well what are you waiting for? Get to work." He turned to me and said, "You too, Bob. Get a sleeping bag and lock yourself in your cutting room. I'll have some sandwiches sent in to you, and I'll get Phil Scott assigned to the project to help you." Scott was the best sound-effects editor in Hollywood, and he had worked on many of Ford's pictures. "If anybody from the ONI comes snooping around and asks what you're working on, tell them it's none of their goddam business."

I said, "Suppose they're officers?"

He said, "If they're officers it's even simpler. They'll never suspect an enlisted man of being in charge of a classified project. It's against the law for an enlisted man to even *handle* top-secret material, especially an enlisted man with no orders. If anyone knocks on your door, your best bet is to tell 'em to fuck off and not open the door."

Nichols forgot about his feature in northern California and worked day and night for two days. During this time Phil and I organized the film into a workable condition. We had a 35mm black-and-white blowup dupe made, and I arranged for Technicolor to do our laboratory work. I cut the film into a rough version of what Ford and I and Nichols had talked about, and Phil cut in some temporary sound effects.

When we were ready I notified Ford. He called Nichols and the four of us screened my rough assembly while Nichols narrated what he had written. The projection room was locked and an armed Marine guard stood outside. Ford insisted on an armed guard outside my cutting room twenty-four hours a day all the time I was working on *The Battle of Midway*. He also had a Marine pacing around my mother's house in the valley. She made a chocolate cake for him and told the neighbors he was a "secret SOS man."

When the screening was over, Ford asked Nichols for a copy of his narration. Nichols said that it wasn't typed, he had read it from his handwritten notes. He had a two-day growth of beard and was very tired, but he was excited by the film and anxious to do anything Ford wanted—revise, rewrite, start over —anything. He realized he had overwritten, but this was a first draft, it needed to be cut, but if the basic ideas were OK, he would write a proper script.

Ford said, "I'll get Meta to type this up and I'll look it over. She'll send you a copy and you can work on the next draft after you've had some rest. Then I'll call you and we can do the final job after Bob's done a bit more cutting work. In the meantime you get some sleep."

Nichols gave Ford his handful of notes and left. Ford and I went to Ford's office on the Twentieth Century-Fox lot. He gave the notes to Meta Sterne and said, "Type these, send a copy to Dudley, and get Jim McGuinness on the phone."

James Kevin McGuinness was a writer who had worked with Ford on *The Black Watch* and *Men Without Women*. Politically he was an archreactionary, the opposite of Nichols. At that time he was a senior executive at M-G-M, in charge of much of the product. A very busy and important man. When he came on the phone Ford said, "I realize you're having to work especially hard these days what with a lot of the able-bodied men off fighting, but I wonder if you could spare me a few minutes?" There was a pause, and Ford said, "Well it would be better if you were here now, but if you could get over to Fox in fifteen or twenty minutes, I guess it would be OK."

McGuinness arrived a half hour later. I ran the film with him and we went to Ford's office. McGuinness was enthusiastic and full of ideas. As he talked, Meta copied his remarks in shorthand. When he finished, Ford said, "What are you doing over at M-G-M?"

McGuinness said, "I'm producing five pictures."

Ford said, "Oh, then you're not very busy. Why don't you forget your five, uh . . . uh . . . *commercial* pictures and do something for the war effort?" He said the word "commercial" as though it were an obscenity. "Write up your ideas and bring them in to Bob tomorrow. You two can run the film again, see how your stuff fits, and then after you've worked it over together, we can sit down and make a movie for the mothers of America." He paused to light his pipe. "They're not against mothers over at M-G-M, are they?"

McGuinness said in fact he was pro-mother and he thought Ford's film was great, and he would start immediately. When he was out of earshot, Ford said to Meta, "Type up his remarks and see if you can get Hank Fonda and Jane Darwell in to do some recording this afternoon. They're working for Bill Wellman on *The Ox-Bow Incident*. Talk to Bill. Also get Irving Pichel and Donald Crisp. And get me a priority on a flight to Washington tonight."

When Nichols's and McGuinness's notes were typed, Ford stuck them in his hip pocket and told me to get an hour's recording time. Fonda, Jane Darwell, Donald Crisp, and Irving Pichel arrived on the stage at five o'clock sharp. They sat in a semicircle, with a microphone overhead. Ford took the notes from his pocket and said, "When I point to you, say what I tell you to say."

He then had the actors record bits from each of the two writers' suggestions. The session lasted about twenty minutes. He thanked the actors and said to me, "Well, Bob, there's your narration. Al Newman says be will write some music for you. Don't let him do too much. Use about half of whatever he gives you. Be sure you use "Red River Valley" and "My Country 'Tis of Thee" as well as "Anchors Aweigh," "The Air Force Song," and "The Marine Hymn." Get it all together and bring it to me in Washington."

I said, "What about my orders? If I get picked up with no orders they'll toss me in some crummy Navy brig in Chavez Ravine and the mothers of America will be disappointed, especially mine."

He said, "You're not going to get picked up if you stay on the job. The Shore Patrol doesn't cover cutting rooms. You'll get your orders when you need them. In the meantime, don't let anyone see any of the film, especially anyone from the Navy Department."

I said OK and he turned to go. When he got to the heavy soundproof door, he stopped and said, "When Dudley and Jim come in with their rewrites, tell them how much we appreciate their help, but don't use any of the new stuff, just use what we've recorded."

I asked if we shouldn't tell them now that we had already recorded the narration.

Ford said, "No. Dudley's resting and I don't want to disturb him and it will be good for Jim's character to do some work for the war. Just tell 'em I'll get in touch with them after I've read their stuff. But don't tell Dudley that Jim is involved, and don't tell Jim about Dudley."

He went to Washington that night.

McGuinness came in the next day with a full script. He had worked all night. He waited in Ford's office for over an hour because he wanted to deliver it personally. Finally he came to the cutting room and asked if I knew where Ford was. I told him Ford had been called to Washington on an emergency and that his help was much appreciated. He gave me the script and said if we needed any more work done to call him.

Nichols sent his rewrite in a few days later. It was beautiful, poetic. Despite Ford's orders, Phil and I recorded some of it and used it in the picture.

While I was cutting and rerecording the picture, the word got out that a secret Navy film was being made. Several officers from the ONI came looking for the officer in charge of the project. The only person around was a petty officer second-class in dungarees, with no orders. There was no officer in charge, so technically there was no project. On their last visit they said they were coming back the next day to take all the film. And me.

I left that night for Washington with the first print, complete. I put the negative under the bed at my mother's house.

I ran *The Battle of Midway* for Ford and he seemed quite pleased. "It's a good job, Bob." He wanted to know Nichols's and McGuinness's reactions when I told them we had already recorded the narration before receiving their scripts. I said McGuinness was upset but that Nichols was more philosophical and had said, "Ford probably knows what he's doing."

"He probably does," Ford said. "Now all the services are claiming credit for the victory at Midway and they'll try to keep our picture from being released to the public if they're not equally represented. Go measure the footage and let me know how much each service has."

I had been warned about the possibility of this petty checking up. I thought I had given each service equal representation, but I was five feet off on the Marine Corps. When I told Ford this, he reached into his pocket and took out a five-foot close-up in 35mm color of the president's son, Major James Roosevelt of the Marine Corps. "Put this in the memorial-service sequence along with Captain Simard of the Navy and Colonel Shannon of the Army," he said.

I explained that we had a composite print and that the cut of Major Roosevelt would cause a bump in the sound track, that Al Newman's chorus was singing "land where my fathers died" at that particular time and that the sound track would go silent for 3⅓ seconds. He said, "Good. It'll give the audience time to think."

I asked him if Major Roosevelt had actually been at the Battle of Midway. He said, "I don't know if his records will show it, but this shot was made on Midway Island, so I guess he was there. Sometimes men travel around without orders."

This reminded me that I still hadn't received my orders for the trip to California. I told Ford and he said, "You see. That's what I mean. Just because you don't have orders doesn't mean you haven't been someplace."

I put the clip of Major Roosevelt in the film. Ford took it to the White House that night and ran it for the president and Mrs. Roosevelt, Admiral Leahy, Stephen Early, and certain members of the Joint Chiefs of Staff. The president talked throughout the screening until the silent close-up of his son appeared and saluted the burial at sea of the heroic dead of the Battle of Midway. From that moment to the end (2 mins. 21 secs.) the audience sat in complete silence. When the lights came up, Mrs. Roosevelt was crying. The president turned to Admiral Leahy and said, "I want every mother in America to see this picture."

My mother took the negative from under her bed and delivered it to Technicolor where a record 500 prints were made and rushed to theaters across the country. I attended the opening at the Radio City Music Hall in New York on my way to join Ford in London. It was well received and won the Academy Award as the best documentary short subject of 1942. I saw a number of women actually sobbing, and most of them looked like mothers. I don't know how many other mothers saw *The Battle of Midway*, but I know one who didn't. Two years later, when I next saw my mother, she said, "Whatever happened to that dungaree movie you were making for the SOS?"

22

Do Good by Stealth, Etc.

FORD was born Sean Aloysius O'Feeney in Cape Elizabeth, Maine, the thirteenth child of Sean O'Feeney and the former Barbara Curran. His parents had come to America from Galway, Ireland. The original family name had been O'Fearna, now anglicized to O'Feeney. Ford started calling himself Jack Ford when he came to Hollywood, but deep down he remained an O'Feeney, and even deeper down, an O'Fearna, from the Emerald Isle.

When I told him I had met a Red Cross girl and wanted a weekend pass to get married, he said, "Not a chance. You shouldn't get married in the middle of a war. Besides, you're going with me to Chungking. How long have you known the girl?"

I said, "Two weeks, sir. If you don't give me the pass, we'll go to Baltimore tonight and get married anyway." He looked up. I said, "Sir" again.

Out came the handkerchief and the pipe. He spend the next four long minutes chewing the handkerchief, stuffing tobacco, and lighting up the pipe, while I stood at attention and sweated. Visions of court-martial, disgrace, demotion, dismissal from the service for insolence.

Finally, he said, "What's the girl's name?"

"Kathleen," I said. Then, with desperate inspiration, "As in Kathleen Mavourneen."

Ford said, "Why didn't you say so in the first place? If I'd known you were marrying a nice Jewish girl, we needn't have wasted all this time. I'll give you the pass if I can be the best man."

I told him Phil Scott and Mike Luciano had agreed to stand up for me, and Ford said, "Then tell 'em to sit down. Tell 'em they've been out-ranked." I said I'd rather not, and he said, "OK. Luciano, Scott, and I will share the duties, we'll be co-best men." That seemed a fair compromise, so I accepted the arrangement.

He said, "We'll still be leaving for Chungking on September nineteenth, so you can have the wedding on the eighteenth. When can I meet Kathleen?"

I said, "Have dinner with us tonight," and he said OK.

I saluted and started to leave his office. He said, "Wear civilian clothes. Officers are not supposed to dine with enlisted men." I saluted again and said "Yes, sir" again.

Kathie looked beautiful. I don't remember what she wore, but I wore a wide-lapelled, gray, chalk-striped, double-breasted suit. Ford wore his dress uniform. He charmed Kathie and she charmed him, and as I took her home on the streetcar that night she said, "I don't understand you. You told me to be wary of him, when in fact he's a charming, delightful, wonderful man. I think you've misjudged him."

We were married on a rooftop on a beautiful clear September 18th in New York. I had arranged to have Lieutenant (Junior Grade) Loungeway, a Navy chaplain from the Brooklyn Navy Yard, perform the ceremony. To this day, I don't know what faith he preached, but I guess he did a good job. The marriage has lasted more than thirty years.

At the wedding reception, our executive officer, Lieutenant Ray Kellogg, presented me with new orders. I opened them to discover that I was not going to Chungking after all. I was directed to take a two-week leave, then report, "with dependents" (my brand-new wife), to the Coast Guard to make a documentary recruiting film for the SPARS, the women's branch of the Coast Guard.

I realized this was Ford's doing, so I sought him out among the guests. He was deep in conversation (in Gaelic) with my wife's aunt, Kathleen Norris, the novelist. When I thanked him for changing my orders he said, "I don't know what you're talking about. I have no control over the Bureau of Personnel. Sorry to hear you won't be going to Chungking with us. We're sailing on a slow munitions ship tomorrow night, unescorted." And he returned to his conversation with Mrs. Norris.

After a two-week honeymoon on Fire Island, we dined with Aunt Kay at the Chatham Hotel in New York. She was a wonderful, warm, intelligent lady, one of the most successful writers of her time. As a journalist, she had met presidents, heads of state, popes, artists, industrial leaders—practically every newsworthy person for the past thirty years, and she was charmed by Ford. "He's one of the most delightful men I've ever met. What a pity he didn't continue his studies for the priesthood."

Ford was a Catholic, but to my knowledge he had never spent much time studying to be a priest. In fact, I think his academic education ended after high school in 1913. When he

154 GROWING UP IN HOLLYWOOD

failed to win an appointment to Annapolis, he went to Hollywood to join his brother Francis in the motion-picture industry. He began his higher education when he became a prop man for his brother. He graduated to assistant director, grip, stunt man, cameraman, and editor, and finally matriculated as director. There's nothing in the record that hints at the priesthood.

But Aunt Kay was a devout Catholic and believed that he really wanted to be a priest and that he was somehow led astray at the last moment. I was not about to disillusion her with the truth.

Some years later, Ford asked me about Aunt Kay. He said she was a wonderful woman, a fine writer, and that she spoke very good Gaelic. I told him that she had been impressed with his Gaelic too, and that she thought it a pity he hadn't continued with his studies to become a priest.

He looked me right in the eye for a moment, then took out his handkerchief and wiped away an imaginary tear.

"I've always regretted it too," he said.

23

Détente with Russia

HE ASSIGNED me and Budd Schulberg and Joe Zigman and Bob Webb to Justice Jackson's Office for the Prosecution of the Major Nazi War Criminals at Nuremberg. We were given copies of the legal briefs indicting Goering, Von Schirach, Doenitz, Keitel, Streicher, Hess, and the rest. We were to scour Europe trying to find photographic evidence to confirm the accusations against each man and then present our film at the trials four months hence.

We found some of the material in the UFA library at the Afifa lab in Berlin. Other bits came from Warsaw, Cologne, Zurich, Munich, and wherever else we could winkle it out of the shambles that was Europe in May 1945.

In the "Crimes Against Humanity" brief, great stress was placed upon the abortive July 20, 1944, plot on Hitler's life. We knew the Nazis had photographed every detail of the bloody reprisals, and we knew our allies, the Russians, had the film. What we didn't know was how to get it away from them. We had explained at every level that we were all in it together, that our common cause was to punish the villains who had bombed Stalingrad, persecuted the Jews, and generally made life miserable for the past ten years. The Russians were polite but firm. They drank and talked with us for hours, but when it was all sifted out it was still "Nyet." We had lots of conversation, vodka, and bourbon, but no film.

The Russian liaison officer with our little group was a Major Gromoff. We wined and dined him and tried to bribe him with everything our overstocked PX offered—cigarettes (more valuable than currency), cameras, film, watches, field glasses, etc. He accepted all the gifts, but I guess we didn't officially bribe him because when you bribe somebody, they're supposed to deliver something from their side. The major took it all in like a sponge but gave nothing. He spoke perfect English, and when we asked him about the July 20 film he clammed up and said he had never heard of it.

He was a nice guy and liked to visit our headquarters in

Wannsee, a beautiful suburb of Berlin. It had been in the Russian sector at first, but after Potsdam the areas were changed and we inherited a fine German mansion with staff which had belonged to the Baron Von Hanfstaengel. The staff included a great cook who spoke some Russian and wasn't bad-looking. Major Gromoff used to hang around eating our rations and talking to the cook.

One night, Schulberg and I were talking about John Ford, our absent commander. Gromoff overheard us and said, "You don't mean John Ford the great film director?"

I said, "That's right."

He couldn't believe it. "John Ford who made *The Informer* and *The Grapes of Wrath*"?

"And *Young Mr. Lincoln*. And *Stagecoach*," Budd said.

"And *The Iron Horse* and *Four Sons* and *Men Without Women* and *The Lost Patrol* and . . ." He went on naming, in chronological order, every picture that Ford had directed, some that Schulberg and I hadn't heard of. He knew more about Ford, I think, than Ford knew about himself. He flavored his recital with names of the cast and crew of each picture and little-known bits of information: "Ford changed his billing from Jack Ford to John Ford in 1923, when he directed *Cameo Kirby*, starring John Gilbert and Gertrude Olmstead. George Schneiderman was the cameraman, and some of the sequences were tinted, a process used by Ford again in *Mother Machree* in 1928."

"Yes," I said, "but Chester Lyons was the cameraman on *Mother Machree*. I know because I worked in it as a child."

"You've met John Ford?" said the unbelieving Russian.

"Of course. He's our commanding officer, our boss. He's actually in charge of this operation."

"Will he come to Berlin?"

"Probably. We're expecting him any day." That was true, but we had no idea when or if he would actually appear.

"He's my hero," said Gromoff. "I'm writing the definitive book about him. In Russian. I'd give anything to meet him."

"Would you give us the July twentieth film?"

"Of course," he said, without batting an eye. "I didn't know it was for John Ford."

The next day, we took a four-wheel weapons carrier to a warehouse in the Russian zone, and Major Gromoff personally supervised the loading of thirty thousand feet of film, everything we needed.

Ford never appeared in Berlin, but I got a photograph of him directing George O'Brien in *The Iron Horse* from the ruins of the bombed-out Fox exchange and forged his signature on it:

"To Major Gromoff
With gratitude,
John Ford."

24

In Memoriam

AFTER the war, I had a disagreement with Ford. He wanted to extend his OSS–U.S. Navy unit into civilian life and I didn't. I felt that five years had been enough. I was anxious to get out of uniform and back into the movie business. I still wanted to be a director.

When the war was almost over, Ford went to Louis B. Mayer, the head of M-G-M, and said, "I'll direct *They Were Expendable* for you if you'll pay me the highest price ever paid to a director. I'll contribute all of it to the Field Photo Farm and I want you to contribute an equal amount."

Mayer said, "What's the Field Photo Farm?"

Ford told him that while he (Mayer) was making movies and money, others (including Ford and his OSS unit) had been fighting the Nazis. Now it was time to pay the bill. The Field Photo Farm was eight acres in the San Fernando valley owned by Sam Briskin, an executive at Columbia Pictures. There was a nice five-bedroom house, a swimming pool, stables, and a tennis court. Ford wanted to buy it and use it as a clubhouse for the men who had served with him in the war. Any ex-member of his OSS unit could live there, without paying, for as long as he wanted.

Ford said to Mayer, "Just pay me two hundred fifty thousand dollars. That will be my contribution. Then you throw in another two hundred fifty thousand to show that you are grateful to the lads for suppressing Nazism, and I'll direct *They Were Expendable* and get John Wayne to star in it. We'll get Cliff Reid as associate producer."

Wayne was at the height of his career, a genuine Hollywood star; that is to say, millions of people throughout the world would buy tickets if John Wayne was in the movie. And Wayne would do practically anything Ford asked.

Cliff Reid was the associate producer of *The Informer*. After working with Ford on *The Lost Patrol, The Informer,* and *The Plough and the Stars,* Reid's luck had changed. His credits away from Ford included *You Can't Fool Your Wife, Mexican Spitfire at Sea,* and *Mexican Spitfire Sees a Ghost.* He hadn't worked for some time and had quietly faded into semiretirement.

"Wayne, yes, but why do you want Cliff Reid?" asked Mayer.

Ford said, "Because he's the best goddam associate producer in the business. Did a hell of a job on *The Informer.*"

Mayer accepted Ford's terms, and *They Were Expendable* was made. Ford got the highest fee ever paid to a director, and he gave all of it to the Field Photo Farm. As soon as the Farm came out of escrow, a sign appeared at the entrance—NO WOMEN EXCEPT ON VISITORS' DAY.

Some of us were newly married and were more interested in homes for our families than in an all-male extension of the Navy. Property prices were high, salaries were low, and a lot of us were living in one rented room or with our parents. I visited the Farm a couple of times and then got on with my life.

After a while, Ford invited Kathie and me to his house for dinner. He said, "We're making some improvements at the Farm and I'd like your suggestions. We're converting the old stable into an all-denominational chapel. We'll keep the basic structure. I've got an art director coming out from the studio to make some sketches. He'll probably want to keep a couple of the horse stalls intact for the Christmas Nativity play. He'll put a steeple and bell on the roof, and I think Zanuck will give us some stained-glass windows from the *How Green Was My Valley* set. We'll leave the hitching rail in front in case someone wants to stop and pray when they come in from riding. Anyone and everyone will be welcome—Protestants, Jews, Catholics, Communists—everyone. What do you think of the idea? Do you have any suggestions?"

I said, "I have a suggestion. I think you should bulldoze the farmhouse, the chapel, the hitching post, the stained-glass windows, the swimming pool, the stables—the whole thing. Then I think you should subdivide the eight acres into fifty-foot lots and build low-cost duplex houses for returning veterans."

I blurted it all out, forgetting that I was a guest in his house and not caring that I was hitting him below the belt. I waited for him to hit back. He refilled his pipe instead. Then he lit it. Four times he lit it, and each time he would let the long kitchen matches he used burn right down to the end. I became fascinated, wondering why he didn't burn his fingers. He finally got the pipe going and blew out the last match.

"Like I said before, everyone will be welcome, regardless of race, creed, or color."

One of Ford's dreams was to have a wedding or a funeral at the Farm. His first opportunity came when his good friend Harry Carey died. When Ford was a novice director of twenty-two, he directed westerns with Carey. They had remained friends since, and although Carey had been too old to join Ford's Navy unit, his son Dobie had served under Ford. As far as Ford was concerned, Harry Carey deserved a memorial service in the Farm's new chapel.

Dan Fuchs, the writer, had been with me in the unit, but during the years since the war we both had been too busy with our own lives and families to spend much time at the Farm. I hadn't been there since the dinner at Ford's house. Dobie Carey was a friend of ours, so when he asked us to come to the memorial service, I collected Dan and off we went to the valley. Sure enough, the old barn was now a chapel with a bell on the roof and a hitching post in front. Harry Carey's horse was tied to the hitching post.

He had been standing there all night along with an honor guard of four sailors in uniform. Mike Luciano was one of them. By the time Dan Fuchs and I arrived the next day, they were all pretty tired. The strains of "Red River Valley," Carey's (and Ford's) favorite tune, greeted us as we approached the chapel. I recognized the familiar tone of Dan Borzage's accordion. Borzage was one of Frank Borzage's brothers, and he had played "Red River Valley" for Ford many times, both in his pictures and on the sidelines for "mood."

After the service, we gathered outside the chapel to talk about Harry and to renew old acquaintances. Some of the old comrades had kept their Navy uniforms and had stuffed themselves into them for the occasion. Buttons strained, bellies sagged, but the medals and shoes were all polished and those in uniform managed to whip up a smart salute for Ford (now a retired rear admiral) and the other Navy brass who had shown up for the service.

A warrant officer was telling Fuchs and me about the success of the Field Photo Farm, when Ford came up to our group. As Ford approached, the warrant officer saluted and said, "Good afternoon, sir." He then introduced me and Fuchs. "You remember Parrish and Fuchs, sir. They were in the outfit. Parrish edited

The Battle of Midway for us." Ford looked at Fuchs and me for a few seconds but showed no sign of recognition. I said, "Good morning, sir."

He took out his pipe and started to feel around in his pockets for a match. When he found none, he turned to the warrant officer and said, "Have you got a match, Guy?" The warrant officer gave him one, and he lit the pipe (58 secs.) and puffed up a cloud of black smoke. Without looking at me or Fuchs again, he said, "Guy, as soon as the morbidly curious civilians leave, we'll break out the beer and start the wake." Then he turned and walked away.

As I left the Farm for the last time, I heard the sad tones of "Red River Valley" being squeezed out of Dan Borzage's accordion.

25

Linoleum OOgie

KATHIE and I and Pat Kelley and his wife, Judy, bought a fifty-foot lot on Fair Avenue in the valley, three miles from Ford's farm, and built a duplex dwelling with a loan from the U.S. government's GI Bill of Rights. Kelley and I had served together in the OSS and we had both married during the war. When the paint was almost dry (and before the carpets were laid and the curtains hung), Pat moved into the bottom half of the duplex with his beautiful pregnant Judy, from Uxbridge, Middlesex. Since the war, they had been living with Pat's parents.

A week after they moved in, Kathie and I said good-by to my mother and politely listened to her reasons why we should continue living with her and not move into the brand-new, sunshiny duplex top floor that we had been sweating out for eleven months. She said we could stay in her guest room (my room before the war) until the duplex was completely finished and furnished ("Sometimes it takes months, you know"), and that in the future we could have complete privacy, that she promised not to come in and talk at us for several hours every night. We both told her that that was not the reason for the move to our new home, that we both loved her very much, that Fair Avenue was only four blocks from her house on Farmdale Avenue, and that she could come over and see us as often as she liked. She burst into tears and said, "I understand."

As soon as we were settled into the new duplex and Kathie read the terms of the GI loan, she said, "We both have to work." I said, "Nonsense, I can support my family." She said, "Not if we want carpets and a refrigerator."

Universal Studio was a few blocks from our duplex. Kathie got a job there in the story department. I asked her what she would have to do, and she said, "Read scripts and I must join the story analysts' union." I said, "If you read scripts you are a reader—why don't you join a readers' union instead of the story analysts' union?" She said, "For the same reason that cutters join the film editors' union instead of a cutters' union, except that readers are affiliated with the carpenters and plasterers, and cutters are affiliated with the projectionists and hairdressers." The next day I got a job at the same studio, and Kathie and I settled down to the happiest period of our lives.

I had been in the editors' union for nine years, and although I had actually edited films during the war and even before, I was still classified as an assistant and it was very difficult to make the jump from assistant editor to editor. The studios and unions co-operated on a seniority system that made advancement almost impossible. Most of the top technicians (cameramen and editors, for example) were older men, and the camera operators and assistant editors were slightly younger older men. In the studio system, the really young men were apprentices for three or four years before being promoted to assistant. Then, unless they got an unusually lucky break, like suddenly becoming the son or nephew of the head of the studio, they lived out their middle age as well-paid assistants until an old editor or cameraman became senile or drunk or both. Then the assistant could take over the number-one spot; but he was still an assistant until the older man died. Even then, the assistant would have to remain an assistant if another senior man at the studio was available. A very frustrating business.

I was assistant montage editor, assistant montage director, and assistant head of the montage department at Universal. The department consisted of me and my boss, Harry Kaufman. Our job was to fill in the gaps on the cheap movies Universal was turning out. The writers would write "Montage of Gold Rush" or "Montage of World War I" or "Montage of Lon Chaney, Jr., changing into the Wolf Man," and Harry and I would make these sequences out of stock footage and/or the few cheap scenes we were permitted to shoot—newspaper inserts, close shots of hands and feet, calendar pages fluttering, and so on. We were not allowed to shoot faces because the Screen Actors Guild rate for faces was $7.50, too high for our budgets. In fact, we often used our own hands and pocketed the $2.00 allotted by the production department. On one picture we delivered the Middle Ages and the Industrial Revolution for $275.00. The Renaissance on another picture came to $695.75, but that was in color.

Kaufman had been a fixture at Universal for years. The montage department had originally been created for the serials that Universal specialized in, and Kaufman had done the whole job himself. He was the cameraman, editor, director, and prop man. The boss of the serials died at about the same time that the serials died, and Kaufman, a very insecure man in the best of times, thought he and his montage department would die too.

In anticipation of this, he had built up a cut-rate carpet company on the side. He called himself "Linoleum OOgie," because there was a giant chain of carpet merchants called "Linoleum LOOie." Kaufman thought the name similarity would give his cheap operation some fallout business from the well-advertised Linoleum LOOie.

When Universal stopped making serials, instead of firing Kaufman they increased his budget, doubled his staff (me), and told him to make montages for their low-budget features.

When I reported to him in his matchbox-sized cutting room-*cum*-office-*cum*-film library he said, "Hello, are you related to anybody in the front office?" I said, "No," and he said, "OK, then, here's how we work."

He pointed to a cigarette holder, which was attached to a rubber tube. The tube extended along his cutting bench and out of a neat hole that had been cut in the window. "When I yell 'puff,' you puff on this cigarette holder," he said. Before I could question him, he scurried out of the door and put a cigarette in the other end of the rubber tube, struck a match, held it to the cigarette, and yelled, "PUFF!"

I wasn't a smoker, but I puffed away like an addict until the cigarette was lit. Kaufman bustled back into the cutting room, jumped into his chair, and took over the cigarette holder. "We're not allowed to smoke in the cutting rooms," he said.

I said it didn't matter because I didn't smoke, and he said, "I don't care if you smoke or not, the important thing is to follow the rules of the department: first of all, and most important, stay out of everybody's sight. Don't say hello to anybody in the morning. Don't say good-by to anybody at night. After you punch in, come right here. Never mind the cups of coffee and the social bullshit. Those are the guys that the guys running the studio notice, and those are the guys who get fired. Be invisible like me and you'll last longer. Don't have lunch in the studio commissary and don't go on the sets. Don't sit in on runnings of pictures and don't get to know any executives. They change every six months or so, and if you know them, they'll change you too. OK?"

I stared at him. I was an eager young assistant cutter who wanted to go on the sets *and* eat in the commissary *and* drink coffee *and* say hello and good-by. But I also wanted to hang on to my job, so I said, "OK."

Kaufman said, "Fine. In the montage department, we come in early and we leave late. That way, fewer people see us punch in and out and fewer people ask questions about what we're doing here. It also means we put in more hours and thereby get more pay.

"We're supposed to make montages to plug up story holes and to add production value to low-budget pictures. Therefore *we* operate on a low budget. Vorkapitch at M-G-M and Don Siegel at Warner Brothers can spend more on one montage for one picture than we can spend all year. They have real departments, with art directors, writers, cameramen, et cetera. We have you and me and a lot of old stock film."

He sat on his cutting chair and paused long enough to let me absorb this, his feet dangling eighteen inches from the floor. He glanced into the mirror over his cutting bench and smoothed down his pencil-line mustache. He discovered a couple of wild hairs and trimmed them with his cutting scissors. He became interested in his face, turned the mirror over to the magnifying side, and trimmed the hairs in his nose and ears. He always wore a shirt and tie and suit, unlike most of the other studio workers, who usually dressed quite informally. He kept his tie knotted very tightly under his jutting blue chin, and he had a habit of tightening it from time to time during the day so that by the time he went home he could hardly breathe. After I got to know him better I pointed this out to him, and he said, "I *want* to look uncomfortable when I go home. I want my wife to think I've had a tough day."

"Do you go to the movies a lot?" he asked. I told him that I saw practically every movie that came out of Hollywood, and a lot of foreign films.

He said, "Good. Keep going as often as you can, but from now on watch out for montages, especially in M-G-M and Warner Brothers pictures. When you see a particularly good one, let me know and we'll steal it."

I thought he was joking, so I gave him a kind of patronizing, chickenshit smile and said, "How do we do that?"

He said: "We borrow the print, clean it up, and knock off a dupe negative and put it in my library here." He pointed to some long flat film cans that had labels in his pinched handwriting— "Building the West," "Police Car Chase," "Roman Empire," and

"City on Fire" were among them. One was marked "Sunrises and Sunsets—Kaufman Personal." I found out later that it contained various little rolls of pornographic film which he had squirreled away over the years.

I said, "Can we get away with that, stealing some other studio's film? For example, won't M-G-M recognize Spencer Tracy and Clark Gable if we use Vorkapitch's montage from *Boom Town*?"

Kaufman said, "We don't use Gable and Tracy. When we come to the parts that might be recognized we cut them out or optically superimpose an oil gusher or a close-up of one of our actors, Rod Cameron or Bill Lundigan or somebody. Let me worry about that. You just keep going to movies and looking for montages, and when you see a good one let me know. OK?"

I said, "OK, but don't we shoot anything ourselves?"

He said, "Of course we do. But only if we can't find it in somebody else's pictures."

We worked together for about two years. As I learned more about making montages, Kaufman spent more and more time as Linoleum OOgie. Sometimes he would punch in in the morning and sneak out to peddle linoleum all day, returning at six-thirty or seven o'clock to check my work and punch out.

One Sunday night I called him at his home. He answered the phone in a disguised voice, the way Marlon Brando sometimes does to avoid fans and reporters. Kaufman did it because he was naturally sneaky. I knew who it was, but I said, "Is Mr. Kaufman there?"

The voice said, "Who's calling?"

I said, "The studio," and he hung up. I called back and when a different voice answered I said, "Harry, for chrissakes, it's Bob, come off the Greek accent."

"It's Serbo-Croat," he said. "Whaddya want?"

"There's going to be a strike at the studio tomorrow," I said.

He said, "Whaddya telling me for? I'm in the linoleum business."

I said, "Yes, I know, OOgie, but you're also head of the montage department at Universal Studio. As you know, my wife is a story analyst at the studio, and she's just been advised by her union that they're being called out with the carpenters and plasterers. She has to report for picket duty in the morning."

Harry said, "What time?"

"I don't know." I turned to Kathie. "What time do you have

to be there, honey?" She said, "Eight o'clock." I relayed this into the phone.

"We can get in ahead of 'em," Harry said.

"That's not the point, Harry," I said. "I've talked to the cutters' union and we're *not* on strike. They *want* us to cross the picket line, but I don't want to, especially if Kathie is one of the pickets. How would you like to be called 'scab' by your wife?"

"That's what she always calls me," he said. "I think I'll be in the linoleum business until the strike blows over. Would you like to come down and help me? You'd have the same job that you have now, you'd still be my assistant."

I told him I'd rather stay in the movie business and would look for a job in a studio that wasn't being picketed. He said to try Walter Thompson at the new Enterprise Studio. I said OK but that we'd probably never work again at Universal. "Nonsense," he said. "The strike'll be over before they even know we're gone. Now do you see why we don't eat in the commissary and don't say hello and good-by to executives?" He hung up after telling me to come to the Linoleum OOgie shop on North Main Street if I changed my mind.

I phoned Walter Thompson, one of the industry's top editors, whom I had worked with at Twentieth Century-Fox. He was now the chief editor at Enterprise. He said there were no picket lines at Enterprise because they had no story analysts—the directors and writers analyzed their own stories. He said I could come to work the next day at 9:00 A.M. as his assistant, with a cut in salary but more chance for promotion. Kathie was washing her hair when I told her. She said, "That's good. You can drop me at the picket line on the way."

26

Tiger, Tiger, Burning Bright

FADE IN:

I T WILL be the true story of Barney Ross, the three-time champion of the world, war hero, and model for young people. We'll get John Garfield to star in it and Robert Rossen, the writer-turned-director, to direct. We'll call it *Tiger, Tiger, Burning Bright* to give it a classy sound, but it will actually be a straightforward, gutsy melodrama, right off the streets. The kind of stuff Zanuck did at Warner Brothers, only better, and we'll end it with Ross making a comeback at Madison Square Garden, recapturing the title for the fourth time."

FADE OUT:

FADE IN:

Headline:

BARNEY ROSS CONFESSES
DRUG ADDICTION
Former Welterweight Champion "Hooked" in
Army Hospital after War Injury

Barney Ross, the former three-time welterweight champion, has confessed to an addiction to heroin. "It started as a painkiller during the war," the short, dark, still well-built boxer told a press conference today.

FADE OUT:

FADE IN:

"The picture's off, we can't make a movie where the hero's a junkie. Declare *force majeure* or deception or something, cancel all the contracts, and we'll swallow our losses. I think we're probably lucky anyway. Prize-fight pictures are box-office poison. Women don't go to see them."

Robert Rossen said, "I think you're wrong. I say we go ahead. It doesn't *have* to be about Barney Ross. Polonsky's script can be about any bum who comes up the hard way. We'll just change the title and change the ending. We'll use the ending from Hemingway's *Fifty Grand.*"

"We don't own the motion-picture rights to *Fifty Grand.*"

"OK, so in our picture the payoff will be sixty grand. The thing is, we have a good story, a good cast, and crew, and we're ready to go."

"You haven't got a good story. You *had* a good story until Ross's press conference yesterday. You know the code won't permit movies where drugs are even mentioned, so the Barney Ross story is out. Period. Forget it. And to invent a new ending, then try to patch up the rest of the script by borrowing from other prize-fight stories, and still meet our contractual dates sounds like disaster to me, like putting Band-Aids on a leper." He turned to the company lawyer. "What do you think, Al?"

Al said, "We're a new studio. We've got most of our money tied up in *Arch Of Triumph*. We know that's a winner. With a best seller, Bergman and Boyer, two of the biggest stars in the business, and a great director, we can't miss. If that were finished and in release it would be different, but it will be a year before we see any money from that one. Our whole publicity campaign on *Tiger, Tiger, Burning Bright* is based on Barney Ross. If we go ahead now, we'll be murdered by the code and the women's clubs and we'll be sued by Ross. I think we should cancel, Charlie, and quick."

"I've always been nervous about boxing pictures anyway," Charlie said. "If it weren't for John Garfield's box-office attraction I wouldn't have gone into this project in the first place. Look, Bob, why don't you give me and Al a couple of hours to go into the legal and contractual aspects, and we'll see you after lunch. I promise we'll consider everything with an open mind and we won't make a decision until this afternoon."

Rossen was now pacing the room, his shoulders hunched, his chubby face a cloud of bitter frustration. He was sweating profusely, cornered, fighting for his life as a movie director. He had directed one picture, a successful melodrama with Dick Powell at Columbia called *Johnny O'Clock*. *Tiger, Tiger, Burning Bright* was to be his breakthrough into the big time, and he wasn't going to see it go down the drain just because Barney Ross was hooked on heroin.

He turned on his tormentor, i.e., his employer, the head of the studio. "OK, maybe this'll help you make up your open minds. It's going to cost you as much to cancel as it would to shoot. You gotta pay me and Polonsky and Garfield whether you make the picture or not. The sets are built. We've made deals with Lilli Palmer, Bill Conrad, and the New York actors. You're probably even going to have to pay Barney Ross."

"No we won't," Al said. "There's a morals clause in his contract. We'll save some money there."

"There's one in my contract too," Rossen said, "but it won't save you any money. Mine says 'play or pay.' "

He left the room like a wounded, dangerous bear who was going to call his lawyer.

FADE OUT:

FADE IN:

The picture started shooting three weeks later. The title was changed to *Body and Soul,* and announcements were made saying that the picture had nothing to do with Barney Ross.

Enterprise was a new studio, so there were no seniority problems, and Walter Thompson gave me my first job as a film editor. My assistant was Mike Luciano, Rossen's assistant director was Bob Aldrich. He also had Francis (Pete) Lyon on the set with him as editorial adviser and Don Weis as dialogue coach and script supervisor. James Wong Howe was the cameraman. Abraham Polonsky had written the shooting script.

It was apparent from the first day's rushes that Rossen was a talented director. It soon became apparent that he was also a worried director. He was, of course, worried about the usual things that movie directors worry about, but as we neared the end of the shooting period he seemed to be preoccupied with something else, over and above these normal worries.

After running the rushes one night, he invited Jimmy Howe and me into his office for a drink. Jimmy said, "Bob, you seem worried. What's on your mind? You should be happy. The stuff looks great."

Rossen was a suspicious man who kept his real thoughts to himself. He was happy with Jimmy's photography, but he also knew that Jimmy wanted to direct. This made Rossen nervous and, on some occasions, reluctant to accept the cameraman's advice. He looked at Jimmy and then at me, his eyes shifting from one of us to the other as he made up his mind whether or not to share his problem.

I thought he wanted to tell Jimmy something in confidence, so I swallowed my whisky and said, "Thanks for the drink. I have to get back to the cutting room." I always said that when I sensed a high-level argument coming up.

Rossen poured me another drink and said, "No, you better hear this." He filled his own glass and Jimmy's. "I'm worried about the end of the picture."

Jimmy said, "What's wrong with it? I think Abe has done a hell of a job."

Rossen stopped drinking and looked at me as if he thought I had told Jimmy to say this. Of course I hadn't, because I had learned earlier that Rossen became apprehensive if one member of the cast or crew praised another member. Whenever this happened, Rossen immediately suspected treachery, or, at the very least, collusion. His eyes shifted back to Jimmy, and he said, "Polonsky wants Garfield to win the last fight and tell Lloyd Gough to go fuck himself." (Gough played Roberts, the crooked gambler in the picture.) "I'm not sure Polonsky's right. I may want Garfield to lose the fight or, even if he wins it, I have an idea for an additional scene where Garfield gets shot by the gamblers, falls into a garbage can, and dies." He paused for us to absorb this idea, then added, "Lilli Palmer sees this from across the street and screams."

I glanced at Jimmy's face and it was completely impassive. His Oriental eyes stared straight at Rossen, telling him nothing. I put my glass to my mouth so I wouldn't have to say anything.

Rossen said, "What do you think?"

Jimmy said, "You could end it that way, Bob." (Ever so slight emphasis on "could.")

Rossen then asked me what I thought, and not being as experienced as Jimmy Howe, I said I liked the ending in the script better.

Rossen looked at me for a full ten seconds before he got up and started walking around the office. After he had made three laps, Jimmy said, "Why don't you shoot it both ways?"

Rossen said, "That's no good. I hardly have time to shoot *one* ending." He turned to me as though he and I were collaborators. "I've got three days to shoot five days' work, and this guy" —he pointed at Jimmy— "comes up with the bright suggestion that we 'shoot it both ways.'" He mimicked Jimmy with the last four words and added, "Christ!" Then he said, "You guys don't seem to understand the problem. I have to shoot the big stadium sequence next week and I haven't made up my mind how I'm gonna end the picture. Garfield's trained and ready. The other guy's trained and ready. Johnny Indrisano has coached them both to a fine edge."

Indrisano, Mae West's former bodyguard, was now a prize-fight coach and stunt arranger for movies. After I had been on the picture a few weeks and gotten to know him, I told him about how I had followed him around the Italian restaurants on North Broadway, and he thought it was very funny. Or, at least, I think he thought it was funny. In any event, he laughed. I had the feeling he thought I was making up the story.

"It's an expensive set with a lot of extras," Rossen went on, "and I don't know how we're going to get the coverage we need within the schedule, even if we don't shoot my new ending."

Jimmy said, "I've got an idea for you."

Rossen eyed him suspiciously, then growled, "What's the idea?"

The wily cameraman knew exactly how to handle Rossen. He had worked with practically every top director and star in Hollywood and had learned a few things. "No, I don't think it would work," he said.

Rossen snapped at the hook. "What won't work?"

Jimmy said, "A way to solve your problem," and then he let Rossen run with the bait.

"What's your idea, for chrissakes? We're all in this together, we're all making the goddam movie. Don't be so coy."

Jimmy started to reel him in. "Well, it's a way to shoot the stadium as scheduled next week and have it work for whatever ending you and Abe come up with."

Rossen said, "Go on." He turned his back on Jimmy, ostensibly to pour another drink, but I thought it was so that Jimmy wouldn't see his mouth watering.

"The war produced a lot of good cameramen, but none of them can get in the union unless his father is a cameraman."

Rossen's eyes narrowed and again started to shift from Jimmy to me and back. He was a very insecure fellow, and he suspected Jimmy was making him the butt of some joke yet to be revealed. "What the fuck does that have to do with the end of our picture?" he said hoarsely.

Jimmy continued as if Rossen hadn't spoken. "I'd like to pick four good ex-combat cameramen and get them waivers from the union to work on this one job. I'm sure I can do it. You and I will go ahead shooting with the first unit, but we'll give each of these guys an Eyemo hand-held camera and a thousand feet of negative each morning. We'll tell 'em they can shoot anything they want as long as they don't turn in any unexposed negative. So, aside from our regular footage, we'll have four thousand feet of surprises to choose from each day. The law of averages will make most of it unusable, but the same law will give us some shots that we could never get, shooting in the normal way."

Jimmy paused while Rossen eyed him, still suspicious. "Parrish and I will run the stuff each evening and put the good footage aside. Then, when we're all finished shooting in the stadium, we'll run everything with you and Abe and Francis Lyon and make an ending to the picture from it. The combat guys I pick will give us some unique material, I'm sure of that, and when cut with what you and I shoot, we'll have a hell of an ending." He looked at Rossen with his expressionless eyes. "It'll work, Bob, and this way you'll have enough stuff for any ending you want. You just make it in the cutting room instead of on the set."

Rossen said, "And what are you and I doing while these four combat cameramen are running around shooting stuff that's mostly unusable?"

Jimmy said, "We'll be shooting close-ups of Garfield and the other principals. I'll put on a pair of roller skates and let the grip pull me around so that our stuff will have the same quality as the combat footage."

"And each combat man has an assistant to pull focus and hold slate. We'll be falling over each other."

"No. Each guy works on his own, the way they did at Guadalcanal and Normandy. You won't even know they're there. They'll slate each hundred-foot roll at the beginning, and if a few shots are out of focus, so much the better. We'll have a real fight on the screen for the first time."

Rossen finally agreed and it all worked out just the way Jimmy predicted. I got twelve thousand feet from the combat cameramen and five thousand feet from Rossen and Jimmy Howe. We cut the seventeen thousand feet down to six hundred feet and shot two endings. When it came time to decide which one to use, Rossen and Polonsky had their private fight and Polonsky won. The movie ended the way he wrote it and we wound up with a rousing finale. Charley Davis (John Garfield) double-crossed Roberts (Lloyd Gough), the Mr. Big of the syndicate. The gamblers lost sixty thousand dollars.

REVISED 1/13/47
Scene no.   *Page no.*
                                                                    121

294   CLOSE SHOT—CHARLEY IN RING
       his face dazed, sweaty, bloody.

295   FULL SHOT—RING
       as the pandemonium moves from the crowd into the ring,
       the disappointed gamblers, the squad of cops surrounding
       the winner.

296   CLOSE SHOT—RINGSIDE
       As Charley comes through the ropes and down and is
       congratulated by the joyous Arnold.

297   AISLE PANNING SHOT
       Peg fights her way through the crowd.

298   CORRIDOR AND RAMP IN ARENA
       As policemen form a line to keep the excited crowd from
       pouring through the corridor, which leads to the dressing
       rooms. Charley and his entourage come through the police
       line and down the steps into the corridor. As Peg reaches
       him, locks arms with him, Roberts is waiting. As Charley
       comes by, Roberts turns to him. In the b.g. we see Quinn
       and Alice looking over the line of police. The spectators
       yell to Charley as they pass.

                         ROBERTS
                       (*ironically*)
              Congratulations, Champ!

       Still at the height of his emotion, Charley wheels, looks
       furiously at Roberts, and takes a swing at him. Roberts
       catches Charley's gloved hand and pulls him in close.

299   TIGHT TWO SHOT—ROBERTS, CHARLEY
       To the bystanders an ordinary conversation.

                         ROBERTS
              What makes you think you can get away
              with this?

                         CHARLEY
                        (*smiling*)
              Whatta you going to do, kill me?
              Everybody dies.

       He and Peg break away from Roberts through the
       reporters and into the depth of the corridor.

                                        FADE OUT:

                      THE END

Body and Soul was a hit, commercially and critically. The little picture that almost wasn't made had saved the studio. Francis Lyon and I had won Academy Awards and the script that Polonsky had fought so hard to preserve became a kind of textbook for screenwriters. I decided to pay more attention to writers in the future, whether Billy Hamilton liked it or not.

When I received the Oscar I wanted to thank the many people who had helped me—Chaplin, Fairbanks, Jane Loring, Hamilton, John Ford, Al Jolson, Linoleum OOgie, Rossen, Jimmy Howe, Walter Thompson, Mike Luciano, and the rest. It was my first and only chance to address all of the top people in Hollywood, but I was so nervous, I just muttered, "Thanks," and walked back to my seat with the Oscar clutched tightly in my hand, hoping that nobody would take it away from me.

27

Oscar

SHORTLY after I won the Academy Award, John Ford's secretary called and invited me to have lunch with Ford. He was shooting *Fort Apache* at the Selznick studio in Culver City. Lunch was set up in his office. The other guests were John Wayne, Merian C. Cooper (Ford's favorite producer), and Bob Wise, the director, a friend of Ford's and mine.

During lunch, Ford dominated the conversation with reminiscences of incidents that he and I had experienced during the war. This was slightly embarrassing, because, for various good and sufficient reasons, the other guests, except for Merian Cooper, happened not to have been in the war. After lunch, I got up to leave, and Ford muttered, "Stick around. I've got some information I'd like to give you."

When we were alone, Ford said, "How's Kathie?" I said, "Fine." He said, "Where are you living now?" I said, "On a fifty-foot lot in the valley."

He smiled and lit his pipe (1 min. 40 secs.). Then he decided he wanted a cigar instead. He selected a butt from the ashtray and lit it (1 min. 10 secs.). "I hear you won an Academy Award," he said finally.

"Yes, I did."

He relit the cigar butt. "I've won seven."

There was nothing much I could say to that without sounding insolent or petty. In fact, at that time he had won three Oscars for direction—*The Informer* (1935), *The Grapes of Wrath* (1940), and *How Green Was My Valley* (1941). He didn't show up at the awards ceremony to collect any of these first three Oscars because, he explained, "Once I went fishing, another time there was a war on, and on another occasion, I remember, I was suddenly taken drunk."

In addition to his awards for direction, *The Battle of Midway* had won an Academy Award in 1942, and *December 7th*, another OSS-Navy documentary, had won one in 1943. That was still only five; but a lot of actors, cameramen, musicians, writers, cutters, and art directors had won Oscars because of Ford's inspiration, so I guessed it was all right for him to say he had won seven Oscars. In any event, I wasn't going to bicker about an Oscar or two. Ford deserved every award he received and some he didn't receive.

He went on, "There's a place downtown on Hill Street between Fifth and Sixth where, if you take your Oscar in and give them fifteen cents, they'll give you a cup of coffee."

I think I got his point, but there wasn't much I could say. "Do you have the address?" was the best I could do.

"No, but I've got the Oscars, and they don't mean a thing. The only thing that's important is to keep working. And even that's only important when you're actually doing it. OK?"

I said, "Yes. That's OK."

He said, "Congratulations," and I said, "Thanks." He said, "Good luck," and I said, "The same to you."

I didn't have an occasion to talk to Ford again for twenty years.

28

Interior Columbia Studio — Day

EVERY time an Oscar was awarded to someone working at Columbia Studio, Harry Cohn had a copy made for his office. He sat at his desk backed by thirty-eight gold statues standing on terraced platforms built by his prop department. Robert Rossen stood at the window, his back to Cohn, staring glumly out at the traffic on Gower Street.

"The preview last night was a disaster," Cohn said. "The fuckin' picture is almost three hours long and it still doesn't make any sense." He turned to Rossen and pointed at me. "What makes you think this schmuck can salvage it when the best cutter in the studio has been working on it for five months?"

Cohn was a Hollywood legend. He had risen far above his "poverty row" title, and Columbia now made "quality" pictures as well as "B" pictures. As the quality of the pictures rose, so did Cohn's determination to remain uncouth and vulgar. He was a well-built man with a rather handsome face and penetrating blue eyes. He could be charming and he could also be odious and ruthless.

If he suspected that someone had talent, he would charm, bribe, cajole, until he had the talented person on his payroll. Once the talent was locked in, he would set about bullying it into submission. If the talent fought and survived, Cohn respected him and backed him all the way (Capra, Stevens, Sidney Buchman, and Rossen were among those who survived). If the talent caved in, Cohn despised him and fired him.

Rossen wanted me to recut *All the King's Men,* but he had to get Cohn's approval. I had cut three pictures after *Body and Soul* and was now considered a cutting prodigy. I decided not to take a regular job at any studio. I picked directors I wanted to work with (Ophuls, Milestone, Cukor) instead of studios. By maintaining this approach, I worked with the best directors, and I also made more money.

From time to time I was called in to give editorial advice after pictures were shot. For this kind of second-guessing work, I set a fixed fee—a hundred dollars a week more than the highest-paid cutter on the lot. For a short, heady time I became known as a "hot editor." "Pictures are made in the cutting room, you know" was the "in" attitude. The fact is that no picture was (or is) "made" in the cutting room. It starts with the writer. If he writes a good script, that script must run a gauntlet like a newborn child starting out in life. It has to hurdle producers, agents, bankers, actors, musicians, cameramen, directors, editors, and, finally, even laboratory technicians and projectionists. An editor can make it better or he can make it worse, but he can't "create" it. It comes to him already created. The movies are collaborative. The editor is one of the important collaborators.

Rossen had warned me about Cohn. "He'll try to insult you, but don't take it personally. Just think of him as a foul-mouthed diamond thief in the rough who respects talent and pays well. Besides, you won't be working for Cohn, you'll be working for me. Let me handle him." Rossen got up and walked over to Cohn's desk. He put both hands on it and leaned across, eyeball to eyeball, monster to monster. "I don't care how long *your* cutter's been working on it. I say there's a hell of a movie in that footage and when it's properly edited, we'll have a hit. Maybe the bum has been working on it too long."

"Maybe you have too," Cohn said.

Rossen ignored that. "Parrish hasn't seen a foot of it," he said. "He can come on it fresh, with no preconceived notions. He'll recut it and we'll take it out again. And this time, we'll go to Huntington Park or Torrance instead of Santa Barbara."

Cohn looked at him for a moment, then he smiled his happy-go-lucky, scorpion's smile and said, "What does that have to do with it?"

Rossen said, "How can you expect those retired fat cats in Santa Barbara to understand a movie about Huey Long? *All The King's Men* is a story of the people, the working stiffs, the Roosevelt voters. They live in factory towns, not in Palm Beach or Santa Barbara."

Cohn got up and went into the toilet in the back of his office. He left the door open and yelled back at Rossen. "Half the audience walked out last night and the other half stayed to boo or to sleep." He came back into the office zipping up his fly. "My own ass got tired halfway through, and when my ass gets tired, I know I got a flop."

Rossen's face turned beet red. He pointed his finger at Cohn and said, "You're full of shit, Harry."

Cohn turned to me and said, "Would you mind waiting outside?" I got up and left the office. As I closed the soundproof door, I heard Cohn say, "Now listen, you prick . . ."

I sat in the outer office with the male secretary while the two dinosaurs continued the discussion. I took a copy of *Variety*, the trade paper, out of my pocket and started to read it. The male secretary said, "You'd better not let Mr. Cohn see you reading that. He's barred *Variety* from the lot and anyone caught reading it or smuggling it in is liable to instant dismissal." I said he couldn't fire me because he hadn't hired me yet. I asked why *Variety* had been banned, but before he could answer, Cohn's voice came over the intercom, "Ask Mr. Parrish to come back in." The secretary said, "He wants to see you. You'd better put the paper back in your pocket." I followed his advice, but I let it stick out so that the *Variety* banner could be seen.

Both men were amiable, friendly. No hint of any disagreement. Rossen said, "Bob, Mr. Cohn has agreed for you to look at the film as it is now cut and give us your opinion. Would you be able to run it this afternoon?"

I looked over to Cohn, expecting him to call me a schmuck again, but instead he said, "I liked the job you did on *Body and Soul* and *A Double Life*. Rossen says you will look at the picture with no obligation and tell us what you think."

I agreed to run it, provided Al Clark, the editor then on the picture, ran it with me.

I had lunch with Clark, an old friend of mine, a fine editor with a good record. He said nothing would make him happier than for me to come onto the picture. He was fed up. Rossen was disenchanted with him and he couldn't do anything right for Rossen. Rossen had shot the entire picture on James Wong Howe's law-of-averages theory, the one we had been successful with on the prize-fight sequence in *Body and Soul*. Consequently, there were thousands of feet of superfluous film and Rossen couldn't make up his mind which parts to use. Al suggested that if I accepted the job, I do it on the condition that I actually take over the picture and recut it with no interference from Rossen, Cohn, or anybody else. "If you do it that way, Bob, I will pitch in with you, and I think we can come up with a good picture. The trouble now is that Rossen wants to hang on to every foot of film."

I ran the picture with Al Clark and Frank Keller, his assistant. As a movie it was a mess, but as film much of it was very exciting. The trouble was that the story made no sense whatsoever. I asked Al and Frank about the "outtakes" and "lifts," i.e., the film that had not been used in this cut version. Al said there were tens of thousands of feet of film but that it would take a week to organize it for viewing and a full day to view it. I told him I would not give Cohn and Rossen a decision until I had viewed every foot of film that Rossen had shot.

Back in Cohn's office that night, I put my proposition to Cohn and Rossen. I was very excited about what I had seen and I thought a good picture could be made out of it, but I would have to see everything Rossen had shot before making up my mind whether or not to take on the job. And then I would have to have carte blanche until the next preview.

Cohn stared straight at me. Rossen shifted his eyes back and forth from me to Cohn the way he had done in the meeting with Jimmy Howe on *Body and Soul*.

Cohn said, "How much do you get?"

I said, "A hundred dollars a week." Both men looked at me suspiciously. The union minimum salary for editors was $245.00 per week. Rossen said, "Bob, uh . . ." and I went on, ". . . plus what you pay the highest-paid editor on the lot."

Rossen blanched visibly, and Cohn smiled. "You got a deal, kid," he said. I found out later why he smiled. My salary would be charged to Robert Rossen Productions, not Columbia Pictures.

Al Clark and Frank Keller assembled all of the printed footage and I ran it—lots of unusable material and lots of brilliant, but formless, material. I read Robert Penn Warren's novel on which the film was based and all the scripts that I could find—material by Norman Corwin, John Bright, Hans Viertel, Walter Bernstein, and Robert Penn Warren himself. Then I read hundreds of pages that Rossen had put together using bits of the book plus the various other scripts. When I finished reading everything, I was more confused than ever and kept thinking of Billy Hamilton. I phoned him at the Grotto and told him my problem.

He said, "Is the film itself any good?" I told him it was, and he said, "Then why are you wasting time reading pieces of paper? You should be sitting at the moviola." I heard him ask the bartender to turn the music down. "Tell Rossen you think you've found a way to recut his film. If he asks for details like story line or motivation or characterization or any other crap that those guys like to talk about while someone else is doing the work, recite the book to him. The original material is usually the best, and he's probably forgotten it. If you need any help, let me know and I'll come in and help you at night."

I thanked him, brushed up on the book, and told Rossen I thought I saw a way to recut the picture. I waited for him to say "What is it?" Instead, he said, "OK, go ahead. I'm too close to it. I've been working on it for over a year. I'm taking a holiday. I'll be back in a month and we'll preview your cut in Huntington Park, a tough factory town. They'll understand it."

And that's what we did. I recut the entire picture, redubbed it using music from the film library, and we previewed in Huntington Park.

The fat cats from Santa Barbara must have been in touch with the working stiffs in Huntington Park, because the reception wasn't any better. In fact, it was worse. The Santa Barbara audience was simply bored. The working-class audience in Huntington Park hated it, as did Cohn and the other Columbia executives. Rossen alone still believed in it, and he somehow convinced Cohn to let us carry on.

We worked on the picture for six months after the Huntington Park fiasco. We had seven more disastrous previews with all kinds of audiences. After each flop preview, Cohn threatened to ship the picture. Each time, Rossen talked him out of it. We discovered that Mercedes MacCambridge, a new actress from New York, was particularly well received by each audience, so we went back into production and made more of her part. Cohn grumbled, threatened, bullied, and used obscenely abusive language to Rossen. Rossen sweated, threatened, bullied, cajoled, and cursed right back at Cohn.

But the picture was still over two and a half hours long and we somehow couldn't capture the cohesive story line of the novel.

Finally, Cohn called me in and said, "I want you to cut the negative and get ready to ship, but don't tell Rossen until the negative is already cut." I said I would have to tell Rossen. Cohn said, "Why?" and I said because he had directed the picture and I was being paid by him. "Besides," I said, "we're in the middle of getting ready for another preview. We'll waste a lot of money if we abandon and cut the negative now."

He said, "You really believe in this picture, don't you?" I said I did, and he said, "OK, this is the last preview. After this, we ship."

I told Rossen about our conversation. He scowled and mut-

Author and mother, 1942.

(Top left) Commander John Ford, best man, and groom, USNR.
(Top right) The chapel, OSS Field Photo Farm. (Bottom) Groom,
bride, and best man John Ford.

(Top) Universal Studio, with Hollywood in background. (Bottom)
John Wayne, Mark Armistead, John Ford, and Ward Bond.

Cutter's copy

"BODY AND SOUL"

ORIGINAL SCREENPLAY

by

ABRAHAM POLONSKY

SHOOTING SCRIPT - FINAL
Revised 1-13-47

PLEASE SIGN ON BOTTOM LINE, TEAR AT PERFORATION, AND RETURN TO MAIL ROOM.

ORDER	SIGNATURE	ORDER	SIGNATURE
Editorial			

SIGNATURE _B.B. Parrish_   DATE 16 JAN 1947

(Top left) *Body and Soul* poster. (Right) Screenplay, cutter's copy.
(Bottom) *Body and Soul:* James Wong Howe with camera, John
Garfield at right.

Body and Soul Academy Awards, 1947: author and Anne Baxter.

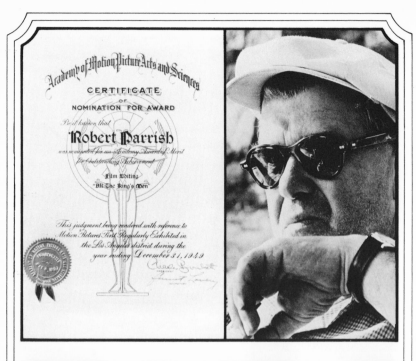

(Top left) Oscar nomination for *All the King's Men.* (Top right) Robert Rossen. (Bottom) Broderick Crawford, Willie Stark in *All the King's Men.*

Paramount

RELEASE AUGUST 13, 1957 OR THEREAFTER

KINGLY PAIR -- Cecil B. DeMille, king of film-makers and Hollywood's most honored citizen, is caught on his 76th birthday (August 12) on the Paramount studio lot with a ranking representative of the animal kingdom. Leo the Lion, symbol of DeMille's own birth sign Leo, has been accepting through the ages as denoting nobility, strength and leadership, qualities for which the celebrated producer-director has been hailed throughout his motion picture career which spans 45 years and reaches its peak with his 70th and latest motion picture, the monumental "The Ten Commandments." For his continued demonstration of high principles and devotion to God and country, he has been aptly described as the modern "Spirit of 76"

(Top left) Cecil B. DeMille and Leo the Lion. (Top right) Paramount publicity release. (Bottom left) *Variety*. (Bottom right) Joseph L. Mankiewicz.

To Bob Parrish
with gratitude —
John Ford
Wash. D.C.
~ '44

John Ford.

tered, "Fuck 'im." He came to the dubbing room where I was working and brooded all afternoon. He didn't seem to pay much attention to the dubbing. At about six o'clock, he turned to me and said, "Did you ever see *The Roaring Twenties,* the picture I wrote for Raoul Walsh?" Rossen had collaborated with Jerry Wald on the screenplay, but I could see he was in no mood to have this pointed out to him. I said, "Yes, I saw it. Good picture. Walsh is a hell of a director." He shifted his eyes over to me and said, "You and I are running *The Roaring Twenties* tonight."

After the running, Rossen and I went to the Naples Italian restaurant near the studio and he said, "The reason that picture works is because it's imperfect. It gallops along from scene to scene like one big ninety-minute montage. The audience never gets a chance to relax and think about the story holes. They're into the next scene before they have time to think about the last one." I agreed and he said, "I've got an idea for our picture." I suggested that we not make any drastic changes in the middle of dubbing, that we wait until after the preview.

"Bullshit," said Rossen. "It'll be too late then. Cohn's going to take the picture away from me. It's gotta be done now."

"What's your idea?" I said.

"I want you to go through the whole picture. Select what you consider to be the center of each scene, put the film in the sync machine and wind down a hundred feet before and a hundred feet after, and chop it off, regardless of what's going on. Cut through dialogue, music, anything. Then, when you're finished, we'll run the picture and see what we've got."

It sounded like a good idea to me, because up until now Rossen had been reluctant to lose footage. The picture was still a slow two hours and ten minutes.

I went straight back to the cutting room, followed Rossen's instructions to the letter, and when Frank Keller and I measured it, at 5:00 A.M., we had a ninety-minute picture. We ran it for Rossen and discovered that his brainstorm had worked. It all made sense in an exciting, slightly confusing, montagey sort of way. We went back and added bits to three scenes. Then we dubbed it, took it out for our final preview in Pasadena (more fat cats than in Santa Barbara), and were relieved at the audience's enthusiastic reaction. When Willie Stark (Broderick Crawford) was being tried, and delivered Huey Long's famous speech to the Louisiana State Legislature ("I've been accused of stealing one million dollars. It's a lie. I stole *three* million! But I stole it for *you!* To build your hospitals, your schools, your roads . . ."), the audience was with him all the way. The demogoguery poured out of the screen at the Queens Theater, and the Pasadena fat cats stood up and applauded. It was the most successful preview I ever went to—except *Body and Soul.*

By now we were all so nervous about the whole operation that we decided not to touch it again. After the Pasadena preview we cut the negative with all the imperfections, the mismatched cuts, and the jumps in the sound track.

All the King's Men won the Academy Award for the best picture of that year, and Cohn added Oscar number thirty-nine to his collection. He and Rossen were now fighting again, so Cohn gave me credit for saving the picture.

29

You Don't Want to Go
to Europe . . .

I'M OFFERING you the job as head of my cutting department for the same money that Rossen paid you to cut *All the King's Men* and you're turning me down, is that right?"

"That's right," I said.

"OK," he said, "how much do you want?"

"It isn't the money, Mr. Cohn. It's just that I don't want to sit at a desk and sign the time cards for the real cutters."

"So what do you want?"

"I want to go to Europe and I want to be a director," I said.

"You don't want to go to Europe, I just got back," he said. "There's nothing over there." From anyone else, this might have been a joke, but Cohn said it straight.

"So much for Western Civilization," I thought. The Holy Roman Empire, the Glory of Greece, the Renaissance, Voltaire, Heine, Beethoven, Balzac, Picasso, Tolstoy, Auguste Renoir's paintings and his son's films—all dismissed by an ex-streetcar conductor on North Gower Street.

"As for directing," he said, "you're not ready yet. You need more experience in the cutting room."

"Fair enough," I said, "But I want to actually cut. I'd rather work on one good picture than oversee a lot of mediocre ones. Besides, I can make more money if I choose my pictures. Rossen paid me more to recut *All the King's Men* than you pay your head cutter to supervise forty pictures."

He reached over and flipped the intercom switch. "Send Cahane, Briskin, Fier, and Arnow in." These were his four top executives. He got up from behind his massive desk and paced around the office. He stopped at the window and looked out onto the parking lot across Gower Street. Buddy Adler, one of his producers, was getting out of his car and crossing toward the studio front gate. Cohn jumped back to his desk, flipped the intercom, and said, "Get me Adler." When Adler's secretary came on, Cohn said, "Let me speak to him." Pause; then Cohn said, "Well, when he comes back from the toilet, ask him to call me." He turned to me and said, "What time is it?" I told him it was 11:45.

At that point, the four executives were announced by the male secretary, and Cohn said, "Send 'em in." Cahane was a dignified lawyer, Briskin was executive assistant to Cohn, Arnow was the casting director, and Fier was a very good production boss.

Fier became famous at Columbia when Orson Welles was shooting *The Lady from Shanghai* with Rita Hayworth. At the last moment, on a Saturday, Welles wanted a complete set repainted for shooting on the following Monday. Fier told him it was impossible. Welles and some friends came in on Sunday night, broke into the paint department, and repainted the set. They also painted a huge banner which they hung over the studio entrance: THE ONLY THING WE HAVE TO FEAR IS FIER HIMSELF.

As the early-morning workmen arrived Monday, they saw the sign and all had a good laugh. That is, all but the members of the Motion Picture Set-Painters' Union, Local 729 (IATSE). Instead of laughing, they closed the studio with picket lines and threatened to keep it closed until a full crew was paid triple time for the work done by Welles and his chums. Fier agreed, put the cost on Welles's personal bill, and had the union painters paint a banner saying: ALL'S WELL THAT ENDS WELLES, which everyone saw as they left the studio Monday evening. When Welles saw it he charged into Fier's office, threw his arms around Fier, and the two enemies became friends for the rest of the picture.

Fier led the other three executives into Cohn's office and started to sit down. Cohn said, "Who the fuck told you to sit down?"

Fier settled into his chair and said, "Nobody has to tell me, Harry. I learned it when I was a little boy."

Cohn knew a good production man when he hired one, so he let the remark pass. He pointed at me and said, "I want you to take a look at this guy." I knew them all, so they nodded or smiled and I nodded back. Jack Fier was the only one who spoke. He said, "How are you, Bob?"

Before I could answer, Cohn said, "I've now got a schmuck cutter who only wants to work on good pictures. It isn't enough that writers, directors, and actors give me that "quality" shit, now I'm getting it from a fuckin' cutter."

Jack Fier stood up and said, "Is it OK if I say something, Harry?"

Cohn looked at him suspiciously and said, "It depends on what you're going to say. Say it and then I'll tell you if it's OK." He walked to the window and looked out.

Fier said, "The 'quality' shit didn't hurt *All the King's Men*."

Cohn turned and pointed his finger at Fier, but before he could think of anything to say, the intercom buzzer cut him off. He went to his desk, flipped the switch, and the male secretary said, "Mr. Adler returning your call." Cohn said, "Put him on," and waved the four executives out of the office. I started to follow, and he said, "You wait, Bob."

He said into the phone, "Where the fuck were you?" Pause; then Cohn said, "So your secretary told me. Do you always take a crap in the parking lot at eleven-forty-five in the morning? Get your ass down here." He hung up the phone and turned to me.

"Now, let me give you some facts of life. I release fifty-two pictures a year. I make about forty and buy the rest. Every Friday, the front door of this studio opens and I spit a movie out onto Gower Street." I pictured him in the small reception room every Friday, sitting, Buddha-like, under large photographs of Rita Hayworth and Bill Holden, waiting for the front door to open so he could belch and spit ten cans of film out onto Gower Street.

"If that door opens and I spit and nothing comes out, it means that a lot of people are out of work—drivers, distributors, exhibitors, projectionists, ushers, and a lot of other pricks."

I wondered if that last category included cutter, but I didn't say anything.

"How many of those fifty-two pictures do you think that *I* think are good?"

"Well, Mr. Cohn," I mistaked, "I assume you want them all to be good."

"Never mind the bullshit," he said. "I want one good picture a year. That's my policy. Give me a *Mr. Deeds* or a *Jolson Story* or an *All the King's Men* or a *Lost Horizon* and I won't let an exhibitor have it unless he takes the bread-and-butter product, the *Boston Blackies*, the *Blondies*, the low-budget westerns, and the rest of the junk we make. I like good pictures too, but nobody knows when they're going to be good, so to get one, I have to shoot for five or six, and to shoot for five or six, I have to keep the plant going with the program pictures."

I said that I understood but I still wanted to be a director, even if I directed one of the program pictures—maybe I could make it into one of his "good" pictures.

The intercom buzzed and the male secretary said, "Mr. Adler is here." Cohn said, "Tell him to wait." He turned to me and became paternal, charming, seductive.

"Here's a proposition for you. I have six pictures in various stages of production or postproduction. I'd like you to take charge of them as you did on the Rossen picture. They're all crap and I want them shipped as soon as possible. You can call yourself the executive producer or head cutter or anything you please, but you'll actually be my personal cutter and you won't have to sign time cards or count paper clips or answer to anybody but me. All you have to do is get those six pictures into preview condition as soon as possible. I'll pay you what Rossen paid you, and I'll give you a picture to direct and a bonus if you meet the shipping dates."

I still wanted to be a director, and nobody else had offered me a picture. I also liked cutting. Here was my chance to break through. It was true that Cohn was considered a tough customer, but I felt I knew him now and could handle his eccentricities. Also, we had something in common, an obsession with picturemaking. It was the only thing either of us really wanted to do.

I accepted the job and completed the last picture, *Woman of Distinction*, well ahead of schedule. Up to now, Cohn had kept his word and treated me with a certain amount of respect. When I was ready to screen something for him, we usually screened it at his home at night. He didn't particularly like any of the six pictures, so as soon as I said they were ready to be shipped, we shipped them.

We previewed *Woman of Distinction* at the Queens Theater in Pasadena and returned to Cohn's office for the preview postmortem. As usual, Cohn dictated notes to his male secretary en route back to the studio. Then, while the producer, director, cutter, composer, etc., told him their ideas and counted the preview cards, the male secretary typed Cohn's notes. When he finished and brought the copies in, Cohn passed them around and said, "Let's stop the bullshit. Here's what we're doing with the picture. We're shipping it tomorrow. You can all go home. You did a good job, Bob."

As the others left, I said, "Thank you. May I see you alone for a few minutes?"

He said, "Sure, kid. I gotta take a piss. Come on in." I said I would wait until he finished and he said, "No, come on. You can pee too."

I followed him into his toilet, and as he relieved himself he said, "What's your mind?" I said, "That's the last of the six pictures. Now I'd like to talk to you about directing." I hadn't peed, but I nervously washed my hands, figuring that's what he would be doing next and it would show a spirit of friendly co-operation. Instead, he walked back into the office and said, "What the hell are you doing?" There were no towels, so I came in drying my hands with my handkerchief.

He was putting his papers in his briefcase and said, "Hollywood's full of directors. Good cutters are harder to come by and they're worth more. I've got six more pictures I want you to push through. When you've done those you'll be more experienced and I'll know you better. In the meantime, I'll be on the lookout for a picture for you to direct."

"That wasn't our deal," I said. "You said you'd give me a directing assignment if I supervised your six sick pictures."

He closed his bag and said, "How about giving me a lift?" He lived in Beverly Hills and I lived in Brentwood, so it was on my way home. We drove in silence until we got to his house, a Spanish-style mansion in back of the Beverly Hills Hotel. I stopped the car and kept the engine running. "If you want to direct, go direct for somebody else," he said. "You're not ready yet. You'll fall on your face. After you've got it out of your system, come back and cut for me. I'll raise your salary." He closed the car door and disappeared into the gloomy house without waiting for an answer.

30

Is It Fun Yet?

W HENEVER I hear the phrase "the Golden Age of Hollywood," I think of Joel McCrea. McCrea was a well-paid actor—about five thousand dollars a week before taxes and still several thousand after taxes. He bought a working ranch, which, under his management, showed a net profit of $28.31 the first year, $8,401.63 the second year, $31,248.09 the third year, and so on. When I worked with Joel, a few years after he bought the ranch, he was negotiating with the Union Oil Company of California to lease them a small section of the ranch for over one million dollars plus a royalty. You can see that he knew what he was about, capital gains-wise.

He loved Hollywood. He loved making movies. He loved the beaches of Santa Monica, where he had been a lifeguard with his friend Andy Devine. He loved horses. And he loved his family. He was always trying to teach his sons lessons of thrift, frugality, and industry. He also loved his ranch.

It was a relaxing place to go to, especially when you were out of work and needed a change from Harry Cohn. I called Joel and asked if I could come out and see him. He always made me feel better than I was. "Sure," he said. "Come early, I have something I want to talk to you about." Loosely translated, that meant, "So you can help me with the chores around the ranch." Of course we could talk too. There was no rule against conversation.

He handed me a shovel and said, "We're going to take these horseapples out of the stable and spread them on the alfalfa field."

I said, "You mean before lunch?"

"Yes. I want to do it now, I'll tell you why later." He looked around to see if anyone was listening. "I'll tell you why later" was always muttered conspiratorially so that you didn't dare question it at the time for fear of being overheard by some enemy. If you asked Joel about it later, he would say, "Well, that was because I know you're a busy man and I didn't want to

190

waste your time explaining." What he really meant this time was that by Tom Sawyering me, he could save two hours of the hired hand's labor. No, four hours—two for me and two for Joel. He always worked harder than anyone else.

On this occasion, he also wanted to teach his son David the virtues of hard work. Joel had bought a toy shovel, which the four-year-old was using to make mud pies. Joel couldn't see any profit in mud pies, so he said, "Come on, David, help me and Uncle Bob clean out the stable." David glanced at his father and continued making mud pies. Joel said, "Watch me, David." He took David's toy shovel, scooped up a large horseapple, carried it to the wheelbarrow, dropped it in, and gave the shovel back to David. Joel said, "Go on, David. Now you try it. It's fun."

Without a word, David got up from the mud puddle and copied his father's actions, one horseapple at a time, for just over an hour. Joel and I were working like hell, sweating, straining, shoveling, wheelbarrowing, covering ourselves in horseshit. Finally, David stopped work, turned to his Dad, and said, "Is it fun yet?"

31

Anybody Can Direct

T HIS is Dick Powell. Could we meet?"
I said, "Certainly. Any time." And he invited
Kathie and me to his house for dinner that night.

Dick Powell was an unusual movie star. When he called me, he was enjoying his second movie-star career. He first rose to fame as a crooner in Warner Brothers musicals. He was always *Shuffling off to Buffalo* with, or *Only Having Eyes* for, or *By a Waterfall Calling* to, Ruby Keeler. He had wavy hair, and my friend Jack McHugh said he had a face like a plucked chicken's ass. McHugh's was a minority opinion, because most people, especially women, thought Powell handsome.

I had worked extra in some of the Warner musicals, but the one I remembered best was *Shipmates Forever*. In that picture Dick Powell and I and fifty other midshipmen had graduated from the Naval Academy at Annapolis. We were sailing away on our first cruise, standing in our uniforms on the deck of a destroyer built in front of a back-projection process screen on Stage 6 at the Warner Brothers Studio. As the special-effects men rocked the destroyer, the Annapolis shoreline on the process screen got smaller, and waves appeared.

We were all supposed to be feeling sad about leaving the Academy, so we were singing a song called "Shipmates Forever." The camera moved in to a close-up of Dick Powell about halfway through the song, because (a) he was the star, (b) he was the only one of the midshipmen who could carry a tune, and (c) he was sailing away from Ruby Keeler and the director wanted the camera to be close enough to see Dick's eyes mist up. Frank Borzage, my old friend from *History Is Made at Night*, was directing. He was an expert on shipboard tears.

After the first rehearsal, somebody came up with the idea of blowing water in our faces and putting heavier seas with white-caps on the process screen when we came to the line in the song about "fair or *stormy* weather." We broke for lunch while this dramatic change was organized. Jack McHugh and I tried to get into the "green room" at the studio restaurant but were told that all tables were reserved and that extras were supposed to eat in the big "regular" restaurant. We knew from past experience that only stars, directors, and executives were allowed in the green room, but we always gave it a try.

The "James Cagney Special" on the menu that day was "Shrimp Cocktail, Large Bowl of Chili and Beans with Onions, Pistachio Ice Cream, Coffee, Tea, or Milk—45 cents." McHugh and I washed the pistachio ice cream down with milk, then each ordered a slice of apple pie (five cents extra). I figured to spend sixty cents for lunch. I bought an Oh, Henry! chocolate bar (five cents) and was still five cents under my budget.

When we got back on the set, the special-effects men had brought in wind machines and gallons of water to blow in our faces. The cutter had found a piece of stock film in the library labeled *"Captain Blood*—Rough Seas—Whitecaps," and he gave it to the background projectionist. Lew Borzage, the assistant director, herded us onto the destroyer deck, and we spent the next two hours trying to co-ordinate the playback words "stormy weather" with the "Rough Seas—Whitecaps" stock film, the wind machines, the spray water in our singing faces, the rocking of the destroyer, and the glycerine tears in Dick Powell's eyes. I thought about suggesting my well-tried soap-under-the-fingernails formula to Dick, but I was having other problems.

We were supposed to keep our eyes on the process screen and look sad as we mouthed the words to the playback sound recording. I was OK on the rehearsals, but at four o'clock, when we were finally ready for a take, I began to feel seasick. Every time I mouthed "fair or stormy weather" and felt the destroyer roll under my feet as the special-effects man blew water in my face, I became woozier and woozier. Lew Borzage kept yelling, "Watch the process screen!" and the more I watched it, the sicker I got. I was standing in back of Dick Powell, and when we finally made a take, and the camera was moving into his close-up, I vomited all over his U.S. Navy midshipman uniform. The James Cagney Special sprayed out onto his neck and rolled down his perfectly fitted navy-blue jacket, followed by the apple pie (five cents extra) and the Oh, Henry! bar.

I will say this for Dick Powell. He was a pro. Only a pro could sing "If you have to take a lickin', carry on and quit your kickin'" with lukewarm shrimp cocktail, chili beans, onions, and pistachio ice cream rolling down his back. Frank Borzage yelled "Cut," but the wind machines drowned out his voice.

They also blew the James Cagney Special, the apple pie, and the Oh, Henry! bar back onto me and the other midshipmen. Powell followed the playback as though nothing had happened. He sang the last, drawn-out, dramatic line—"Don't gi-i-ive up thuuuuh ship!"—with great feeling and a warm neck.

In the meantime, the special-effects men were sloshing buckets of water in front of the wind machines, and Frank Borzage sat quietly smoking his pipe, knowing that eventually his brother Lew would get everything under control. Frank Borzage was not a yeller, he was a waiter. He waited patiently until the playback ended and the "*Captain Blood*—Rough Seas —Whitecaps" film ran out on the process screen and the wind machines stopped and the James Cagney Special was cleaned off the uniforms. Then he said, "OK, let's go again." I thought I was going to be fired, but instead he said, "You'd better come sit here with me. The weather's calmer."

Dick Powell's second acting career started with *Murder My Sweet*, a Raymond Chandler private-eye story with Powell playing Philip Marlowe and Edward Dmytryk directing. Powell agreed to cut his wavy, crooner's hair, and the picture was a success. The new Dick Powell was tough, ruthless, and crew-cutted. He would give up the ship or Ruby Keeler or anything else for a buck. With the crew cut, Jack McHugh said, his face no longer looked like a plucked chicken's ass.

After *Murder My Sweet*, he crew-cutted through *Cornered*, *Johnny O'Clock*, *To the Ends of the Earth*, *Pitfall*, *Rogue's Regiment*, and *Right Cross*—all successful and all songless. Powell was no longer a crooner. He was a "tough guy." Dashiell Hammett had Bogart (or vice versa), and Raymond Chandler had Powell.

I took my wife to his house for dinner. After dinner, his movie-star wife, June Allyson, and Kathie went up to June's bedroom. June had to set her hair for the next day's shooting and thought Kathie might like to watch her put the curlers in. Dick and I went to the "den" that all fancy Bel Air homes had in those days. This one had a bar and a lot of flying and sailing trophies that Dick had won.

"Would you like to direct a picture?" he said.

I said, "Yes," and he said, "OK."

I knew that it couldn't be that easy, that there must be a Harry Cohn catch somewhere. I said, "How did you happen to pick me?" I didn't think it could be just because I had vomited on him fifteen years before.

"There's this little guy named Sam Wiesenthal. He's got a script called *Cry Danger* and he's got a theater owner from the Middle West with some of the money. Howard Hughes has promised him distribution and the rest of the finance if he can get me and a director. I believe in new directors. I called the new directors I've worked with recently and none of them is available. Rossen's too important to direct an inexpensive melodrama, John Sturges is under contract to M-G-M, and Panama and Frank are directing *Callaway Went Thataway*. When I talked to them, they all recommended you. That's why I called you."

"How's the script?" I said.

Dick said, "Terrible. But we'll get Bill Bowers to rewrite it." Bowers was (and is) one of the best writers in Hollywood. "Do you want to read it, or can I tell Sam you'll do it?"

"Both," I said.

He took me to meet Sam Wiesenthal, a very nice, worried little man. Maybe he wasn't really worried, but he looked worried. "Howard Hughes wants to meet you," he said. He took me to Hughes's office and left me with the secretary while he went in to see Hughes. The door was left open and I heard a nasal, slightly southern voice say, "Hi, Sammy. What's on your mind?"

Wiesenthal said, "I've brought Bob Parrish in to meet you."

"Who the hell's he?" the voice said.

"He's the director I told you about. Dick Powell likes him, and I thought you said you wanted to meet him."

"I didn't say I wanted to *meet* the sonofabitch, I just said I wanted him insured."

The door closed, and I couldn't hear Sam's answer. He came out a few minutes later and said that Hughes liked my work and would be pleased to meet me some other time. He then took me to the RKO studio medical department, where I had an insurance examination.

That's as close as I came to meeting Howard Hughes. As I worked with Powell and Bowers on the rewrite, I kept thinking that the whole thing was a plot. I imagined that Wiesenthal and Hughes never intended to make the picture, that they had had me heavily insured and were waiting for a chance to push me under a truck and collect double indemnity for my accidental death.

Bowers was bright, realistic, and talented. He knew enough not to try to make a silk purse out of mediocre script. We all settled for a sow's ear with Bowers's sharp dialogue.

Two weeks before shooting, I got cold feet. It was obvious that nothing was going to come together. Wiesenthal was a nice man, but he was no Irving Thalberg. His financial partner from the Middle West arrived and was a constant pain in the neck to everybody. Bowers hadn't finished the script. The art director, Richard Day, and I were desperately looking for "live locations," because the total set budget was $7,500, just enough to furnish Wiesenthal's office. The only calm one was Powell. I had lunch with him at The Players, Preston Sturges's restaurant on Sunset Boulevard, and I blabbed out my fears, my insecurities. "Do you really think I can direct this movie?" I asked him.

"Of course you can," he said. "Anybody can direct a movie, even I could do it. I'd rather not because it would take too much time. I can make more money acting, selling real estate, and playing the market." This was true. He was a very good businessman, one of the richest actors in town, along with Fred MacMurray and Joel McCrea. The latter two stars *saved* their fortunes. Powell *made* two or three fortunes with an acute business sense and limitless energy. "Just hang on and pretend you know exactly what you're doing. I'll back you to the limit if you'll promise to do one thing."

"What's that?" I said.

"Just remember what Hitchcock said. 'It's only a movie.' It's not real life. It's shadows on a screen. It's nothing. It's dreams. You can't put it in your pocket. You can't put it in the bank. You can't even touch it. As you reach for it, it's gone. You start with a bare white screen and you put something up there that you hope will be interesting. If only your wife and your mother like it, you're a flop. If fifty million people like it, it's worth while. So let's stop this 'can I do it?' nonsense and make the movie."

I thought about D. W. Griffith and Ford and Milestone and Walsh and wondered if they said, "It's only a movie."

Dick said, "We'll make a quality movie for the price. That's what it's all about. We'll start on schedule in two weeks and we'll finish on schedule twenty-two days later. Then you can cut it with Bernie Burton, we'll ship it, and then we can start thinking about something else. OK?"

It all sounded so simple, so routine. I said, "Sure, let's get back to work."

"What do you think of the Hollywood Ten?" he said.

This question, out of the blue, surprised and worried me. We were in the midst of the McCarthy era, and the Hollywood

Ten were un-co-operative congressional witnesses for the Mc-Carthy-Nixon witch hunt. They had all been sentenced to jail, and some would start serving their terms on the day we started shooting *Cry Danger*. I had only met one of them personally, but I admired some of their work and felt that they had been treated unjustly. I also knew that Powell was a close personal friend of Congressman Richard Nixon and had contributed large sums to his political campaigns from the beginning of Nixon's career. Powell and I had never discussed politics, but I knew that he was conservative and that compared with him I was left wing. In fact, the only politics I was deeply interested in was the politics of moviemaking. So now the two had come together at Preston Sturges's restaurant.

"I think they got a rotten deal," I said.

Dick called for the bill, and while he was paying I wondered who he would get to direct *Cry Danger*.

"I want to go see Eddie Dmytryk," he said. "He lives in an apartment on the other side of Sunset, and I want to see him before he goes to jail. His house is probably being watched, so I don't want you to come with me unless you want to."

Dmytryk was one of the Ten. The temper of the times made many people nervous about associating with those who resisted the witch hunt. Guilt by association was in the air. When I was working for Harry Cohn, my agent had asked me if I was a Communist.

"For chrissakes, Bernie, you're my agent. You're supposed to be on *my* side. What kind of a dumb question is that?" I asked him.

Bernie's impassive face was tanned a mahogany brown. His hair was neatly combed. He wore a dark suit and a thin black tie. He wore lifts in his shoes, but he was still short. His eyes were like smoldering icicles behind his glasses. His teeth were white, especially in contrast to his expensive dark skin. He had his initial embroidered on his Sulka silk shirt—not both initials like the cheaper agents, just "B." With all that going for him he should have been a good agent, but the question he asked me raised grave doubts.

"I'm not asking you to tell *me* whether or not you are a Communist. It's the studio. You're under contract to Columbia, and they want to know. We're asking all our clients to sign a loyalty oath so that we can honestly say we don't represent any subversives."

"Bernie, look at me. Do I look like a guy who wants to throw a bomb at Harry Cohn?"

"Of course you do. Everybody at Columbia wants to do that. That's not the point. With the current political climate it's just better to clear the air. Besides, you worked on *Body and Soul.*"

"What in the hell does that have to do with it?"

"They're suspicious of Rossen, Polonsky, and Garfield, so they're suspicious of everybody who worked on the picture. Jesus Christ, Bob. Don't make such a big deal of it. I'll send you the goddam paper, you sign it, and we'll forget about it."

The next day, I asked Harry Cohn if he was suspicious of me. He said, "I'm suspicious of everybody. What have you done?" I told him that my agent wanted to know if I was a Communist, that he wanted me to sign a loyalty oath.

He said, "Tell him to go fuck himself. It's none of his goddam business. Ask him if he's a Jew." I said I didn't care if he was a Jew or not. He said, "Ask him anyway." He got up from his desk and went to the bathroom adjoining his office. When he came back, he said, "By the way, are you a Communist?"

I said, "No. Are you a Jew?"

He said, "It's none of your goddam business. Now let's get to work."

Powell was grateful to Dmytryk for casting him in *Murder My Sweet* and starting him off on his new, noncrooning career. He said, "I'm not going to see Eddie as a politician, I'm going to see him as a friend. He's a very nice guy and a good director. I'd like you to meet him."

"OK, let's go," I said.

When we arrived at Dmytryk's apartment, he was working out with heavy bar bells. He greeted Dick warmly, said he was glad to meet me, and asked his pretty wife to make us coffee. He gave Powell some scripts, which Dick said he would get his agent to sell without using Dmytryk's name. Powell also said that he would personally option one of them and pay the money to Dmytryk's wife while Dmytryk was in jail.

As we drove back to the studio, Powell said, "How about giving Eddie's wife, Jean Porter, a job in the picture?"

I said, "Is she an actress?"

Powell said, "Anybody can act."

I didn't quite believe this, because I knew, for example, that I couldn't act. However, in Jean Porter's case, Dick was right. We gave her a big part and she did it beautifully. Sam Wiesenthal's midwestern banker kept muttering, "Are you sure she's not a Communist?" And Powell kept saying, "I don't know, Bill. Why don't you ask her? If she says yes, we can reshoot her part and you can put up another hundred thousand dollars."

Our first set was a run-down trailer camp overlooking the slum section of downtown Los Angeles. Richard Day had done a first-rate job on the trailers. Joe Biroc, the cameraman, and I had gone down the night before and worked out all our shots for the first day. Powell, Bill Conrad, Jean Porter, Richard Erdman, and Jay Adler had come to my house and rehearsed the whole picture. We were better prepared than on any picture I've ever worked on.

I had been around movie sets since I was ten years old, so I knew the normal routine. The director usually rehearses the scene, works out the camera shots, and then prepares to shoot the first setup. The make-up and wardrobe is checked, the assistant director yells, "QUIET!" and then turns to the director and says, "OK?" The director nods, and the assistant director says, "Turn 'em," or "Roll 'em." The camera operator throws a switch, which starts the camera and sound equipment running in synchronization. He says, "Running." The sound mixer watches a dial, and when the equipment reaches the right running speed (ninety feet a minute), he says, "SPEED." The assistant cameraman holding the slate identifying the picture, director, cameraman, date, scene number, and take number says, "Scene one, take one," and claps the clapper board so that the cutter can synchronize the sound and picture. He scurries out, and at that point the director is supposed to take over and say, "Action."

Our first setup was a medium shot of Dick Erdman and Jean Porter lying in the sun near one of the trailers. Dick Powell, just out of prison (Bill Bowers gave him the name "Rocky"), was offstage at the beginning of the shot. He stood between me and the camera, waiting for his cue to enter.

The ritual I had watched and heard so many times as an extra started. The assistant director, Lowell Farrell, got the set quiet and said, "Stand by." I crossed my fingers and hoped the siren noise from downtown Los Angeles far below wouldn't drown the dialogue. Dick Erdman picked his nose and the make-up man ran in and powdered his upper lip. A fly lit on Jean Porter's cheek and the prop man sprayed her with a Flit gun. Lowell Farrell said, "Steady now," which made me more nervous than ever. He turned to the sound mixer and said, "Sound OK?" The sound mixer nodded. Farrell then said, "Camera OK?" and the camera operator gave him the thumbs-up sign. Farrell said, "OK, roll 'em." I looked up at Dick Powell's face, and for the first time, from this profile view, I saw that Jack McHugh had a point, even with the crew cut. The camera operator said, "Running." The sound man said, "Speed." The assistant cameraman said, "Scene one, take one," clapped his board, and ran out of the scene.

I was fascinated with the whole performance. I watched it, hypnotized, as though I were watching it on the screen. When the assistant cameraman ran out, another fly lit on Jean Porter's lip. She brushed it away and I breathed a sigh of relief. Dick Erdman sat poised, a whisky bottle in his hand, waiting. I glanced up at the film-speed meter on the camera and saw that the needle was right on ninety. The camera operator had his eyes glued to the finder, and the focus puller had his hand on the focus changer, ready for Dick Powell's entrance. I was delighted that everything was going well. I relaxed and looked out at the tableau. Jean Porter and Richard Erdman were still there, poised like waxed figures, ready. I was wondering when they were going to start doing what we had rehearsed so many times when I felt a tug on my sleeve. I looked up at Dick Powell's calm face and he said, *"You're* supposed to say 'Action.' "

I said it and the tableau came to life and I was a movie director.

32

Petition

THE undersigned, Director Members who have subscribed to the non-Communist oath required by the bylaws of the Guild and who are members in good standing of the Screen Directors Guild of America, Inc., request that the Executive Secretary of the Screen Directors Guild of America, Inc., call a Special Separate Meeting of the Director Membership within ten days of the receipt of this petition.

The purpose of this meeting shall be to the Good and Welfare of the Screen Directors Guild of America, Inc., and to consider the proposed recall of the President and the transaction of such business as may come before it.

Each of us hereby swears for himself alone, "that I am not a member of the Communist Party or affiliated with such party, and I do not believe in, and I am not a member nor do I support any organizations that believe in or teaches the overthrow of the U.S. Government by force or by any illegal or unconstitutional methods."

1. John Huston (Signed)
2. H. C. Potter (Signed)
3. Edward H. Cahn (Signed)
4. Michael Gordon (Signed)
5. Andrew Marton (Signed)
6. George Seaton (Signed)
7. Maxwell Shane (Signed)
8. Mark Robson (Signed)
9. Richard Brooks (Signed)
10. John Sturges (Signed)
11. Felix E. Feist (Signed)
12. Robert Wise (Signed)
13. Robert Parrish (Signed)
14. Otto Lang (Signed)
15. Richard Fleischer (Signed)
16. Fred Zinnemann (Signed)
17. Joseph Losey (Signed)
18. William Wyler (Signed)
19. Jean Negulesco (Signed)
20. Nicholas Ray (Signed)
21. Billy Wilder (Signed)
22. Don Hartman (Signed)
23. Charles Vidor (Signed)
24. John Farrow (Signed)
25. Walter Reisch (Signed)

County of Los Angeles
State of California

Subscribed and sworn to before me on this 13th day of October 1950—

Norman F. Tyre (Signed)
Notary Public

PETITION

The undersigned, Director Members in good standing of
the Screen Directors Guild of America, Inc., request that
the Executive Secretary of the Screen Directors Guild of
America, Inc., call a Special Separate meeting of the
Director Membership within ten days of the receipt of this
petition.

The purpose of this meeting shall be the Good and
Welfare of the Screen Directors Guild of America, Inc.; and
the transaction of such business as may come before it.

1. _____   13. Robert Aldrich
2. H C Potter   14. _____
3. Edward L Cahn   15. Richard Fleischer
4. Michael Gordon   16. Fred Zinnemann
5. Andrew Marton   17. Joseph Losey
6. George Seaton   18. William Wyler
7. Maxwell Shane   19. Jean Negulesco
8. Mark Robson   20. Nicholas Ray
9. Richard Brooks   21. Billy Wilder
10. John Sturges   22. _____
11. _____   23. Charles Vidor
12. Robert Wise   24. John Farrow

25. _____

COUNTY of Los Angeles
State of California

Generally speaking, I think movie directors are not such bad people. A lot of them have homes and mothers and kids and things like that and a lot of them also have bad tempers and numbered Swiss bank accounts and divorces and things like that. They are no better and no worse than bank presidents, football players, steelworkers, or pop stars, still speaking generally, of course. If you were to dissect your average film director, you would find the same number of arms, legs, hernias, dyspeptic stomachs, strong hearts, and weak kidneys (or vice versa) as you would find in your average zeppelin pilot, Catholic priest, nuclear physicist, or United States senator. The point is that, individually, taken one at a time, they can be normal, intelligent citizens who have normal hopes and fears, as we all have. But when a lot of them get together in one room and try to thrash out a political problem, as they did at the Beverly Hills Hotel on Sunday, the twenty-second of October, 1950, it makes one wonder if perhaps some of them shouldn't be kept under lock and key except when they are actually on the set, puttees laced, bald heads shining, and megaphones at the ready.

Cecil B. DeMille was a member of the Screen Directors Guild of America, Inc.; so was Joseph L. Mankiewicz. So was I. DeMille was a charter member, in at the beginning, a founding father. Mankiewicz was president of the Guild. I had just directed my first picture and was the newest, greenest, most naive, most awe-struck member.

DeMille led a faction that wanted to throw Mankiewicz out (the petition said "recall" him). Aside from DeMille, the most active members of his faction were Albert S. Rogell, George Marshall, and Vernon Keays, the paid executive secretary of the Guild. Mankiewicz had no "faction." I don't think he even knew about the DeMille plot.

The reason DeMille wanted to get rid of Mankiewicz was that Mankiewicz didn't think the same way DeMille thought. Under the Taft-Hartley Act, then in effect, all officers of all unions and guilds in America were required to sign the so-called Loyalty Oath. As president of the Screen Directors Guild, Mankiewicz had signed it. DeMille thought it should also be mandatory for every other member of the Guild to sign the oath. He even seriously proposed that every director be required, at the close of every film he directed, to file with the Guild a report on *whatever he had been able to find out* about the political convictions of everyone connected with the film, particularly writers and actors. This information would then be on file at the Guild so that directors could check on the "loyalty" of those who wanted jobs. This bizarre suggestion was soundly defeated by the board.

Mankiewicz's position was that while he had signed the oath required of him by the government of the United States, he wasn't prepared to sign an oath demanded of him by Cecil B. DeMille. Mankiewicz thought this infringed upon a citizen's rights under the United States Constitution. Mankiewicz had read Thomas Paine and had seen *Mr. Smith Goes to Washington*. DeMille apparently had not.

Mankiewicz had won Academy Awards for both the writing and the direction of *A Letter to Three Wives*. He then wrote and directed *All About Eve* and took off for Europe for a well-deserved vacation. As soon as he left, the DeMille faction decided to strike. While Mankiewicz was on the high seas, the board of directors of the Guild, led by DeMille, passed the "Mandatory Loyalty Oath" bylaw. Strangely, under the constitution of the Guild as it was then written, the board of directors was not even required to *notify* the membership of their intent to pass such a law, much less secure the approval of the membership. DeMille said it was out of "courtesy" to the membership that they were granted the privilege of expressing an opinion on a *fait accompli* —on an *open, signed ballot.* You simply marked the ballot "yes" or "no"—*and signed your name.* The measure was adopted by a large majority.

All this was taking place while Senator Joseph McCarthy (Republican, Wisconsin) was riding high in Washington, and Representative Richard Nixon (Republican, California) was campaigning for United States senator. Nixon had already exposed Alger Hiss ("If the American people understood the real character of Alger Hiss, they would boil him in oil") and was making his "plea for an anti-Communist faith." As members of the House Committee on Un-American Activities, Nixon, J. Parnell Thomas (Republican, New Jersey), and others were looking for Communists and Communist sympathizers in every nook and cranny of America. DeMille was helping them with the search in Hollywood.

The "Mandatory Loyalty Oath" bylaw, thus, had been passed and was in effect when Mankiewicz returned to California. There was no way he could oppose, much less repeal, the oath as it stood. What was not expected was Mankiewicz's violent and voluble resistance to the open ballot, and, in particular, his insistence that the membership be afforded an opportunity to discuss openly what was a highly charged and deeply personal issue at that time. His insistence upon calling such a meeting grew as he received an increasing number of letters, phone calls, and telegrams from members who wanted to know what was going on. He notified DeMille and the rest of the board that he was going to call a membership meeting within ten days and lay everything out for open discussion.

An interesting organization called The Cecil B. DeMille Foundation for Americanism was formed. It became the chief source of information for State Senator John Tenney, head of the California Un-American Committee, who then passed the information on to the House Committee on Un-American Activities in Washington.

Items began to appear in the press suggesting that Mankiewicz was a "pinko," a "fellow traveler," and a "Communist-inspired left-wing intellectual," who was not averse to slipping Communist propaganda into his films. Mankiewicz's credits included *Skippy, Million Dollar Legs, If I Had a Million, Alice In Wonderland, The Gorgeous Hussy, Philadelphia Story,* and other pictures, which, I guess, DeMille suspected of having subversive content. A secret Joseph L. Mankiewicz film festival was organized. The pictures were run behind closed doors at DeMille's house for a select audience, complete with stenographers, their pencils poised in case Skippy or Alice in Wonderland or The Gorgeous Hussy said anything that could be interpreted as anti-American. When the DeMille group thought they had sufficient evidence, a ballot was drawn up to recall Mankiewicz.

The recall movement was headquartered in DeMille's office. Keays, the executive secretary, ordered the SDG's paid office staff to take the membership lists to DeMille and mail out the recall ballots. SDG-franked return envelopes were enclosed with the anonymous ballots. On the ballots themselves, there was only a space to vote "yes." It was disclosed later that DeMille, personally, had scratched the names of fifty-odd directors he thought to be particularly friendly with Mankiewicz and who might, therefore, tip him off that a recall movement was under way. As it turned out, DeMille must have overlooked some names on his "enemies list," because we all read about the recall ballots in the trade press the day after they were mailed.

A hard-core group of Mankiewicz supporters was quickly

rounded up. They decided to petition a Special Separate Meeting to "consider the proposed recall of the President." The DeMille group didn't want this meeting, because they had planned to railroad the recall vote through before the Mankiewicz loyalists could organize.

I had only just become a movie director, a dream realized after a long struggle, and I wasn't much interested in a political battle in a Guild I had just joined. I was interested in directing movies. DeMille and Mankiewicz were already important movie directors, each with a long list of successes. Neither of them had asked for my support. I didn't know Mankiewicz personally and I doubted if DeMille remembered me from my pole-carrying days in *Rough on Rats*. However, I was against the mandatory loyalty oath in principle, so I threw my brand-new, untried Guild vote in with the Mankiewicz supporters.

In order to call the Special Separate Meeting and save Mankiewicz's presidency, it was necessary to get twenty-five members in good standing to sign a petition. In order to send the petition out, it was necessary to get the addresses of the members. Unfortunately, when the Mankiewicz defenders arrived at the SDG office on Saturday, October 14—a business day—it was locked. Even stranger, no one answered the phone. We went to the rear door, which was also locked. The parking-lot attendant said that Mr. Keays, the executive secretary, had come in early and that he hadn't seen him leave. "There's his car."

The petition had to be signed, notarized, and turned in to the executive secretary of the Guild before the DeMille recall votes were in and counted, or all was lost. It was a low moment for the Mankiewicz side. They needed those addresses. Someone suggested breaking in, getting the addresses, and then pulling Keays out from under the rug and locking him in the filing cabinet for the weekend. Everybody milled around for a while, not knowing quite what to do, until a wise voice said, "Let's see a lawyer."

We went to see Martin Gang, the best lawyer in Hollywood. He agreed to take our case and stuck with us right through to the end. Then he refused to take a penny for his services, a practice unheard of, before or since, I should think, among theatrical lawyers.

Gang pointed out that according to the current bylaws of the Guild a member was not in good standing unless he had signed a loyalty oath, and that any signatures on our petition would be invalid unless each signing member also swore that he was "not a member of the Communist party and did not support any organization that believes in or teaches the overthrow of the U.S. government by force or by any illegal or unconstitutional methods." He then said, "Can you get twenty-five guys to sign such a statement before the deadline?"

A dilemma. We couldn't save Mankiewicz unless we signed the very thing he was against. Emotional discussions were held. Arguments for and against signing such a document were presented. Somebody said something like, "We're fighting a tough enemy," and another prominent director said, "We must fight fire with fire." An Academy Award winner said, "We can't let DeMille get away with it." (As these clichés poured forth, I thought we needed to recruit some members of the Writers Guild.) A two-time Oscar winner said, "I'm sure Keays is hiding in the office. Why don't we go back there and tear the joint apart?" Another successful director (no Academy Awards, but always big box office) said, "No, that's just what they want us to do. We'd be playing into their hands." He paused for a moment, and then added, "Besides, there's not enough time. I say we get the Gang office to write us up a legal petition, then we find twenty-five guys to sign it, call the meeting, and fight it out with the full membership."

This plan was accepted. Norman Tyre, a partner in Martin Gang's law firm, dictated a petition form, altered it in his illegible lawyer's handwriting, and the Mankiewicz supporters charged out on a signature hunt. We scoured the fleshpots, the gin mills, the Beverly Hills homes, and the fancy restaurants looking for movie directors who hated the non-Communist oath but were willing to sign it to save Joe Mankiewicz's Guild presidency. John Huston was the first to sign. Joe Losey was number seventeen, William Wyler was number eighteen, Billy Wilder was number twenty-one, Fred Zinnemann was number sixteen, Nicholas Ray was number twenty, John Farrow (Mia's father) was number twenty-four, and I was number thirteen, between my friend Robert Wise and Otto Lang, who, before he became a director, had been Darryl Zanuck's ski instructor at Sun Valley. Walter Reisch, the last signator (number twenty-five) was cornered in a booth in Chasen's restaurant and signed with a flourish.

The meeting was to be held on Sunday night in the ballroom of the Beverly Hills Hotel. Both sides had mustered all their forces. Mankiewicz spent most of the day in an upstairs hotel bedroom with John Huston, Elia Kazan, George Seaton, and others, cutting and reshaping Mankiewicz's opening speech as if it were a screenplay each intended to shoot. DeMille drove down from his pink house on DeMille Drive off Los Feliz Boulevard. The entire membership showed up, a record turnout. Everybody cared. It was was my first Guild meeting. Every prominent director I had heard of was there, including some I had worked with and knew well—Lewis Milestone, Robert Wise, George Stevens, Robert Rossen, George Cukor, Mark Robson, William Wyler, John Ford, DeMille—and some whom I knew only through their films—Fritz Lang, Rouben Mamoulian, Billy Wilder, Frank Capra, John Huston. Mankiewicz made an hour-long opening speech in which he made it clear that he had not raised an issue on the loyalty oath itself, but on the undemocratic procedure by which the Mandatory Loyalty Oath bylaw had been passed. Mankiewicz said he was unalterably opposed to an open ballot, a blacklist, and a mandatory oath. He said all three were un-American.

DeMille defended his faction's position as best he could, but he was not a good speaker and soon began to bore his audience, a thing he seldom did with his movies. As his loss of ground became more apparent, he turned his fire on what he charged to be the questionable politics of his opponents.

He singled out the twenty-five directors who had signed our petition. DeMille said that most of the twenty-five directors were affiliated with un-American or subversive organizations and theories and that many of them were foreign-born. When he said this, there was a gasp of disbelief, then some of the members started to hiss and boo. Mankiewicz rapped his gavel, and a thundering silence hung over the ballroom. Mankiewicz said, "Mr. DeMille has the floor." DeMille stood there for a moment and then sat down.

Men who were not among the twenty-five signers of the petition took the floor against DeMille's accusations. Rouben Mamoulian, William Wellman, and John Cromwell, among others, bitterly assailed DeMille's statements. Another director said he was at Bastogne when DeMille was defending his capital gains in Hollywood. That was the polemical level to which the meeting had sunk.

Fritz Lang quietly confessed that, for the first time, the fact that he spoke with an accent made him a little afraid. Delmar Daves, a fourth-generation Californian, broke down while expressing his contempt for DeMille's attack upon the foreign-born directors who had signed the petition.

Al Rogell, DeMille's lieutenant, read a deposition he had filed in support of the recall movement against Mankiewicz. In the deposition, he charged Mankiewicz with leaking information to *Variety*, the trade paper. This accusation got the biggest laugh of the evening. George Marshall, the third leader of the Mankiewicz recall movement, sat silently during the entire meeting. A young second-unit director rose and said, "Mr. DeMille gave me my first job in the business as a prop man. I've learned everything I know from him. He's been like a father to me. But unless he can explain these serious charges made against him and his supporters, I want to state publicly that I am ashamed of my association with him." He looked at DeMille, burst into tears, and sat down.

William Wyler, who had to sit up front because his hearing had been impaired during a bombing raid over Berlin, said that he was sick and tired of having insinuations thrown at him about being a Communist every time he disagreed with DeMille, and he intended to punch the next insinuator right in the nose. He looked at DeMille and concluded with, "And I don't care how old he is." We all sat nervously wondering if we were going to see the most successful box-office director in the world have his nose punched in front of the full membership of the Screen Directors Guild.

Many speeches were made, many charges and counter-charges. For four hours, film directors attacked or defended De-Mille or Mankiewicz. Finally, DeMille was asked from the floor to retract his charges against the twenty-five directors. DeMille flatly refused. George Stevens took the floor and offered his resignation from the board of directors. The members present refused to accept his resignation.

Stevens then launched into an articulate, devastating list of charges against the executive secretary and the anti-Mankiewicz members of the board. He made the most effective speech of the evening so far and finished by asking DeMille to recall the recall movement. DeMille demanded an act of contrition from Mankiewicz in exchange, which Mankiewicz refused. Stevens said, "I have nothing more to say," and sat down.

Except for John Ford and the little group sitting around De-Mille, the entire membership rose to their feet and applauded Stevens's speech.

During all this, Ford had not said a word. As the waves of

emotion rolled over the members, he sat there in his baseball cap and tennis shoes and sucked on his pipe. From time to time he would put the pipe away, take out a dirty handerchief, wipe his glasses with it, and then chew on it for a while. He was an important man in the Guild, and everyone wondered what he thought. He was also a master of timing.

After the applause for Stevens stopped, there was silence for a moment, and Ford raised his hand. A court stenographer was there, and everyone had to identify himself for the record. Ford stood up and faced the stenographer.

"My name's John Ford," he said. "I make westerns." He paused for a moment to let this bit of news sink in. "I don't think there is anyone in this room who knows more about what the American public wants than Cecil B. DeMille—and he certainly knows how to give it to them. In that respect I admire him." Then he looked right at DeMille, who was across the room from him. "But I don't like you, C. B.," he said. "I don't like what you stand for and I don't like what you've been saying here to-night. Joe has been vilified, and I think he needs an apology." He stared at DeMille while the membership waited in silence. DeMille stared straight ahead and made no move. After thirty seconds, Ford finally said, "Then I believe there is only one alternative, and I hereby so move: that Mr. DeMille and the entire board of directors resign and that we give Joe a vote of confidence—and then let's all go home and get some sleep. We've got some pictures to make tomorrow."   .

Walter Lang seconded the motion. Ford sat down and lit his pipe. The membership voted in favor of Ford's motion. DeMille and the board resigned and we gave Mankiewicz a unanimous vote of confidence, with four abstentions. My first Screen Directors Guild meeting was adjourned.

We had saved Mankiewicz's presidency and defied the man who parted the Red Sea twice, once in 1923 with Theodore Roberts and again with Charlton Heston in 1956.

33

The Final Lesson

J OHN FORD'S daughter phoned me in London and said that Ford had terminal cancer and that it would please him if I could come and see him. He had moved to Palm Desert to be near the Eisenhower Hospital. I arrived in a driving rainstorm.

A nurse (one of three on 24-hour duty) met me at the door. "Five minutes, Mr. Parrish. He's quite tired and the doctor says we must limit his visitors to one a day, and then only for five minutes. We've had to turn a lot of people down, but we've made an exception in your case because you've come so far. You must promise to leave after five minutes."

I promised, and she let me in. Barbara, his daughter, who had devoted the past several years to taking care of him, greeted me warmly. She said, "Daddy's pretty sick, but he's remarkably alert and he's expecting you." I asked about Mrs. Ford, and Barbara said, "She has Parkinson's disease and will see you later in her bedroom. Come on, I'll take you in to Daddy."

They had just moved into the Palm Desert house, so a lot of the furniture and things had not been put into place. As we passed through the living room, I saw a large crate full of various awards that Ford had received. All his Oscars had been taken out and placed together on a table, along with miniature Oscars to match each one of the originals—a golden forest.

Barbara showed me into his bedroom. He was propped into a half-sitting position pawing over a plastic bucket of something. Aside from a little statue of the Virgin Mary and some burning candles, the thing that caught my eye was a giant, black, silver-mounted saddle on a sawhorse at the foot of his bed. Barbara said, "Bob's here," and left us alone. I walked around the bed and took a seat on the opposite side. He was still wearing the familiar patch over his left eye, and he was very thin. Otherwise, I thought, he didn't look much different from when I had first seen him, forty-three years earlier.

The plastic bucket was about half full of old cigar butts, and Ford was trying to find one that he liked. He'd plunge his hand in and come up with a well-chewed two-incher, lift his patch, study the butt with the bad eye, sniff it, and toss it back. He rejected four or five, then found one that suited him. He lit it and passed the plastic bucket to me. "Would you like a cigar, Bob?" I said, "No thank you, but I could use a drink." He called the nurse and she went out to get me a Fernet-Branca, the only alcoholic beverage in the house.

He said, "How's Kathleen?" I said, "Fine, she sends you her best." He said, "How's your mother?" I said, "Fine, she sends you her best too." He said, "How old is she?" I said, "Eighty-six." I looked at my watch. I'd been with him almost three minutes.

He said, "What are you looking at your watch for?"

I had discovered years before that it was a mistake to lie to him. "The nurse said I could only stay five minutes."

He turned his unpatched eye on me. "*You* got five minutes? How the hell . . . I mean for chrissakes . . . *Stevens* only got five minutes. *Capra* only got five minutes. *Hawks* only got five minutes. Jesus Christ . . ."

I thought he was going to say *He* only got five minutes too. Instead, he spat in the plastic bucket and relit his cigar (34 secs.). When it was burning well, he lifted the patch, fixed his left eye on me, and said, "I'll tell you what. You came a long way. There was another director in to see me yesterday. He was such a dull sonofabitch, I threw him out after two minutes. You can have his other three minutes."

I stayed with him for over an hour. Every time the nurse came in, he sent her away. We talked about many things. He said, "Do you still live on that fifty-foot lot in the valley?" (A long look and a hint of a smile.) I told him I lived in London. He said, "Do you like living with the limeys?" I said I liked it very much. He asked if London had changed much since we were there in the war. He particularly wanted to know if the Coach and Horses pub in Bruton Street was still standing. He said he had been drinking there when the buildings around it were bombed. I told him it was still there. I asked him if he still had the lucky necklace he was wearing that night. He said, "Yes, it's around here someplace. We just moved in, and it takes a while to get organized. I'll find it if I need it."

It wasn't really a necklace, it was a string he wore around his neck with his Navy identification dog tag and several charms on it—a St. Christopher medal, a Star of David, an elk's tooth, a small black ring made from rhinoceros hair, and several other things that I never got close enough to identify. If he met someone who he thought was Catholic, he would shamelessly pull out the string and rub the St. Christopher medal while he talked. If he thought someone might be Jewish, he had the Star of David standing by. I guess the elk's tooth was for the B.P.O.E., but I could never think of an occasion that might require use of the rhinoceros ring.

He asked me to give his regards to Jack Hawkins, who was then suffering from throat cancer—"A fine actor and a great guy."

We talked about zoom lenses (he didn't approve), John Wayne (he approved), Hank Fonda (he approved), Pat Kelley (he approved but wished Kelley hadn't turned executive—"Terrible thing for a good sound-effects cutter to allow himself to become the president of a successful film-producing company"). He told me that he had known Pat's father, Dan, in the old Buck Jones days at Universal. He asked about his co-best men, Mike Luciano and Phil Scott. I told him they were both in good health. "Good men," he said. I agreed.

He then said, "Have you won any more Oscars?" I told him I hadn't, and he said, "It turns out they're not as unimportant as I thought, so you should go ahead and win as many as you can."

I said, "Yes, sir." He said, "Take care of yourself." I said, "Take care of *your*self," and he said, "Be sure and see Mary before you go." I said, "Yes, sir," again and got up to leave. When I got to the door, I turned for a last look. He said, "God bless you, Bob. You're a good lad."

I left him scrounging in the plastic bucket for another cigar butt.

Mary Ford was lying on her bed, looking quite beautiful. Her hair was brushed off her face, Madonna-like, the way she always wore it. I kissed her and sat beside her bed. She started to tell me the details of her husband's illness. As she talked, Ford appeared in the door in the background. Out of bed he looked dangerously thin. I guess it was because I could see his legs now. They were like matchsticks. Mary couldn't see him, because she was lying on her side, her back to him. He listened a bit and then said, "What are you two talking about?"

I said, "We're talking about you."

He chewed on his cigar for a moment and then said, "I find the subject totally uninteresting." He turned and went back to his bedroom.

Shortly after I last saw him, he put on his rear admiral's uniform and made a final trip to Hollywood. The president of the United States personally promoted him to full admiral for the evening and presented him with the Medal of Freedom, the nation's highest civilian honor.

He died a few weeks later. The New York *Times* quoted a story in which somebody mentioned the films of Ingmar Bergman to Ford.

"Ingrid Bergman?" Ford asked.

"No, Ingmar Bergman—you know, the great Swedish director."

"Oh, *Ingmar* Bergman," Ford said. "He's the fella that called me the greatest director in the world."

34

The Winds of Change

PARAMOUNT Pictures was bought by a conglomerate called Gulf + Western. Charles Bluhdorn, the new boss, came to Hollywood to look over the acquisition and to meet the Hollywood filmmakers—the producers, writers, directors, and actors who had been producing films for Paramount till then. More important, he wanted to meet the agents who would produce the producers, writers, directors, and actors who would produce films for Paramount in the future.

Charles Feldman, a top agent, gave the introduction party, and I was included in the guest list. I arrived at Feldman's home in Coldwater Canyon and found the house full of film celebrities —Hollywood Old Guard and Hollywood New Guard—Mr. and Mrs. Samuel Goldwyn, Mr. and Mrs. William Goetz, Mr. and Mrs. Kirk Douglas, Burt Lancaster, Mel Ferrer, Robert Evans (newly appointed head of production for Paramount), and many, many others. Feldman explained that Bluhdorn's plane was late and that he would come directly from the airport.

We were served an excellent dinner and were sitting in groups talking when Bluhdorn arrived. Feldman took him around and introduced him to each person. When the introductions were completed, Bluhdorn and Feldman walked over to the fireplace. Within seconds they were joined by Robert Evans. Then Kirk Douglas excused himself from the ladies he was talking to and went to the fireplace, followed by Mel Ferrer, Bill Goetz, Burt Lancaster, and practically every other man in the room. I was sitting in a little alcove talking to Mrs. Goldwyn, an intelligent, dignified woman who knows everything there is to know about Hollywood. As the men abandoned their lady companions and drifted over to Bluhdorn she said, "Mr. Parrish, look into the other room."

I looked over and saw about twenty-five women at one end of the room and Bluhdorn surrounded by twenty-five men at the other end.

Mrs. Goldwyn said, "New girl in town."

215

Conclusion

"So endeth this chronicle. . . . When one writes . . . about grown people, he knows exactly where to stop . . . but when he writes of juveniles, he must stop where he best can."

—Mark Twain

Acknowledgments

The author gratefully acknowledges the generous co-operation and contributions of the following: the Academy of Motion Picture Arts and Sciences; the American Cinema Institute; the American Legion, Hollywood Post 43; Harry Ansel; the British Film Institute; Robert Belcher; Kevin Brownlow; City of Los Angeles, History Department; Charles Chaplin; Columbia Pictures; the Columbus *Ledger-Enquirer;* the Directors Guild of America, Inc.; Barbara Ford; Tom Fuchs; Georgia Department of Community Development; Vernon Harbin; Historic Columbus Foundation; Patrick Kelley; Marianne Kingsford; F. Clayton Kyle; Joseph L. Mankiewicz; Martin Theaters, Columbus, Georgia; Metro-Goldwyn-Mayer; Caroline Munro; Natural History Museum of Los Angeles County, History Division; Al Parker; Paramount Pictures Corporation; Abraham Polonsky; *Ring* magazine; RKO-Radio Pictures; Rick Rosenfeld; Arthur Schwartz; Robert Stein; Twentieth Century-Fox Film Corporation; Warner Brothers Picture Corporation; Robert Wise.

The following publications were used for research: *British Film and T.V. Year Book,* edited by Peter Noble; *The Hollywood Reporter; International Motion Picture Almanac;* the Los Angeles *Times; The New York Times Directory of the Film,* edited by Arthur Knight; *The Parade's Gone By,* by Kevin Brownlow; *Twenty Years of American Cinema,* by Jean-Pierre Coursodon and Bertrand Tavernier; *Variety.*

Index

Unless otherwise indicated, entries in italics are titles of films.